Policies for Growth
The Latin American Experience

Proceedings of a conference held in
Mangaratiba, Rio de Janeiro, Brazil
March 16–19, 1994

André Lara Resende
Moderator

International Monetary Fund
Washington • 1995

This book was designed and produced by the IMF Graphics Section.

Library of Congress Cataloging-in-Publication Data

Policies for growth : the Latin American experience : proceedings of a
conference held in Mangaratiba, Rio de Janeiro, Brazil, March 16–19,
1994 / André Lara Resende, moderator.
    p.   cm.
    Includes bibliographical references.
    ISBN 1-55775-517-5
    1. Economic Stabilization—Latin America—Congresses.   2. Latin
America—Economic policy—Congresses.   3. Fiscal policy—Latin
America—Congresses.   4. Monetary policy—Latin America—
Congresses.   I. Resende, André Lara.   II. International Monetary
Fund.
HC125.P637   1995
338.98—dc20   95-33289
                                                    CIP

Price: US$24.00

Please send orders to:
International Monetary Fund, Publication Services
700 19th Street, N.W., Washington, D.C. 20431, U.S.A.
Tel: (202) 623-7430   Telefax: (202) 623-7201
Internet: publications@imf.org

CONTENTS

Foreword

Following years of high inflation, entrenched protectionism, and heavy indebtedness, Latin America in the early 1990s appears poised to exploit its formidable economic potential. The successful implementation of adjustment and reform programs in the region has given millions of people new hope for a brighter future.

The International Monetary Fund, in collaboration with other international organizations, has been closely associated with Latin America's transformation efforts and has contributed to the "silent revolution" in economic policymaking in the region and throughout the world. It has done so through its policy dialogue with country authorities as part of its surveillance function and by providing financial support to economic reform programs.

To extend the policy dialogue beyond official circles, the IMF cosponsored a seminar entitled "Macroeconomic, Structural, and Social Policies for Growth: The Latin American Experience" in Mangaratiba, Brazil, on March 16-19, 1994. The cosponsors were the Catholic University of Rio de Janeiro and the Central Bank of Brazil. Academic and business economists and national and international officials discussed and debated the role of macroeconomic policy in achieving stabilization and sustainable growth. The debate served to confirm the consensus that is emerging among economists and officials alike on the policies that are likely to be most conducive to high-quality economic growth.

The papers and comments presented in Mangaratiba and published in this volume will, I hope, serve as a useful reference for economic policymakers everywhere as they face the challenges of improving the human condition by promoting greater economic efficiency and sustained growth.

> Michel Camdessus
> *Managing Director*
> *International Monetary Fund*

Acknowledgments

The productive and illuminating discussions held in Mangaratiba, Brazil, during the seminar "Macroeconomic, Structural, and Social Policies for Growth: The Evolving Latin American Experience" would not have been possible without the dedicated contribution of a number of staff in the three institutions that cosponsored it.

On behalf of all the participants, I would like to extend our appreciation to Luiz Afonso Simoens da Silva of Banco Central do Brasil, Edward Amadeo of Pontifícia Universidade Católica (Rio de Janeiro), and Hernán Puentes of the International Monetary Fund, who were responsible for planning and implementing the event. Our warmest thanks go also to those at the Banco Central do Brasil who were responsible for the arrangements in Brazil. This team was led by Paulo Miranda da Fonseca and Jane Luiza Fialho F. Santiago and included Mario Bellardi Neto, Pedro Valdenir Pinto da Silva, Miriam Pessoa Braga, Cleyd Soares Teixeira, and Silvia Regina Pinto Netto. Thanks are also due to the IMF's Kathleen White and Patricia Kane for their organizational contribution in Washington and to Elisa Diehl, who painstakingly edited and produced this volume.

In light of the subsequent developments in the Latin American region, the timeliness and relevance of the discussions held in Mangaratiba in March 1994 are, indeed, remarkable.

Shailendra J. Anjaria
Director
External Relations Department

1

Introduction

André Lara Resende

Held in Mangaratiba, Rio de Janeiro, under the sponsorship of the International Monetary Fund, the Central Bank of Brazil, and the Catholic University of Rio de Janeiro, this seminar brought together a large number of economists from different countries and institutions. The purpose was to discuss policies for sustained growth based on recent Latin American experiences. Although, at the time of the seminar, some economies—particularly that of Brazil—could not yet be deemed successful in their efforts to achieve price stability, the discussions centered on themes considered pertinent to the consolidation of stability and the recovery of growth.

The first paper, by Ricardo López Murphy, looks at the general characteristics of recent stabilization programs in Latin America. Next, Edward Amadeo discusses distributive and social costs associated with the stabilization process. Thus, these first two papers address the specific themes of overcoming the inflationary episodes that all Latin American economies have experienced in recent decades.

The following papers are dedicated to the themes of the institutional reforms associated with stabilization. Roberto Steiner discusses financial liberalization and international capital flows. Tomás Baliño analyzes the problems of coordinating monetary and fiscal policies within a framework of enhanced central bank independence. Parthasarathi Shome examines recent trends in the fiscal area. Sebastián Edwards concludes with a discussion of trade liberalization and industrial policy.

These are rich, complex, and highly relevant themes, and the discussants do not claim to have exhausted them. The papers are, however, of fundamental importance to the discussion of the still incomplete process of stabilization undertaken in the aftermath of the inflationary crises in the Latin American economies in the 1980s. They are required reading for anyone wishing to understand the themes associated with the consolidation of price stability.

The panel discussions were extraordinarily vibrant and rich. The moderator had the difficult task of ensuring that the time frames, always insufficient, were at least minimally respected. The inevitable impression that the discussions could have been prolonged with no loss of interest is made easier to accept only when one recalls that there will be other opportunities to continue them within the cycle of debates periodically sponsored by the International Monetary Fund.

An even harder task was to prepare a summary worthy of the discussions. The feeling that much has been left aside grows into certainty. The summary that follows can only be a pallid attempt to summarize the wealth of the debate. With no intention of reconstituting the debates or obviating the reading of the papers, I have tried to set out the general lines of the discussions. To avoid even greater unfairness in capturing the richness of the arguments raised by each of the participants, I have opted to provide a general overview of the various arguments. Despite the moderator's efforts to remain neutral, the result is inevitably subjective. I have tried to avoid at least what one of the participants described at the end of the meeting as "the risks of an excessively Brazilian vision" of the Latin American experience.

Pillars of the Stabilization Program

There is a consensus today on what could be termed the four great themes, or pillars, of price stabilization programs. These are, first, re-establishing fiscal equilibrium; second, overcoming chronic inflation inertia; third, implementing institutional reforms; and, finally, recovering credibility.

Eliminating the fiscal deficit was unanimously seen as a fundamental condition for the success of a stabilization program. Two aspects of the fiscal balance requirement deserve mention. The first is the definition of the deficit itself. It should not be restricted to the treasury's budget deficit. The deficit must be viewed in its broad sense, encompassing all spheres of government, the social security system, and financial and non-financial public companies. The second aspect is the distinction between transitory balance and permanent balance. To re-establish permanent fiscal balance is crucial. Sustained price stabilization requires that intertemporal fiscal balance be achieved. It is not sufficient to generate a temporary fiscal surplus through transitory efforts to cut expenditures and increase revenues. These efforts are perceived to be unsustainable over the longer term. Already, the complex question of credibility, which permeates the entire theme of stabilization, comes to the fore.

Still on the theme of fiscal equilibrium, an important question has recently been raised. It deals with the functionality of inflation in reducing the deficit. According to the well-known "Tanzi effect," fiscal revenues are reduced when inflation accelerates because of the erosion of the real value of revenues between the moment the tax is due and the moment it is effectively collected. However, a recent line of argument states that, after many years of chronic inflation, the combination of indexed fiscal revenues and shorter periods between the moment the tax is due and the moment it is collected creates what could be termed an "inverted Tanzi effect." Fiscal revenues would be sufficiently indexed so as to be relatively immune to any significant degree of inflationary erosion. Government would, on the contrary, use inflation to reduce the real value of approved budgetary expenditures by postponing their release. In this case, a sudden reduction of inflation would increase the fiscal deficit, instead of reducing it as the Tanzi effect would suggest. According to this hypothesis, inflation helps a politically weak government, incapable of imposing, a priori, a balanced budget to reduce the ex post budget deficit. Although certainly controversial, the hypothesis was considered relevant for countries that have been exposed to long periods of inflation, have developed sophisticated indexation mechanisms, and have been saddled with weak governments in the face of a congress with power over the budget. Brazil and Israel are examples of countries where these conditions have prevailed.

Insofar as the second pillar of price stabilization—overcoming inflationary inertia—is concerned, there is a reasonable degree of consensus. Deep-rooted inflation, including moderate but chronic inflation, demands measures aimed at eliminating the inertial element of generalized price increases. Here, a distinction should be made. There are countries that have developed formal and informal indexation but are still using the national currency as a means of payment; there are also countries nearing open hyperinflation in which currency substitution has reached a significant degree. These circumstances have different implications and require distinct therapies.

The third theme is that of institutional reforms. Four great reforms were emphasized and unanimously accepted as fundamental to stabilization programs: trade liberalization, international financial integration, privatization, and, finally, the creation of a more independent central bank.

The complex and elusive theme of reclaiming credibility is the last of the four great stabilization topics. Once more, there is a solid consensus on the importance of credibility but a great deal of difficulty in defining the conditions capable of guaranteeing it. Credibility seems to be associated with the three great themes treated above, particularly with that of institutional reforms. An inflexible institutional structure that would grant independence to the central bank, or the extreme case of a "currency board," would seem to contribute to regained credibility. But here the discussion takes on a polemical character. It was stressed that the homogeneity of the government team and, more specifically, of the team responsible for economic policy was important to credibility. The importance of policy continuity was also stressed. Above all, the importance of a conviction within society that stabilization is a national priority emerged as the main determinant of credibility. Society's option for stabilization based on the conviction that inflation has become fundamentally dysfunctional is the single most important determinant of credibility, without which stabilization is not possible.

A fifth theme was briefly discussed. It is whether stabilization requires or is facilitated by an authoritarian political system. Although the question is complex, it seems that society's conviction as to the need for stabilization weakens in the face of the suggestion that authoritarian regimes are necessary to the stabilization process.

The panel that followed upon the opening session examined these major themes.

Social Costs of Stabilization

What are the social and distributive costs of stabilization? Experience demonstrates that the recessive or distributive costs of the period immediately after the reduction of inflation are low or nonexistent. There is no evidence of recession or of a significant worsening of income and wealth distribution in the immediate aftermath of stabilization. Quite the contrary, stabilization generates increased consumption, recovery of investments, and a strong growth surge. Although a consensus existed in this regard, Amadeo questioned whether the costs had not been incurred previously. The debate called attention to the fact that, once the question is formulated in this manner, the analysis runs the risk of confusing the costs of high inflation—recognizably high—with the costs of stabilization. There was unanimity with respect to the perverse social and distributive effects of inflation. The brutally regressive character of the inflationary tax was insistently recalled. The fact that stabilization does not eliminate poverty cannot be used as an argument against stabilization, just as it does not permit one to conclude that stabilization causes poverty. In order to judge stabilization from the point of view of equity and social justice, one must compare it with the alternative of not pursuing stabilization. The consequences would be unmistakably worse.

Tax Reform and Stabilization

Recent tax reform trends in Latin America were discussed next. From the more aggressive cases, such as the Argentine experience, to the more gradual reforms, as carried out in Colombia, the reforms were geared toward simplification. The tax systems that emerged from these reforms are less sophisticated and conceptually more rudimentary than the ones that preceded them. They are based less on direct taxes and more on indirect taxes. For practical reasons, there has been a tendency to reduce income tax rates and broaden the range of exemptions in all Latin American countries. Direct taxes are operationally more complex and more expensive to collect. With respect to the income tax, the motivation has been "let's not worry the small taxpayer," for whom collection costs are excessively high. The overriding emphasis of the reforms has been on simplification and the reduction of collection costs. The neutrality and equity aspects of the value-added tax were questioned and the tax proposed as the theme of future analyses.

The fiscal reforms of the stabilization programs, which can be characterized as emergency measures, were considered far from adequate. Innumerable difficulties remain to be solved. The social security system is the first one. It is a broad and complex question that must be an essential element of future discussions. Among the other thorny issues raised were the questions of federalism; the distribution of revenues and responsibilities among the various levels of government; fiscal incentives, exemptions, and waivers; and the challenges created by the irreversible trend toward internationalization and economic integration. The discussion went on to encompass the question of how to tax primary products, which are still so relevant to Latin American countries.

The panel came to an unequivocal conclusion: recent tax reforms have been implemented with the limited objective of price stabilization. Much remains to be done. A careful analysis of how to act with respect to tax matters is imperative.

Trade and Industrial Policies

Trade and industrial policies were the next theme. Since the mid-1980s, Latin American countries have undertaken the unprecedented process of unilateral trade liberalization. The elimination of quantitative restrictions was followed by across-the-board reductions in import tariffs. The early experiences, such as Chile's, have been very successful. Costs in terms of industrial output and employment were much lower than initially feared. Consequently, the more recent experiences of Brazil and Colombia were implemented at a faster pace than the earlier programs. The chronological sequence once considered imperative—stabilization, followed by trade liberalization, and, finally, financial liberation—now seems open to question. The Brazilian case stands as evidence that there is no rigid chronological order because trade and financial liberalization started well before inflation could be said to be under control.

The topic is still being hotly discussed. There is considerable disagreement on the effects of trade and capital account liberalization on productivity. The difficulty of measuring productivity gains adds to the difficulty of the discussion. The Mexican case is cause for some perplexity. At least from the point of view of the economy as a whole, significant gains were not achieved. Some would even question whether any productivity gain at all was attained.

A comparison was drawn between the Latin American industrial policy experience of the last three decades and the highly successful experience of the countries of Southeast Asia. It was argued that Latin America attempted to combine stimuli specific to particular industries, sectors, or technologies, with a generalized system of tariff protection for domestic industry. The successful policies adopted in Southeast Asia were quite different. More generalist policies were used to promote exports. The decision as to which industries and technologies had comparative advantages, and what would actually be exported, was left to market forces.

No definitive conclusions were drawn in this regard. Trade liberalization is no panacea and does not necessarily substitute for an indicative industrial policy. However, because liberalization exposes inflationary and excessively protected economies to foreign competition, it is a fundamental element of stabilization. But even though most participants agreed with this statement, some participants called attention to the fact that liberalization had occurred within a favorable international economic environment. According to them, those years were marked by abundant foreign credit and the absence of adverse external shocks.

The compatibility of regional trade agreements with multilateral trade liberalization was questioned. It was recalled that the trade unions in industrial countries might bring pressure on Latin America to impose certain standards of "ecological correctness" that could well be extremely burdensome. It was also argued that, given a rigid structure of wage and exchange rates, trade and financial liberalization could aggravate adverse external shocks. These arguments are not new. Some participants argued that the unusually favorable environment of recent years has given rise to an excessive optimism in relation to the risks inherent to trade and financial liberalization.

Financial Liberalization

The opening of capital accounts and international financial integration are today a reality. In recent years, capital flows to Latin America have been abundant. Against this background, two major questions were discussed. The first one was whether these flows were permanent or transitory. The second one was whether these capital flows were driven mainly by internal attraction or by external expulsion. The predominant view was that capital flows are transitory—at least at current abundant levels— and that external factors are dominant or at least as important as internal factors.

The old distinction between speculative flows and long-term investments was considered pertinent and still deserving of attention. Mention was also made of the distinction between flows mediated by the banking system—such as those that preceded the foreign debt crisis of the 1980s—and the more recent flows, dominated by securitization and stock markets. However, no consensus was reached as to whether this distinction was relevant or had major implications.

The fact that deficit and surplus countries must adjust their current accounts over the course of time was recalled. Consequently, interest rates in industrial countries should rise in relation to the levels of recent years, and the flows of foreign capital to Latin America should decline. The relevant question is just how traumatic will be the landing forced by the reduction—or the end—of these flows.

Countries' experiences with a fixed exchange rate—using the gold standard or currency boards—were the subject of much controversy. It was argued that the convenience of adopting a fixed exchange regime was intrinsically linked to the abundance of external capital flows. Recent experiences were greatly facilitated by the abundance of capital and the absence of external shocks. There was, however, considerable wariness with respect to the ability of fixed exchange regimes to adjust to a reversal of foreign capital flows or to a deterioration in the conditions of the world economy.

A fixed exchange rate regime and financial liberalization require the abdication of any active monetary policy and—when taken to the limit of the currency board—of the right to have a lender of last resort. It was argued that to eliminate risks of financial distress, countries would additionally have to abdicate having a national banking system. Most participants considered that this would be terribly difficult to justify.

Central Bank Independence and Policy Coordination

The discussion of exchange and monetary regimes leads to the topic of the structure of the monetary authorities and to the final theme of the seminar: central bank independence and monetary and fiscal policy coordination. The need for coordination is self-evident. The compatibility of monetary, exchange, and public debt policies would not even be a subject of discussion were it not for the recent trend—some would term it a fad—to emphasize central bank independence.

What do we mean by "independence"? First, it was argued that there is a lower correlation between formal, or legal, independence and practical independence of central banks than one would suppose. There is, however, a positive correlation between formal independence of the central bank and an enhanced fiscal austerity and lower rates of inflation. The direction of this causality was questioned. Is it the formal independence of the central bank that leads to fiscal discipline and price stability? Or is it the opposite? Isn't it true that countries that have made the political choice to adjust and stabilize have, a posteriori, instituted formally independent central banks?

Once more, there was a high degree of consensus as to the conclusion that central bank independence—no matter how one may define the term—is not a panacea. However, it was agreed that the central bank must have a single, well-defined objective: to preserve the stability of the national currency. This is essential for credibility. It was questioned whether "lack of independence" might not be the more correct expression, because the central bank, under this definition, actually has less freedom.

The relevant alternative is not between "dependence" and "independence," but rather between rules and discretion. The advantages and disadvantages of a central bank with no freedom to deviate from a strict policy in defense of the purchasing power of the national currency were discussed. Would it be desirable to simply abandon the idea of a central bank and adopt a currency board? On this subject, the discussion was heated and opinions divided. However, even those who defend the currency board recognize that it is not the ideal regime. They argue that its complete lack of flexibility is the price to pay for regaining the credibility lost after many years of fiscal and monetary irresponsibility. It is, therefore, important to distinguish between the ideal system and the necessary system until the price stabilization is consolidated.

There was general agreement that central bank independence cannot, by itself, ensure stability. On the contrary, if independence were to mean a lack of coordination between monetary, fiscal, and public debt policies, it could be extremely costly. A central bank institutionally protected from circumstantial political pressures was, however, unanimously considered a sign of the political decision to stabilize. It is, therefore, an important factor in the effort to recover credibility.

Finally, it was noted that recent experiences in Latin America with independent central banks have not yet been submitted to the test of adverse circumstances. They have neither seen a period of adverse external shocks nor had to cope with the fiscal policies of populist governments uncommitted to price stabilization or with a crisis in the domestic financial system. Consequently, definitive conclusions cannot yet be drawn.

2

Stabilization Programs:
Recent Experience in Latin America

Ricardo López Murphy

This paper discusses stabilization programs in Latin America, with an analysis of the general conceptual framework and of a few practical experiences that demonstrate the main points. The viewpoint will be that of a policymaker, with an emphasis on those issues that experience has generally shown to be the most controversial.

The paper begins by discussing why governments try hard to attain stability and then defines stability and focuses on what is required, and the instruments typically used, to achieve it. Next, it examines institutional difficulties or pre-existing problems, the real scope of which can be assessed only in a climate of stability. The conceptual discussion concludes with a presentation of a few problems that recently arose in connection with stabilization plans that have otherwise been very successful. Finally, comparisons are made between experiences in Argentina, Chile, Mexico, and Uruguay. Given the brevity of this paper, remarks on each topic are confined to the most salient points.

Objectives of a Stabilization Program

Short-term programs typically involve three competing objectives: general price stability, the economic growth rate, and balance of payments equilibrium. Stabilization plans normally focus primarily on the general level of prices. However, it is recognized that price stability cannot be achieved during a prolonged recession or in a situation of external imbalance. To some extent, stability depends on whether economic activity realizes its long-term potential and on the expectation that the external accounts will require no drastic adjustments.

The demand for financial assets—money, bonds, or deposits—depends on the viability of the current situation. To a large extent, for stabilization programs to succeed, capital markets must operate normally, and that goal can be extremely difficult to achieve without a coherent short-term policy. In the context of stabilization, it is important to recognize that inflation is a monetary phenomenon in the strict sense: to measure it, one must use monetary concepts. This view is not an attempt to reopen an old Latin American debate between structuralists and monetarists in that it does not take a position regarding the causes of inflation: whether it is due to an initial monetary imbalance; cost pressures, external shocks, and relative price rigidities; or indexation phenomena. The statement refers exclusively to the fact that continuous changes in the monetary base are required to convert a rise in prices into an inflationary process.

The second major issue is to recognize inflation as a form of taxation. When a tax increases for an individual, to a large extent it increases the government's net wealth. As the definition implies, a deficit position in the current sense is not required; what is required is a disequilibrium that is financed by the issuance of money. Thus, for example, an inflation tax can be used to reduce domestic or external debt or to accumulate reserves or claims on the private sector through loans. The increased government wealth will imply less need for taxation in the future. The monetary and fiscal characterization of inflation must then refer to the need to create a new system in both areas if stabilization is to be achieved.

Reasons for Stabilizing

The launching of stabilization plans has generally provoked opposition from some social groups because of the adjustment the plans imply. For example, experience shows that they sometimes generate declines in the level of activity and in real wages and a rise in real interest rates. However, in spite of opposition, governments make bold efforts to overcome high inflation and should be strongly supported. They are motivated by a number of considerations.

First, comparisons are usually made between the stabilization period and previous periods. This methodology is inappropriate. The correct comparison would be one based on an estimation of what might have happened had stabilization not been attempted. Considering the destructive effect of hyperinflation on the level of activity, real wages, and investment inflation in Argentina, Bolivia, Nicaragua, and Peru, there is no need for lengthy argument.

Second, the high inflation rates experienced by Latin American countries have decreased the efficiency of the price system in allocating resources because the rise in the variability of relative prices makes them less reliable as a source of information and a greater source of risk. In turn, the loss of nominality makes past prices irrelevant for establishing contrasts, and a vital factor in domestic competition is lost. This clouding of the data caused by inflation has created quasi-monopolistic factors in markets that, by their nature, should be highly competitive.

Third, mega-inflation destroys the various functions of the local currency (unit of account, store of value, and transaction facility), resulting, at best, in its replacement by a foreign currency for which the economy must surrender resources (without remuneration) and, at worst, in episodes of hyperinflation that block transactions (as occurred in Argentina when sales were suspended). The severe demonetization causes a loss of resources and creates hardships: unending lines at banks and time and effort wasted in arbitration, re-marking prices, and preparing budgets.

Fourth, the sharp regressiveness of the inflation tax is noteworthy. There is no need to stress the inequity of access to anti-inflationary coverage or the disproportionate impact of inflation on monetary reserves for transactions, which make up a greater portion of the net worth of the poorest social sectors compared with other social sectors. The inequity of the inflationary tax also has a negative effect on the social climate and discourages productive efforts.

Fifth, inflation decreases the effectiveness of the tax system, particularly of those taxes that are more distinctly progressive, thus worsening the situation described above.

Sixth, the most affected markets are those having to do with growth, such as the investment, capital, and financing markets. Owing to price volatility, the breakdown of financial intermediation, and the loss of relevance of accounting statements and economic information, growth possibilities dry up. This outcome increases discouragement and fosters pessimism.

Finally, using inflation as a tax not established by law gives a sense of illegitimacy to all government activities. Ultimately, the authorities are induced to confront the upsurge of inflation by launching stabilization programs, in spite of all the difficulties and institutional reluctance.

Stabilization Program Requirements

The closing of the fiscal gap is the first component of any stabilization program. For the closing of the fiscal gap to be effective, it must be permanent; if temporary measures are used, they will not generate the credibility required and will be an obstacle to the forces cooperating to build the stabilization pyramid (rapid monetization, a decline in interest rates, and greater financing that will make the economic recovery possible). Because stabilization plans in Latin America used fiscal measures that were temporary, a number of the stabilization attempts were short-lived, which, to a large extent, explained their failure in spite of the fact that they were initially conceived with great technical virtuosity (for example, Argentina's Plan Austral). Generally, the fiscal gap to be closed is of a recurrent nature and must be addressed with resources that are similarly recurrent.

Second, nominality must be re-created; that is, a nominal magnitude must be set that is invariable whatever the trends in the other economic variables. In other words, the other variables should not cause the nominal magnitude to change. The nominal anchor can take various forms. Generally, there is a tendency to choose a variable that is clearly under the control of the monetary authorities, for example, the money supply and the exchange rate. The chosen variable and the rate at which it is altered must be essentially sustainable. Sustainability is determined to a large extent by the fiscal position and compatibility with other nominal policies. For example, setting an anchor that implies excessive real interest rates would be far from suitable.

In most stabilization processes, the preference has generally been for a fixed exchange rate because the lengthy inflation process and the high level of currency substitution make it difficult to use a monetary target as a primary gauge. Monetization can give rise to a very strong real appreciation, with serious consequences for competing sectors because of the high interest rates implied. A fixed exchange rate makes it possible for economic agents to establish internally the desired level of the local currency and, thus, to avoid excessive flexibility in general price levels, with the difficulty that this implies for wages and nominal government expenditure.

It is extremely important to note that levels fixed for other nominal variables, as well as their rate of change, must be compatible with the chosen anchor. Two numbers are vital: total government expenditure and the nominal wage. It is difficult to believe that the fixing of the anchor is sustainable when nominal changes in these variables are well above international inflation and the increase in productivity (generally, failure has been related to this problem). Careful attention should also be paid to the initial level because financing through high taxation of (sunk) investment is not enough. There must be profits and investment possibilities with the rates of taxation established.

A point that is often underestimated is that the stabilizing adjustment process is usually accompanied by a need to correct any strong external disequilibrium caused by an excess of absorption. The most contractionary phase of adjustment is generally due to this problem. Inflation, especially mega-inflation and hyperinflation, can destroy economic activity. Its reduction should therefore result in economic recovery (this was very obvious in Argentina).

According to the recent literature, stabilization processes are usually accompanied, in their initial phases, by a fall in real wages and a rise in the real interest rate. With respect to the former, a distinction must be made between purchasing power and real wages in an environment of mega-inflation, since at such inflation rates, the deterioration that occurs between the time wages are earned and the point at which they are actually received is substantial. Consequently, the normal decline resulting from a fall in wages because of a slowdown in the growth of nominal expenditure compared with the prices implicit in aggregate supply must be adjusted with the latter statistical component.

It is noteworthy that the interest rate effect will be all the more significant when credibility is low. Here, the distinction between ex post and ex ante is highly relevant. A slowdown in inflation generally occurs sooner than expected, thereby causing such high rates. This factor is very important if domestic debt is high. One of the reasons for the relatively smaller adjustment in Argentina is that the hyperinflationary process practically eliminated domestic debt. This outcome influenced the Plan Austral, Primavera, and President Carlos Menem's first stabilization attempt, and, in turn, the Chilean and Mexican plans.

Designing the Plan

Stabilization plans are generally constructed on the basis of policies formulated to control aggregate demand. In this way, the rate of growth of nominal expenditure is reduced in an attempt to bring it closer to the rate of growth of real output.

Supply and Demand Policies

To a large extent, emphasis is placed on demand policies because it is easier to quantify them and to set targets and controls for them. They are more readily perceived by the public, the specialized press, and the international agencies that normally support the policies. Commitments are relatively simple to establish when they involve quantifiable targets, and this is indispensable when conditionality motivates domestic and external agents, such as when debt must be restructured at the same time.

However, supply policies have recently begun to acquire more importance. Naturally, no one thinks that inflation at three digits or more can be corrected with increased production. Supply policies are popular for other reasons. The persistence of high inflation and poor economic organization were generating a profound distortion and an inflexibility that, if not removed, could substantially increase the cost of stabilization. Supply polices include the following:

(1) Flexibility of factor mobility and prices. To adapt to the new demand structure, flexibility is essential in matters of employment (contracting, maintenance, functional versatility, and terms of labor contracts), availability of capital, and rights to capital. The delays caused by commercial (company) and bankruptcy laws that prevent the rapid restructuring of production are often underestimated.

(2) Elimination of distortions. The barely competitive and strongly sub-sidized behavior of a closed and highly inflationary economy implies that there is less potential for activity and adaptation, both of which are en-hanced by stability. If this effect is not corrected, the capacity to adapt to the new demand structure is minimal, and the underutilization of re-sources that the slowdown in nominal expenditure growth suggests is likely to be exaggerated.

(3) Protection. One of the mechanisms most often used to obtain flexi-bility, competition, and financial resources is to transfer to the state re-sources that benefited some sectors in the private area through excessive protection. The reduction in protection enables the economy to change the production structure, through a low and standard tariff, to one that is more adaptable to domestic and external demand. This makes it possible to reallocate resources rapidly when the level of domestic absorption changes. In the small economies of the region, this reform may well be the most complementary to the stabilization process. Even in the larger economies, it contributes greatly to the design and control of stabilization programs by imposing considerable self-discipline. It should be remem-bered that, following many years of disorder and inflation, no one knows what relative prices are appropriate.

(4) Inertia and deindexation. In the literature, this is perhaps one of the most analyzed supply policy components. Correcting the structure of contracts is unavoidable and is now generally accepted. Breaking with the past is an absolute must if stabilization is to be successful. Moreover, the existence of constitutional requirements for backward indexation perhaps explains why Uruguay is not successful in reducing its inflation rate to international levels, in spite of its reasonable fiscal and monetary situation.

(5) Incomes policies. These are generally placed under the same head-ing as inertia although some think they are a different matter. Incomes policies involve coordinating trends in wages and in controlled or regu-lated prices from the start of stabilization. There is always an incomes pol-icy, whether it is explicit or implicit. The key is to acknowledge that such a policy seeks to avoid repeated attempts to achieve macroeconomic equilibrium with a high cost in terms of economic downturn. It cannot be claimed that these policies are effective at income distribution. In the final analysis, this objective falls in the domain of fiscal policy. The com-patibility of an incomes policy with an exchange policy is perhaps the major test of the viability of the stabilizing adjustment.

(6) Reorganization. A critical feature of recent stabilization programs in Latin America has been a dynamic reorganization of the institutional and administrative structures. Privatization, with three important elements, must be understood in this context of new regulation: (a) less manipula-tion of prices and subsidies in the future and, therefore, a lower deficit;

(b) the expectation that there will be a set of actors who will feel keenly committed to stability and its success; and (c) the possibility of using resources from sales to bridge the fiscal gap in the short term or to settle the external and internal debt, for example, in Argentina.

An essential aspect of stabilization is credibility, which is difficult to define and quantify. Credibility is not easily gained, and, like a reputation, can be lost in a moment. It is well known that both individuals and communities find attempts at stabilization hard to believe, particularly following various failures in that area. Evidence shows that credibility is based on the consistency and internal logic of the program; the character, reputation, and cohesion of the technical team appointed; and political support that is expressed both in word and in deed.

These characteristics can be demonstrated by consistency between announcements and actual practice and the viability of measures suggested at the technical level in terms of instrumental feasibility and political support. Initially, the reorganization program will be tested and challenged. There should be no doubt about its irreversibility. Another criterion for credibility is the transparency of data. When in doubt, those with the most liquid funds are naturally extremely fearful and expect failure. A lack of transparency is the enemy of success in stabilization. Any effort that provides as much information as possible, with the widest coverage possible, will enhance credibility.

A Few Basic Requirements

It has already been pointed out above that when inflationary crisis lasts for many years, it is difficult to have a notion of what is normal. Generally, a workable solution to such a crisis is to think of the program targets expressed in foreign currency. First, this provides a simple mechanism to correct for inflation that makes it possible to standardize data for different periods; second, it reflects a recognition of the role of government expenditure as an input in the productive process and the viability that this expenditure must have in an open economy (financing cannot be provided for an unlimited level of government expenditure).

Once expenditure and revenue have been calculated at the appropriate rate of exchange, the net revenue from the elimination of subsidies and quantitative trade restrictions, the generalization of the tax bases, and the equalization of rates should be incorporated. This exercise should make it possible to close the fiscal gap. If this is not possible, a different ratio of wages to the exchange rate should be used.

Once the fiscal gap has been closed (ratio of wages to exchange rate and taxes), the nominal problem, that is, the ratio of base money to external reserves, should be addressed. Generally, a low initial ratio (high reserve levels) at the beginning averts the need for a traumatic initial jump in taxes. The initial high inflation tax generally makes it possible to enjoy a lower interest rate and less vulnerability to capital flows. Even though building up greater reserves by means of a significant fiscal effort eases the initial trauma of the correction, it leads to continued uncertainty and high domestic interest rates that conspire against closing the fiscal gap if there is domestic debt and against improving the level of activity and tax collection if the debt is marginal. The initial trauma can be considerable if, in addition, the real adjustment required to close the fiscal deficit is significant. At any rate, these principles will depend on each country's actual situation and previous monetary history.

Following the initial effort and once the lack of transparency created by inflation has been corrected, a highly complex development in stabilization experiences is a particularly disagreeable reality that, in some cases, can be clearly perceived. For example, the low real wages that are part and parcel of undercapitalized, inefficient economies, the lack of competitiveness of domestic activity, and the problems of extreme poverty become highly visible and generate needs that are generally incompatible with macroeconomic discipline. In this perspective, regional and social disequilibria must be evaluated and a program developed to deal with them, so as to avoid creating conflict between the stabilization effort and social needs.

Another factor, which is positive but may create new problems that will be discussed in detail later, must be included in any contingency plan. This factor is the return of capital, which exerts very delicate pressure on relative prices. In this sense, tight fiscal policy and careful control of domestic credit expansion are vital.

Institutional Difficulties

The requirements described above generally relate to an economy with a simplified, timeless institutional structure. In practice, institutional setup and history make the design of stabilization programs much more complex. Three aspects of this problem will be discussed.

(1) Countries with a federal system. In federal countries, there are generally three levels of government (federal, provincial, and local). Among these levels of government, some transfers are related to tax collection, and disequilibria at the lower levels of government have repercussions at the federal level and for the monetary authority. In principle, a well-designed federal organization gives macroeconomic responsibility to the central government, so that transfers to state and local governments and their debt policies are not linked to the economic cycle. In practice, a large part of the adjustment to be carried out involves precisely this task. If transfers are linked to tax collection and if the behavior of tax bases is

also cyclical, it is highly likely that a large portion of the effort to increase revenue will be diluted in this filtering process.

This type of difficulty could create the temptation to design faulty instruments with the objective of avoiding the problem of federalism. To some extent, correcting this malfunction is vital for the orderly management of the macroeconomic question. In particular, expenditure decisions should be decentralized as much as possible, so as to implement the principle of fiscal responsibility to the maximum. (Each marginal expenditure decided upon must be financed by the local community receiving it.) This would make it possible to establish a relationship between the availability of tax resources and the level of spending.

(2) Social security. In the midst of the inflationary crisis, one of the sectors in which expenditure must be adjusted is the social security system, where payment arrears, retirement postponements, and actuarial nonviability accumulate. Once prices have been stabilized, this problem rises brutally to the surface, and, because of the magnitude of the problem, fiscal balance can become impossible to maintain. Consider, for example, that in Uruguay the system's actuarial disequilibrium was calculated at 200 percent of GDP (in some European countries it is in excess of this figure). The dimension of this problem goes beyond the normal problem of government indebtedness.

A program to deal with social security is crucial, above all because social security diminishes the aggregate savings that are vital for the modernization of the economy and for solving employment problems. The potential solution should avoid high rates of taxation on those individuals who will receive no return on these services and should maintain the definition of actuarially viable rights. It is vital to restore the legal rights of all participants in the social security system, but to accept the budgetary restrictions (between crisis periods) if an economic recovery is to be achieved and a loss of confidence in the stabilization plan is to be avoided. In particular, institutional arrangements should not accommodate the use of implicit debt.

(3) External debt overhang. The existence of government debt that is disproportionate to output and exports, with a market value well below its face value and a significant accumulation of arrears or constant renegotiations, can become a major obstacle to the design of a program to achieve stabilization and revive investment. In practice, the interest rate implicit in such government debt renders investment nonviable. Stabilization plans have therefore generally been accompanied by a major external debt-restructuring program, which both clears the fiscal horizon and reveals the implicit cost of investment. External debt arrangements must be complete and the domestic effort consolidated.

The cooperation of multilateral agencies and of official agencies in industrial countries is generally required for a solution to be found, implying a program of conditional assistance that will provide an additional guarantee for capital flows. This is vital to the credibility of the program and to the recovery of the credit rating required to finance investment and expand trade.

A Few Recent Problems

The above sections provide a broad overview of stabilization programs that reflects, to a large extent, the experience of the 1980s and early 1990s. It is also useful to highlight a few recent problems that individual countries have experienced with their stabilization programs, which they developed in specific external circumstances. These experiences will greatly influence future developments in the region.

(1) Currency overvaluation. Considerable currency overvaluation has been a common feature in Latin American countries and stabilization programs and will be referred to in the examination of individual experiences. According to local authorities, currency overvaluation represents the strong recovery of confidence, owing to the aptness and pertinence of the plans used. An alternative explanation is that worldwide circumstances and the over-indebtedness of the industrial economies have produced a disinclination on the part of solvent individuals to borrow, which in turn has generated an abundance of available resources that have caused the collapse of interest rates worldwide. This not only dramatically facilitated the Latin American adjustment (one would have to see how many Brady Plans could have been possible at the interest rates prevailing in the 1980s), but also made investment in the paper issued by many countries extremely attractive.

This exceptional process, which was lucidly described by Calvo, Leiderman, and Reinhart,[1] generated high capital inflows that, in countries with strong protectionist policies and limited capacity to absorb such flows, resulted simultaneously in considerable overvaluation and slow growth in the current account deficit. If there were no substantial protectionist structure, the problem of capital inflows would be less relevant, first, because the exchange lag experienced would not exist, and, second, because the level of domestic activity would not depend exclusively on domestic absorption. Goods produced by local producers could be exported without difficulty to the rest of the world, which the protectionist structure in some of these countries does not permit.

There is speculation on the direct impact the reduction of capital flows and the raising of interest rates will have on public sector expenditure.

---

[1]See Guillermo Calvo, Leonardo Leiderman, and Carmen Reinhart, "The Capital Inflows Problem: Concepts and Issues," IMF Working Paper 93/10 (Washington: International Monetary Fund, 1993).

However, the major problem will be the considerable restructuring of aggregate demand, and its consequences (for government revenue) will be the major difficulty. It must be borne in mind that domestic tax collection is generally structured on the basis of domestic absorption, and industrial activity encounters serious difficulties in reorienting its production in world markets.

(2) Low aggregate savings. Stabilization programs have been accompanied by changes in the composition of external savings flows and a structural weakening of domestic savings. Various hypotheses can be tested to explain what occurred. First, the falling inflation tax, which had mainly affected the low-income sectors and those with the greatest propensity for consumption, was replaced by taxes that affected the population's capacity to save, which had an impact on the overall savings ratio (taxation of households was transferred to the enterprises).

The second, temporary feature of hyperinflation was that consumption was massively postponed in favor of increasing private claims against the rest of the world. When the return to normalcy was felt, these emergency provisions began to decline; excessive consumption is probably a temporary aspect of the process. One result of this effect is that a significant portion of external government debt was owned by citizens of the countries in default for whom the recovery then produced a windfall, owing to a revaluation of their securities.

The third possible explanation is that there was a fall in the relative price of capital goods, while real volume did not decline. This can be appreciated from comparisons of capital goods at current prices and at constant prices and from the substantial rise in the cost of services compared with goods (services are very labor intensive).

The fourth factor, also applicable to a number of cases, is the strong rise in social security transfers that, by their nature, lead to a major increase in the propensity for aggregate consumption. In Argentina, this was aggravated by the settlement of a significant amount of payment arrears financed through the sale of government capital goods.

(3) Financial problem. The strong expansion of financial markets that accompanied the stabilization programs and a significant growth in private indebtedness at extraordinarily high interest rates are cause for concern in the future. It is clear that the share of private debt in GDP is minimal and that previous experiences have led economic agents to be extremely cautious. Reforms of the financial system's regulatory framework and the experience of international banking and capital markets has led to more prudent risk assessment than in the recent past.

However, given the rate of growth of financing, and especially its high cost, a note of warning is warranted. The possibility of distress borrowing by official banks or an inadequate level of provisioning in private banks is a matter that should receive policymakers' most careful attention. To some extent, assiduous implementation of the Basle recommendations may alleviate this problem. One unavoidable question is why economic agents assumed debt at exceptionally high rates. One reason may have been the lack of credibility of the ongoing program; another, the high profits generated in the consumption boom that came with stabilization; and, finally and most important, that in spite of their high cost, these rates reveal a dramatic decline in the cost of capital compared with the cost borne during periods of mega-inflation and capital flight.

Whatever the case, the emergence of rating agencies, their rating of risk, an unprecedented research effort, and greater attention to regulation should prevent a recurrence of the disregard for principles seen in the 1980s, which was at the bottom of the failure of stabilization plans in the financial sectors.

Comparative Experiences

Argentina

For Argentina, it is important to provide the historical background because most adults have no memory of a period of prolonged stability. Demonetization had reached extremely low levels in 1988–90, and currency substitution had made it normal for the most elementary transactions to be performed in foreign currency. The losses incurred by economic agents operating in pesos had reached magnitudes for which it is difficult to find comparable figures in other countries.

It was in this context that the Argentine authorities launched the convertibility plan in March 1991, which involved essentially fixing the exchange rate by law (the capacity to devalue by surprise was thus lost), and establishing full currency backing (convertibility into foreign currencies and into bonds in foreign currencies valued at market prices). Thus, funds could be provided neither to the nonfinancial public sector nor to the banking system, which had, in the past, received enormous transfers from the Central Bank of Argentina.

In practice, convertibility meant abandoning two influential instruments of the past: the inflation tax and exchange policy flexibility. This move implied, for the future, fiscal equilibrium or noninflationary financing of the disequilibrium—which amounts to almost the same thing (over time, a difference could emerge between the two)—as well as an absence of the massive rediscounts that were used intensively to ease financial crises in the past. With respect to flexibility, it became mandatory, in the face of any external shock, for domestic prices and wages to be adjusted in the manner of the gold standard. The crucial point was that the monetary anchor determined the fiscal side and that the political authority was to make the necessary adjustments to implement convertibility.

This change was possible because, among other reasons, the crisis had become so acute that it was possible to remove most institutional restrictions and overcome the antireform coalitions of the past. Stabilization was accompanied by a dramatic economic restructuring that affected the country's integration into the world economy, government ownership, financing, and all aspects of economic organization. Briefly, the convertibility plan comprised the following main reforms and restructuring measures:

(1) The federal issue. Unlike past stabilization programs, the fiscal deficit was now to be eliminated using traditional taxes (by widening the base, removing exemptions, and applying the withholding procedure generally), with an emphasis on reducing evasion and improving tax administration.

The difficulty of this strategy was that the national treasury received only 42 percent of the increased collections, while the rest went to the provinces under the revenue-sharing mechanism, and at the same time expenditure increased. This explains why past stabilization plans used export taxes and surcharges on government fees, which cannot be legally transferred to the provinces. The mechanism used to solve this problem was to transfer federal spending obligations, through subsequent laws, to the provinces and to allocate resources from the revenue-sharing fund to finance the social security system. This procedure made it possible to overcome a serious institutional limitation. Its implementation reveals, in addition to exceptional transparency, enormous political power (the government party controlled two-thirds of the senate).

(2) Outstanding debt. Three elements deserve special attention.

• External payments. Argentina had, for all intents and purposes, been in arrears with its external payments since 1982 and ceased payments totally to private banks in April 1988, although it began to make small payments (a fraction of interest) in June 1990. Considerable external payments arrears—more than $8 billion—accumulated. This problem was resolved within the framework of the Brady Plan and involved the cooperation of the multilateral agencies, the Paris Club, and Japanese financial institutions. Agreement was reached after considerable control of the inflationary and fiscal situation had been achieved and after IMF support had been received under an extended Fund facility arrangement. Success in this area consolidated and strengthened favorable expectations. In particular, it facilitated a clear definition of the sacrifice to be made by the country in the future and how best to take advantage of any additional effort that might be made.

• Domestic debt. In the hyperinflationary process, the first item that ceased to be paid was Argentina's entire debt to suppliers, along with tax subsidies and tax refunds on exports. This debt was consolidated in March 1991 and refinanced over 16 years in the form of consolidation bonds that paid no interest or debt service for a long period (grace period). Another portion of the debt was refinanced with banks, also for a medium term. To a large extent, this approach worked like forced financing that placed extreme restrictions on expenditure, at least until the debt became liquid (that is, paper was issued). In the Argentine fiscal accounts, many of these outlays are not included in the yearly expenditure flows. In other words, changes in the debt are not taken into consideration in deficit measurements (this being especially significant for social security).

• Social security. The program had three types of problems to deal with. First, social security benefits paid out were lower than established by law, causing an accumulation of debts and legal claims. The debts calculated under this heading reached some $7 billion in March 1991. Second, new debts were falling due because of the system's actuarial imbalance; this situation worsened from year to year. The first and second issues were resolved with two debt consolidations, under which retired persons were paid in ten-year bonds resolved with six years of grace, covering the debt accumulated as of March 1991 and at a fraction of revenue-shared collections. In addition, the system was capitalized with a portion of government shares from the sale of public enterprises and part of the tax on profits, which should make it possible to settle pending lawsuits. Third, a social security reform provided for the actuarial debt to be eliminated upon achievement of steady state, making it possible to meet social security commitments without the need for exorbitant payroll contributions.

Among the crucial reforms carried out by the Argentine government were normalization of the tax situation, a change in the budgetary structure, social security reform, the settlement of domestic and external debt, the creation of a new regulatory framework, and privatization.

A surprising feature in Argentina's stabilization effort, compared with that of other countries, is the low public sector primary surplus. This is due, above all, to the fact that the lengthy inflationary and hyperinflationary experience practically eliminated domestic indebtedness. In addition, the external debt is not significant in GDP terms, although it is more so in relation to exports. This low primary surplus was not, in any case, neutral. To a large extent, it explains the substantial overvaluation of the local currency. If the settlement of the social security debt is included as an expenditure, there is no primary surplus. This, in turn, explains the persistence of high spreads on debt in international securities although net capital inflows exceeded exports for more than two consecutive years. The tasks that remain to be accomplished in terms of productive restructuring and opening up the economy are still considerable, and it is perhaps in these areas that the weakest point of the plan is found.

The quantitative data with respect to both Argentina's experience and that of other countries are provided in the appendix tables to illustrate some of the comments made.

Chile

Chile figured for a very long time among the high-inflation countries of Latin America. Indeed, on the basis of Chile's experience, the first discussions were held in that country between monetarists and structuralists. Chile's history of high inflation, with hyperinflationary characteristics, erupted during the government of Salvador Allende, when the deficit finally reached almost 30 percent of GDP, and the disequilibria generated a supply crisis throughout the country.

The authorities addressed this runaway situation in 1974–75, during the first period of military government, with an orthodox shock treatment. Although their approach made it possible to restore the flow of goods and finance the external sector, it did not succeed in substantially reducing the domestic inflation rate. The reason given in the literature is the authorities' persistence in applying a system of indexation and, especially, the need to rebuild the state's net wealth, which was adversely affected early in the decade. The persistently high rates of inflation and the consolidation of macroeconomic trends (balance of payments, fiscal control, and level of activity) gave rise to the second stabilization effort, launched in 1978, with a system involving prior announcement of the exchange rate. Although this plan succeeded in slowing down the inflation rate, this result was achieved at the cost of an exchange rate appreciation and a strong deficit on the current account, which finally collapsed in 1982.

Following a traumatic adjustment process in 1983 and 1984, by 1985 there was consolidation of a stabilization effort toward the end of the decade that was outstanding in the Latin American context. Its achievements included not only the decline in the inflation rate, but also the rapid recovery of investment, maintenance of the real parity of the exchange rate, and a robust growth in exports. The trend is toward even more success, in that the country has survived two difficult political transitions, and the economy remains solid after more than eight years of growth.

The crucial factor behind this result is firm fiscal discipline, which made it possible to apply a large portion of the growth toward investment and exports, and to build up massive savings from the improved terms of trade in the late 1980s.

In general, the maintenance of public expenditure and real wages in real terms made it possible for the economic expansion to ease the burden on the private sector by way of fewer taxes, higher levels of employment, and more scope for investment financing, which enjoyed extremely low interest rates compared with other Latin American countries.

A persistent weakness is that it has not been possible to bring Chile's inflation rate down to international levels. This is probably related to the very broad application of the indexation process to the goods and capital markets. Another cause has been the deficit maintained by the monetary authorities, which has been amplified by sterilization operations and by the lack of recovery of the banking portfolios acquired during the crisis of 1982–83.

One result not often mentioned is that the Chilean fiscal situation is healthier than comparative analysis shows, because there is no actuarial accumulation of debt in its social security system, given that estimates for the future are linked to the savings accumulated by citizens in pension funds and not by unrecorded debt in the pay-as-you-go system.

As in the above cases, the quantitative data presented in the appendix tables attempt to illustrate the points made.

Mexico

Unlike Argentina, Mexico had the experience of a lengthy stabilization process, consolidated in the early 1950s and very firmly maintained up to the early 1970s, at which time, and at very high economic and social costs, it began to diverge from a course that had been successful in a number of respects. During this process, the growth rate and monetary stability were very striking, making it possible for the country to make significant progress in comparison with the Argentine experience.

The break with the policy of budgetary equilibrium in the early 1970s finally led downhill to the devaluation of 1976 and the beginning of an inflationary process that would be further heightened by the high level of indebtedness and the fiscal deficit incurred in the late 1970s and early 1980s. These events led to a complete loss of control in 1981–82, which was manifested in major devaluations and the cessation of payments as of August 1982. In December 1982, Mexico launched a program to correct the disequilibrium, involving a lengthy process to clean up the fiscal imbalances. The steps included the restoration of the tax base and a reduction in the level of spending, which led to a strong reconstitution of the primary surplus. The fiscal rehabilitation was made more difficult by various shocks, such as the earthquake of 1985 and the dramatic decline in petroleum prices in 1986.

The lengthy fiscal readjustment ended with the economic solidarity pact concluded in December 1987. The pact involved a speedy stabilization process combining tough, orthodox adjustment with corresponding unorthodox measures in the area of wage and price policies, and an extensive opening up of the economy (a maximum tariff of 20 percent).

Mexico's structural reform has been impressive. It has included restructuring the tax system, opening up the economy, privatizing public enterprises, and renegotiating the external debt within the framework of the Brady Plan, resulting in write-offs and rescheduling.

The tax reform consisted in broadening the application of taxes, with a reduction in the marginal income tax rate to 35 percent. An assets tax was introduced as a payment against income tax liability. However, the key of the reform was tax administration, where, for the first time, a system of intense auditing was introduced, and criminal action was taken against tax evaders. (Between 1929 and 1988, there were only two criminal indictments for tax evasion, whereas between 1989 and 1991, there were more than two hundred sentencings, all of them involving imprisonment.) A basic element of the reform was a special tax scheme for capital repatriation (approximately $10 billion was repatriated under this system).

This reform was vital to consolidation of the stabilization program in that it made it possible for the Mexican authorities to redeem domestic debt, decrease transfers, and reduce hidden subsidies, so as to strengthen the fiscal position.

The features of the Mexican experience that differ from those of the Argentine experience are the persistence of a significant inflation rate; the exceptional level of the primary surplus; and a smaller rate of economic growth, probably owing to a sharp deterioration in the terms of trade and high domestic interest rates. The persistence of inflation and high interest rates is linked to the type of foreign exchange system adopted, which implies a rate of devaluation and a band of fluctuation that require higher interest rates and involve a higher inflation tax. This system provides a degree of flexibility that the Argentine system lacks.

As in the case of Argentina, the appendix tables presented for Mexico provide an overview and serve as a reference for the arguments advanced above.

Uruguay

Uruguay is an interesting case in that it has been unsuccessful in reducing the inflation rate to figures that can be considered normal, in spite of an extraordinary fiscal effort that has made it possible to reduce the deficit to insignificant levels and to accumulate a substantial primary surplus. This point is particularly sensitive because of the profound dollarization that this economy has been undergoing, following decades of high inflation. Currency substitution in such cases maximizes the cost of monetization of the fiscal deficit. A logical question is why this situation has persisted. Perhaps the dominant factor is the formalization of constitutional indexation clauses. These adjust social security payments with a lag, thereby producing a sort of reverse Tanzi effect. According to this effect, a reduction in the inflation rate produces a rise in the level of government spending, which proves impossible to finance for a country that already has relatively high levels of government spending compared with per capita output.

The coexistence of these two numeraires, one fixed by the monetary authority and the other resulting from indexation, makes durable stabilization impossible without significant structural reform. To understand the problem fully, it is important to note that expenditure on social security in Uruguay is close to 17 percent of GDP, and the rate of inflation is nearly 50 percent. A two-and-a-half-month lag implies a dramatic increase in expenditure even if inflation levels off. This is even more significant if the disequilibrium between commitments and the amounts to be collected largely exceeds GDP as a result of the actuarial debt implicit in the system.

In addition to the relevance of inflation for the short-term fiscal balance, the collection of the inflation tax is making it necessary to redeem net government debt in a country that accumulates it implicitly in its social security system. To some extent, today's inflation prevents the inflation of tomorrow.

Appendix Tables

Argentina

Table 2.1. Public Sector Accounts
(In percent of GDP)

Account	1985	1986	1987	1988	1989	1990	1991	1992	1993
I Primary surplus without capital revenue	1.42	1.12	−0.82	−0.99	0.55	0.97	0.51	1.38	1.38
II Capital revenue	0.15	0.07	0.15	0.14	0.24	0.45	1.21	0.79	0.79
III Primary surplus of the nonfinancial public sector	1.57	1.19	−0.67	−0.85	0.79	1.42	1.72	2.17	2.17
IV Nonfinancial public sector interest	4.40	3.20	3.49	3.82	12.30	3.37	2.65	1.49	0.97
V Overall balance NFPS (III − IV)	−2.84	−2.01	−4.15	−4.66	−11.51	−1.95	−0.93	0.68	1.20
VI Central bank quasi-fiscal operations	−2.09	−1.19	−0.67	−0.49	−4.66	−10.75	−0.36	−0.14	0.10
VII Overall balance of combined public sector	−4.93	−3.20	−4.82	−5.16	−16.16	−2.69	−1.29	0.55	1.30
VIII Overall balance without capital revenue	−5.08	−3.27	−4.97	−5.30	−16.40	−3.14	−2.50	−0.24	0.51

Source: Argentina, Secretaría de Ingresos Públicos.
Note: Table 2.1 describes the situation of the nonfinancial public sector (NFPS). Only toward 1993 did the primary surplus net of capital resource make it possible to deal with interest on the debt.

Table 2.2. Summary of Public Sector Operations

(In percent of GDP)

Indicator	1988	1989	1990	1991	1992
General government current revenue	12.8	12.9	12.9	15.4	16.9
National administration taxes	8.2	8.6	8.4	10.0	11.7
Social security contributions	3.0	2.6	3.5	4.3	4.3
Nontax revenues	1.7	1.7	1.0	1.2	0.9
Expenditure (excluding interest payments)	14.3	14.4	12.5	15.3	15.8
National administration wages	2.4	2.6	2.2	2.7	2.5
Other goods and services	1.0	0.9	0.7	1.0	1.1
Pensions	3.7	3.6	4.0	5.0	5.6
National administration	0.4	0.5	0.3	0.4	0.6
Social security	3.3	3.1	3.7	4.6	5.0
Transfers to provinces	4.3	4.5	3.7	5.1	5.6
Other transfers	0.6	0.7	0.6	0.4	0.2
Capital expenditure	2.3	2.1	1.5	1.1	0.8
Operating surplus of the nonfinancial public enterprises	0.8	0.8	0.9	0.3	0.2
Revenue	6.9	7.2	6.7	5.0	4.0
Expenditure	6.1	6.4	5.8	4.7	3.8
Capital revenue	—	0.4	0.4	1.2	0.8
Primary balance of nonfinancial public sector	−0.6	−0.3	1.6	1.8	2.2
Nonfinancial public sector interest	1.9	2.5	3.3	2.6	1.5
Nonfinancial public sector overall balance	−2.5	−2.8	−1.7	−0.9	0.6
Central bank quasi-fiscal operations	−0.5	−4.5	−0.7	−0.4	−0.1
Overall balance of the combined public sector	−3.0	−7.3	−2.4	−1.3	0.5

Note: Table 2.2 deals with the same items as Table 2.1, with a few methodological differences (interest is recorded on a different basis). It takes account of the revival of collections and the growth in social security expenditure and in transfers to the provinces. Another notable feature is the decline in the share of public enterprises and the fall in public investment as a result of privatization. The other significant consequence is the decline in the Central Bank's deficit; owing to lower net indebtedness, the primary balance is very low, particularly if an adjustment is made for capital inflows.

Table 2.3. National Tax Revenue

(In percent of GDP)

Tax	1983	1984	1985	1986	1987	1988	1989	1990	1991	1992
Overall taxation	23.9	23.5	23.8	18.3	17.9	18.0	24.2	18.6	16.3	18.3
Regular taxes	12.4	12.3	16.7	17.0	16.4	14.4	15.1	14.3	15.9	18.1
Tax on income and assets	1.4	0.9	1.4	1.6	1.9	1.8	2.3	1.2	1.2	1.4
Value-added tax	2.3	1.9	2.4	2.5	2.4	1.8	1.6	2.3	3.4	5.8
Turnover tax, other excises	3.3	3.8	4.4	4.6	4.3	4.2	3.7	3.6	4.0	3.4
Social security	3.9	4.3	6.1	6.4	6.3	5.3	4.7	5.7	6.3	6.7
Tariffs	1.5	1.4	2.4	1.9	1.6	1.2	2.8	1.5	0.9	0.8
Inflationary tax and seigniorage	11.5	11.2	7.1	1.3	1.4	3.6	9.1	4.3	0.4	0.2

Source: Argentina, Secretaría de Ingresos Públicos.

Note: Since the convertibility law, the interest earned on foreign exchange reserves is included in seigniorage. Table 2.3 shows a series of actual taxes established by law and what might be called the "tax on issues" (inflation tax and seigniorage). The most noteworthy aspect is the strong expansion of the VAT and the significant decline in the tax on external trade and on issues. The tax on issues, especially, should be compared in the Plan Austral and in the convertibility plan.

Table 2.4. Liquidity Coefficient

(In percent)

Year	M1/GDP	M2/GDP
1985	2.8	9.4
1986	3.7	11.6
1987	3.2	11.7
1988	2.2	10.6
1989	2.2	8.5
1990	1.8	4.0
1991	2.4	4.6
1992	3.4	6.1
1993	4.2	8.2

Source: United Nations, Economic Commission for Latin America and the Caribbean.

Note: Table 2.4 provides monetization indicators, showing the considerable destruction of the local financial system and the sharp decline in velocity that occurred with stabilization.

Table 2.5. Annual Rate of Inflation
(CPI)

Year	CPI General Level
1975	335.0
1976	347.5
1977	160.4
1978	169.8
1979	139.7
1980	87.6
1981	131.3
1982	209.7
1983	433.7
1984	688.0
1985	385.4
1986	81.9
1987	174.8
1988	387.7
1989	4,923.6
1990	1,343.9
1991	84.0
1992	17.8
1993	7.5

Note: Table 2.5 shows consumer inflation rates. In only 2 years of the first 15 years for which records were kept was the inflation rate lower than 100 percent, and then only slightly so.

Table 2.6. National Income, Saving, and Investment[1]

(In percent of GDP; relative price 1986)

Year	GDP	Terms of Trade Effect	Factor Payment[1]	Gross National Income	Consumption	National Saving	External Saving	Nonfactor Payment Current Account	Gross Domestic Investment
1980	100.0	2.3	–1.5	100.8	78.3	22.5	4.1	–4.9	26.6
1981	100.0	3.1	–3.7	99.4	80.2	19.2	4.4	–3.8	23.6
1982	100.0	1.2	–5.2	96.0	78.1	17.9	2.5	1.5	20.4
1983	100.0	1.4	–6.1	95.3	78.4	16.9	2.6	2.1	19.5
1984	100.0	2.2	–6.4	95.8	79.9	15.9	2.6	1.6	18.5
1985	100.0	1.3	–6.2	95.1	79.8	15.2	1.1	3.9	16.3
1986	100.0	0.0	–4.6	95.4	80.7	14.7	2.7	1.8	17.5
1987	100.0	–0.3	–4.2	95.5	79.7	15.8	3.8	0.7	19.5
1988	100.0	0.7	–4.7	96.0	77.5	18.5	1.1	3.0	19.5
1989	100.0	1.3	–6.2	95.1	79.3	15.9	–0.1	5.0	15.7
1990	100.0	0.6	–5.8	94.8	78.9	15.9	–1.8	6.9	14.2
1991	100.0	–0.3	–4.9	94.8	81.6	13.2	3.0	2.1	16.3
1992	100.0	–0.8	–3.5	95.7	83.2	12.4	7.2	–2.8	19.6

Source: United Nations, Economic Commission for Latin America and the Caribbean.

[1]Deflated by import prices.

Note: Data for all years are preliminary. Table 2.6 shows the aforementioned national savings problem. The decline by nearly 10 percent in terms of GDP is the reason for the weakness of the process of accumulation and external disequilibrium.

Table 2.7. Real Effective Exchange Rate

Year	Index, 1980 = 100
1982	51.94
1983	43.80
1984	51.06
1985	45.35
1986	45.27
1987	41.94
1988	38.38
1989	33.60
1990	49.93
1991	67.91
1992	77.26
1993	82.00

Note: The strength of the stabilization is related to the decline in national savings and to the appreciation of the dollar against other currencies in the past two years.

Table 2.8. External Trade: Value, Volume, and Price Indices

Index	1988	1989	1990	1991	1992
			(1980 = 100)		
Export value	1.14	1.20	1.54	1.50	1.53
Export price	0.72	0.81	0.73	0.71	0.69
Export volume	1.60	1.48	2.13	2.12	2.23
Import value	0.50	0.40	0.39	0.78	1.40
Import price	1.04	1.09	1.12	1.11	1.13
Import volume	0.48	0.36	0.34	0.70	1.23
Terms of trade	0.68	0.73	0.64	0.63	0.60
			(Percentage changes)		
Export value	43.6	4.8	29.1	−3.0	2.2
Export price	14.5	12.7	−10.0	−2.8	−2.9
Export volume	25.4	−7.0	43.4	−0.3	5.2
Import value	−8.5	−21.1	−2.9	102.8	79.7
Import price	5.4	4.5	2.5	−0.8	1.7
Import volume	−13.2	−24.5	−5.2	104.5	76.7
Terms of trade	8.6	7.8	−12.2	−2.0	−4.5
Memorandum items:					
Export value					
(in millions of U.S. dollars)	9,134	9,573	12,354	11,978	12,236
Import value					
(in millions of U.S. dollars)	5,324	4,199	4,079	8,274	14,872

Sources: Central Bank of Argentina; National Institute of Statistics; IMF staff estimates.
Note: Table 2.8. shows the foreign trade numbers. Noteworthy here are the deterioration in the terms of trade and the marked increase in the volume of exports in the 1980s.

Table 2.9. External Trade Prices

(1970 = 100 unit value in U.S. dollars)

Year	Exports	Imports	Terms of Trade	Year	Exports	Imports	Terms of Trade
1980	302.3	256.9	117.9	1986	194.0	240.5	80.7
1981	311.0	249.6	124.6	1987	194.3	268.7	72.3
1982	258.2	245.4	105.2	1988	228.9	293.2	78.1
1983	232.7	228.4	101.9	1989[1]	233.8	308.9	75.7
1984	246.0	223.0	110.3	1990[2]	231.7	316.5	73.2
1985	219.4	231.0	95.0	1991[2]	212.9	314.0	67.8

Source: United Nations, Economic Commission for Latin America and the Caribbean.
[1]Preliminary.
[2]Estimated.
Note: Table 2.9, which complements the previous one, shows that nominal export prices for 1991 were 33 percent lower than for 1981. With the nominal interest rates for the decade, this makes any further comments on the external shock unnecessary.

Table 2.10. Exchange Rates

(In November 1993 pesos)

Date	Free Market	Trade Market Goods	Exports of Agricultural Goods	Exports of Industrial Goods
Average, 1982–88	2.7920	2.1300	1.8022	2.2754
Average, 1982–89	2.8714	2.1937	1.8262	2.3016
Full year 1989	3.4274	2.6393	1.9945	2.4060
Martinez de Hoz (tablita December 1978–March 81)	1.1129	1.1129	1.1129	1.1129
Triennial, 1985–87	2.5914	2.1682	1.8115	2.2899
Austral Plan (June 1985–July 1987)	2.5183	2.2614	1.7637	2.2469
Decline of Austral Plan (August 1986–September 1987)	2.5391	2.0244	1.8008	2.2601
Spring Plan (August 1988–January 1989)	2.1169	1.7562	1.6762	1.9975
Hyperinflation (April 1989–June 1989)	5.0157	3.6844	3.0361	3.3782
Rapanelli (August 1989–November 1989)	2.7349	2.4491	1.5511	2.0360
Erman III (March 1990–December 1990)	1.6551	1.6490	1.2218	1.5782
Cavallo (February 1991–October 1993)	1.1337	1.1334	1.0822	1.2245
November 1993	0.9987	0.9992	0.9932	1.1171

Note: Table 2.10 shows a few exchange rate comparisons. The figures tend to confirm a visitor's impression of Argentina; this country is very expensive in dollars.

Table 2.11. Privatization, 1990–94

(Current = millions of U.S. dollars)

Enterprise	Cash[1]	Public Bond[2]	Enterprise Value[3]
YPF[4]	4,935	215	2,017
Petroleum areas	1,852	—	1,852
Asset	165	—	165
Sold in 1993	2,918	215	3,047
ENTEL	2,271	5,000	3,051
North region	100	2,700	521
South region	114	2,300	473
30 percent Telefónica equity	830	—	830
30 percent Telecom equity	1,227	—	1,227
Aerolineas Argentina	260	1,610	511
Enterprise	260	1,610	511
Gas del estado	300	2,865	1,840
Distribution network	172	2,050	1,274
Transport	128	815	566
Agua y energía	49	277	198
Electrical power unit	49	277	198
SEGBA	476	1,884	1,489
Electrical power unit	216	—	216
Distribution network	65	1,884	1,078
Equity (partial sale)	195	—	195
Defensa	256	219	353
Somisa	140	23	152
Petroquimical	53	130	72
Other (Tandanor, Zapla, etc.)	63	66	130
Hidronor	237	953	952
Hydroelectric dam	237	953	952
Other (sale of assets, etc.)	364	395	576
Total	9,148	13,419	10,987

[1]Cash paid when the enterprise was acquired.

[2]Face value of internal or external bonds swapped by public asset.

[3]Cash plus market value of public bonds. The implicit parities are Aerolineas Argentina and ENTEL, 15.6 percent; Petroquimical, 14.4 percent; Zapla, 46 percent; others, 53.75 percent. In 1993, the market value used was 60 percent.

[4]The figure is the sum of the account sold by the provinces and the federal government.

Note: Not included are the liabilities of the public enterprises that were transferred to the buyers, by $2 billion. Table 2.11 gives estimated earnings from the sale of government assets. If transferred liabilities are added to these and the face value of debt is calculated, the total is a little more than $25.5 billion.

Table 2.12. Public Expenditure

	Consolidated Public Sector	
Year	Millions of 1993 U.S. dollars	Yearly change in percent
1980	107,302	44.7
1981	99,409	−7.3
1982	47,096	−52.6
1983	43,960	−6.7
1984	46,819	6.5
1985	39,647	−15.3
1986	44,209	11.5
1987	43,466	−1.7
1988	43,870	0.9
1989	31,080	−29.2
1990	42,322	36.2
1991	50,744	19.9
1992	54,186	6.8
1993[1]	57,013	5.2
1994[1]	60,478	6.1
Increase 1991–94	9,735	19.2
Increase 1992–94	6,293	11.6

Source: Argentina, Ministry of the Economy, Public Works and Services.
[1]Preliminary estimate of *Carta Económica*.
Note: Public expenditure is the sum of the nonfinancial public sector plus mandated health insurance, plus local governments, plus provincial government, excluding treasury transfers. Table 2.12 shows government expenditure measured in terms of the monetary anchor, adjusted for the size of the economy and the international inflation rate. The substantial exchange revaluation and the decline in savings are related to the considerable expansion of government expenditure, which was concentrated on social security. (To make this account worse, payments on the consolidated debt and the sale of YPF, the Argentine oil company, are not recorded.)

Chile

Table 2.13. Economic Index

Indicator	1980	1981	1982	1983	1984	1985	1986	1987	1988	1989	1990	1991	1992
						(In percent)							
GDP growth (real variation)	7.9	6.2	-13.6	-2.8	6.3	2.0	7.4	5.7	7.4	10.0	2.1	5.5	6.0
Inflation	31.2	9.5	20.7	23.1	23.0	26.4	17.4	21.5	12.7	21.4	27.3	18.7	15.0
Nonfinancial public sector deficit/GDP	-3.1	-1.7	2.3	3.8	4.2	2.6	1.9	0.8	-2.3	-4.8	-2.2	-0.7	-0.1
General government current expenditures/GDP	24.5	26.3	31.6	30.3	30.7	29.5	27.3	26.1	23.3	20.6	20.2	21.6	21.6
Real wages (real variation)	8.6	9.0	0.3	-10.9	0.1	-4.5	2.0	-2.0	6.5	1.9	1.8	5.0	4.0
						(In millions of U.S. dollars)							
Exports of goods	4,705	3,837	3,706	3,831	3,651	3,804	4,199	5,223	7,052	8,080	8,305	8,705	9,244
Exports of goods and services	5,968	5,009	4,642	4,629	4,316	4,470	5,120	6,310	8,266	9,479	10,152	10,571	11,324
Imports	5,469	6,513	3,643	2,845	3,288	2,955	3,099	3,994	4,833	6,502	7,037	7,200	8,326
Trade balance	764	-2,677	63	986	363	850	1,100	1,229	2,219	1,578	1,268	1,505	918
Current transactions	-1,971	-4,733	-2,305	-1,117	-2,110	-1,328	-1,137	-808	-167	-768	-824	-502	-1,325
						(In percent)							
Exports of goods and services/GDP	21.6	15.1	19.6	23.7	22.4	26.2	30.4	33.3	37.4	37.3	36.5	36.2	36.5
Terms of exchange index (1980 = 100)	100.0	92.0	83.0	87.0	81.0	77.0	80.0	86.0	98.0	94.0	87.0	89.0	89.0
Real exchange rate (1978 = 100)	89.6	78.1	85.6	103.7	108.3	133.9	147.4	152.8	162.5	157.0	153.1	143.7	—
						(In millions of U.S. dollars)							
GDP	27,578	33,067	23,627	19,491	19,321	17,043	16,825	18,959	22,085	25,932	27,805	30,446	32,425

(In percent)

Annual growth of noncopper exports												
2.1	14.3	12.2	1.1	10.9	11.7	18.9	9.9	10.0	15.1	12.9	14.8	12.6
Capital readjustment rate 90–365 days, December of every year												
6.3	7.4	5.9	6.1	14.7	6.2	3.5	4.5	5.0	8.8	6.0	5.3	4.7
Investment/GDP												
21.0	22.0	11.0	11.1	17.7	17.3	14.6	16.9	17.0	20.3	20.3	18.5	19.0
Domestic saving/GDP												
13.9	7.7	1.6	5.5	6.9	9.4	7.7	12.6	16.3	16.7	17.5	16.9	19.0
External saving/GDP												
7.1	14.3	9.4	5.6	10.8	7.8	6.9	4.3	0.7	3.6	2.8	1.6	3.0
Unemployment rate												
10.4	11.3	19.6	14.6	13.9	12.0	8.8	9.3	8.3	6.3	6.0	6.3	6.0

(In millions of U.S. dollars)

Copper price LME (U.S. dollars a pound)												
0.99	0.79	0.67	0.72	0.63	0.64	0.62	0.82	1.20	1.27	1.21	1.06	0.92
Oil price (U.S. dollars a barrel)												
33.0	34.9	28.2	27.3	27.3	26.4	13.4	17.4	14.6	17.1	21.6	18.7	21.9
Annual variation (U.S. dollars a pound of copper)												
22.6	23.1	26.8	27.6	27.2	29.8	30.2	30.1	29.9	34.0	33.5	36.5	39.1
Annual variation (U.S. dollars a barrel of oil)												
23.5	18.7	9.3	13.9	14.0	15.9	18.5	20.1	31.9	34.3	39.1	36.3	42.8

(In percent)

Tariffs												
10.0	10.0	10.0	18.0	24.7	25.8	20.0	20.0	15.0	15.0	15.0	13.0	11.0

Sources: D. Simone, "Stabilization of the Argentine Economy: The Convertibility Program, 1991–92" (Unpublished, 1993); and R. Arriazu and D. Simone, "Chile: Receiving the Benefit of Structural Reform," *Emerging Market Research*, Salomon Brothers (September 1992).

Note: Table 2.13 shows trends in the macroeconomic indicators, pointing to the high rate of growth, the decline in government current expenditure, the considerable improvement in the terms of trade (unlike what occurred in the other countries studied), and the dramatic recovery of domestic savings.

Table 2.14. Inflation and Devaluation Rates

Year	Consumer Prices	Official Exchange Rate
1978	40.1	47.0
1979	33.4	17.7
1980	35.1	4.7
1981	19.7	0.0
1982	9.9	30.5
1983	27.3	54.8
1984	19.8	24.9
1985	30.7	63.3
1986	19.5	19.9
1987	19.9	13.7
1988	14.6	11.9
1989	17.0	9.0
1990	27.0	13.7
1991	18.7	11.0

Source: Central Bank of Chile.

Note: The asymmetry in the late 1970s is noteworthy, as is the successful real devaluation achieved after 1982. The persistence of inflation and devaluation in spite of economic successes is linked to the desire to have a way out in case of a serious deterioration in the terms of trade.

Table 2.15. General Government Expenditures and Nonfinancial Public Sector Financing Requirements

(As a percentage of GDP)

Year	Current Expenditures	Capital Expenditures	Total Expenditures	NFPS Deficit (Surplus)
1985	29.5	3.0	32.5	2.6
1986	27.3	3.3	30.6	1.9
1987	26.1	3.4	29.5	0.8
1988	23.3	3.2	26.5	−2.3
1989	20.6	2.7	23.3	−4.8
1990	20.2	2.7	22.9	−2.2
1991[1]	21.6	3.1	24.7	−0.7
1992[2]	21.6	3.2	24.8	0.9
1993[3]	—	—	—	−0.1

Sources: Chile, Ministry of Finance; private research institutions; and R. Arriazu and D. Simone, "Chile: Receiving the Benefit of Structural Reform," *Emerging Market Research*, Salomon Brothers (1992).

[1]Estimate.

[2]Projected budget law for 1992.

[3]Adjusted in January 1992.

Note: NPSF = nonfinancial public sector. Table 2.15 gives a broader view of the fiscal accounts, which show that the contraction in expenditure does not affect government investment.

Table 2.16. Summary Operations of the Nonfinancial Public Sector

(In percent of GDP, unless otherwise indicated)

Category	1988[1]	1989	1990	1991	1992[2]
Total revenue	32.6	32.6	29.3	28.3	28.6
Current revenue	31.4	31.1	28.4	27.8	28.2
General government	29.8	29.9	26.1	26.0	26.3
After-tax surplus of public enterprises[3]	1.6	1.2	2.3	1.8	1.8
Capital revenue	1.2	1.5	0.8	0.6	0.4
Total expenditure	30.1	27.4	25.5	26.0	25.4
Current expenditure of the general					
government	24.4	22.0	21.1	21.4	20.5
Fixed investment	5.7	5.3	4.4	4.6	4.9
General government	3.2	2.7	2.5	2.7	3.0
Public enterprises	2.5	2.6	1.9	1.8	1.9
Overall surplus or deficit (−)	2.5	5.3	3.8	2.3	3.2
Deposited to Copper Stabilization Fund	3.4	3.4	2.5	0.7	0.3
Underlying overall surplus or deficit (−)	−0.9	1.9	1.3	1.6	2.9
Financing	0.9	−1.1	−1.3	−1.6	−2.9
Foreign, net	1.8	1.2	0.2	−1.8	—
Foreign, total	1.9	1.6	0.2	−1.7	0.2
Net amount on-lent to private sector	0.1	0.3	0.1	0.1	0.2
Domestic	−0.9	−2.4	−1.4	0.2	−2.9
Central bank cash results	−3.0	−1.8	−2.2	−1.1	−1.2
Combined public sector results	−0.5	3.5	1.6	1.2	2.0
Memorandum items:					
Current account balance	7.0	9.1	7.4	6.4	7.8
Nominal GDP					
(in billions of Chilean pesos)	5,411	6,777	8,478	10,939	13,740

[1]Adjusted to exclude privatized enterprises.
[2]Preliminary.
[3]Net of taxes and transfers.
Note: Table 2.16 provides another version of the fiscal accounts, in which it is useful to note the effect of the Copper Stabilization Fund, although its operations were canceled, and the persistence of a fiscal surplus. This occurs even when the Central Bank's losses are included. Particularly noteworthy is the size of the government's current savings and how they contribute to the country's overall savings.

Table 2.17. Saving and Investment in the Economy

(in percent of nominal GDP)

| Year | Investment | Saving | | | | |
		Foreign	Domestic	NFPS	Central bank	Private
1980–89[1]	16.9	7.0	9.9	5.3	−2.4	7.0
1990–91	19.5	1.3	18.2	7.1	−1.7	12.8
1990	20.2	2.8	17.4	7.5	−2.1	12.0
1991	18.8	−0.2	19.0	6.6	−1.3	13.6
1992[2]	21.0	1.5	19.5	—	—	—

Sources: R. Laban and Felipe Larraín, "Continuity and Change in the Chilean Economy" (Unpublished, 1992); Central Bank of Chile; Ministry of Finance.

[1]Average.

[2]Projected by the authors (which includes the only commercial bank owned by the Chilean government).

Note: NFPS = nonfinancial public sector. Table 2.17 shows the substitution of external savings for domestic savings and the possibility of financing an increasing volume of investment.

Table 2.18 Evolution of Imports and Exports and the Real Exchange Rate

| Year | Import Volume[1] | | Export Volume[2] | | Real Exchange Rate (1980 = 100) |
	As percent of real GDP	Annual rate of change	As percent of real GDP	Annual rate of change	
1980	30.3	—	23.6	—	100.0
1981	33.1	15.7	20.3	−9.0	87.0
1982	24.7	−35.3	24.6	4.7	97.0
1983	20.9	−17.9	25.3	0.1	116.4
1984	22.3	13.2	24.4	2.3	121.7
1985	19.6	−10.3	26.9	12.3	149.5
1986	20.9	14.1	27.5	9.7	164.5
1987	23.1	17.0	28.3	8.8	171.5
1988	24.1	12.1	27.9	6.1	182.9
1989	27.4	25.3	29.4	15.7	178.6
1990	27.0	0.6	31.0	7.6	185.4
1991	27.7	8.5	33.0	12.9	175.0
1992[2]	30.2	18.1	34.2	12.4	161.8

Source: Central Bank of Chile, national accounts.

[1]In 1977 pesos.

[2]Average for January–October. Assumption of real GDP growth for 1992 is 8.5 percent.

Note: Table 2.18 shows exports and imports as shares of GDP and the real exchange rate. As pointed out, the real growth of exports is observed, together with its increasing share in GDP.

Mexico

Table 2.19. Public Finance Indicators

Year	Public Spending (percent real increase)	Current Investment Spending	Public Sector Borrowing Requirement	Operational Deficit	Primary Deficit (percent of GDP)
1982	−8.0	55.3	16.9	5.5	7.3
1983	−17.3	46.1	8.6	−0.4	−4.2
1984	0.8	43.2	8.5	0.3	−4.8
1985	−6.1	36.4	9.6	0.8	−3.4
1986	−13.3	34.6	15.9	2.4	−1.6
1987	−0.5	33.8	16.0	−1.8	−4.7
1988	−10.3	29.3	12.4	3.6	−8.0
1989	0.4	26.7	5.5	1.7	−7.9
1990	6.1	34.5	4.0	−2.3	−7.9
1991	3.7	37.6	1.5	−2.7	−5.6

Sources: Presidency of the Republic, *Criteria for Economic Policy in 1992;* Pedro Aspe Armella, *Economic Transformation the Mexican Way* (Cambridge, Massachusetts: MIT Press, 1993).

Note: Table 2.19 shows the fiscal indicators, the most important of which is the primary deficit, which changed by nearly 15 percent of GDP between 1982 and 1990.

Table 2.20. Public Finance Indicators

(In percent of GDP)

Indicator	1987	1988	1989	1990	1991
Total revenues	28.4	28.1	27.2	27.5	26.2
PEMEX	11.7	9.9	8.9	9.0	8.0
Federal government	9.5	10.9	12.2	12.2	12.3
Taxes	8.6	9.3	10.1	10.6	10.8
Nontaxes	0.9	1.6	2.1	1.6	1.5
Total expenditures	43.8	40.5	34.4	30.6	26.7
Nonprogrammable expenditures	23.5	21.4	16.9	13.3	9.2
Domestic interest payments	15.7	13.7	9.8	7.5	3.5
Foreign interest payments	4.5	3.9	3.6	2.6	2.2
Programmable expenditures	20.3	19.1	17.5	17.3	17.5
Current expenditures	12.3	11.9	11.1	11.2	10.9
Capital expenditures	4.5	3.7	3.2	3.8	3.4
Deficit of financial mediation	1.0	1.6	0.6	1.1	1.0
Public sector borrowing requirement	16.0	12.4	5.5	4.0	1.5
Operational deficit	−1.8	3.6	1.7	−2.3	−2.7
Primary deficit	−4.7	−8.0	−7.9	−7.9	−5.6

Sources: Mexico, Minstry of Finance. The numbers for 1991 are taken from Presidency of the Republic, *Criteria for Economic Policy in 1991*.

Note: The above numbers exclude expenditures, capital expenditures, and transfers to non-controlled enterprises. Table 2.20 shows complementary public sector indicators, from which the recovery of tax revenue is clear, as are the decline in current expenditure and interest on foreign debt, which are reduced almost by half. Domestic financial outlays are affected by the measurement of inflation, which is why their decline in real terms is overestimated. In any case, the interest burden is five times greater in Mexico than in Argentina; this explains the substantial difference in the primary surplus to be achieved (the cost of maintaining PEMEX instead of redeeming debt).

Table 2.21. Financial Indicators

(In percent)

Year	GDP Growth	Inflation	Nominal Deposit Rates[1]	Financial Deepening[2]	Inflation Tax (percent of GDP)	Net Credit Bank of Mexico to Government[3]
1951	7.69	23.97	8.00	16.74	2.21	0.7
1952	3.94	4.00	8.00	15.74	0.66	0.5
1953	0.29	-1.92	8.00	18.79	0.66	1.0
1954	9.99	7.84	8.00	16.77	1.89	0.7
1955	8.50	14.55	8.00	16.43	1.11	-1.7
1956	6.88	5.29	8.00	15.64	1.17	0.0
1957	7.55	6.03	8.00	14.72	0.68	0.4
1958	5.31	3.32	8.00	14.23	0.76	1.5
1959	3.01	0.00	8.00	14.85	0.57	0.3
1960	8.11	5.50	8.00	18.21	0.38	0.5
1961	4.92	0.00	8.00	18.93	0.46	1.1
1962	4.69	1.30	8.00	20.72	1.28	0.7
1963	8.00	2.15	8.00	22.31	1.63	0.2
1964	11.67	5.04	8.00	22.61	2.36	0.2
1965	6.50	0.80	8.00	23.93	1.23	0.8
1966	6.92	1.98	8.00	25.98	1.24	0.8
1967	6.29	0.78	8.00	28.18	1.72	-0.1
1968	8.14	1.93	8.00	29.76	1.72	0.2
1969	6.32	1.68	8.00	32.08	1.46	1.3
1970	6.91	6.95	8.00	33.97	1.24	0.2
1971	4.19	5.26	8.00	35.08	2.29	-0.2
1972	8.47	5.00	8.00	35.88	2.39	3.7
1973	8.43	12.04	12.91	33.46	2.56	3.3
1974	6.10	23.75	12.44	30.34	3.12	3.7
1975	5.63	11.20	11.97	31.46	3.92	3.0
1976	4.23	27.20	12.12	28.84	3.68	1.8
1977	3.45	20.70	14.04	22.04	3.90	12.8
1978	8.25	16.20	15.88	24.86	3.58	3.7
1979	9.16	20.00	17.52	26.00	4.31	5.1
1980	8.33	29.80	24.25	32.72	4.88	6.0
1981	7.95	28.70	31.81	35.34	5.51	5.9
1982	-0.55	98.80	46.12	38.75	10.00	17.5
1983	-5.28	80.80	56.44	35.56	6.72	11.3
1984	3.68	59.20	47.54	37.87	5.91	8.8
1985	2.78	63.70	65.66	32.84	1.78	9.9
1986	-3.53	105.70	95.33	39.16	3.41	13.6
1987	1.70	159.20	104.30	42.39	3.29	11.3
1988	1.30	51.60	45.48	34.20	1.53	6.1
1989	3.10	19.70	40.11	39.53	0.43	1.0
1990	4.40	29.90	29.20	44.30	1.22	2.9
1991	3.60	18.80	19.90	45.49	0.66	0.0

Sources: Bank of Mexico; Aspe Armella (1993).

[1]Housing bond rates before 1973; after 1973, average cost of funds of the banking system.

[2](M4/GDP); the most comprehensive definition of money at the time is used throughout the series.

[3]As a fraction of GDP; includes the public financial sector.

Note: Table 2.21 provides information on trends in the monetary aggregates (M4/GDP), together with trends in GDP, the inflation rate, nominal interest rates, the inflation tax, and credit to the government. The destruction caused by the increase in the inflation tax in the early 1970s is particularly noteworthy, as its marginal yield falls compared with the rate of inflation. Inflation rates of 20 percent in the 1970s generated income representing 4 percent of GDP; in the 1990s, this has declined to only 0.4 percent of GDP. The other point to be highlighted is the enormous effort required to redress the inflationary situation of the 1970s and 1980s.

Table 2.22. Investment and Savings Performance

(In percent of GDP)

Year	Investment[1]	External Savings	Domestic Savings	Private Savings[2]	Public Sector Savings[3]	Public Sector Balance	Public Investment
1950	13.5	−3.2	16.7	10.8	5.9	−0.2	6.1
1951	14.4	3.2	11.2	6.3	4.9	−0.3	5.2
1952	16.9	3.1	13.8	6.9	6.9	1.4	5.5
1953	15.2	2.8	12.4	8.3	4.1	−0.9	5.0
1954	17.1	3.5	13.6	8.9	4.7	−1.0	5.7
1955	18.1	0.0	18.1	13.4	4.7	−0.3	5.0
1956	20.2	2.3	17.9	13.7	4.2	−0.4	4.6
1957	18.4	3.9	14.5	10.4	4.1	−0.8	4.9
1958	17.4	3.9	13.5	9.2	4.3	−0.7	5.0
1959	16.5	2.2	14.3	10.0	4.3	−0.6	4.9
1960	20.1	3.5	16.6	11.8	4.8	−0.8	5.6
1961	18.1	2.7	15.4	9.7	5.7	−0.7	6.4
1962	16.5	1.8	14.7	9.0	5.7	−0.4	6.1
1963	19.4	1.4	18.0	12.2	5.8	−1.3	7.1
1964	20.9	2.5	18.4	11.3	7.1	−0.8	7.9
1965	20.6	2.3	18.3	13.7	4.6	−0.8	5.4
1966	22.6	2.2	20.4	15.8	4.6	−1.1	5.7
1967	21.9	2.5	19.4	14.5	4.9	−2.1	7.0
1968	20.8	2.9	17.9	12.9	5.0	−1.9	6.9
1969	21.1	2.4	18.7	13.7	5.0	−2.0	7.0
1970	21.1	3.3	17.8	14.6	3.2	−3.4	6.6
1971	20.2	2.4	17.8	15.5	2.3	−2.3	4.6
1972	20.3	2.2	18.1	16.7	1.4	−4.5	5.9
1973	21.4	2.8	18.6	17.7	0.9	−6.3	7.2
1974	23.2	4.5	18.7	18.2	0.5	−6.7	7.2
1975	23.7	5.0	18.7	19.3	−0.6	−9.3	8.7
1976	22.3	4.1	18.2	19.4	−1.2	−9.1	7.9
1977	22.8	1.9	20.9	19.6	1.3	−6.3	7.6
1978	23.5	2.6	20.9	18.4	2.5	−6.2	8.7
1979	26.0	3.6	22.4	19.7	2.7	−7.1	9.8
1980	27.1	5.8	21.3	19.2	2.1	−7.5	9.6
1981	27.3	6.7	20.6	21.8	−1.2	−14.1	12.9
1982	22.9	3.6	19.3	26.0	−6.7	−16.9	10.2
1983	20.8	−4.5	25.3	26.4	−1.1	−8.6	7.5
1984	19.9	−2.7	22.6	24.4	−1.8	−8.5	6.7
1985	21.2	−0.8	22.0	25.5	−3.5	−9.6	6.1
1986	18.2	1.3	16.9	26.8	−9.9	−15.9	6.0
1987	19.2	−3.0	22.2	32.7	−10.5	−16.0	5.5
1988	21.2	1.0	20.2	28.2	−8.0	−12.4	4.4
1989	23.0	2.3	20.7	22.3	−1.6	−5.5	3.9
1990	24.3	2.6	21.7	20.2	1.5	−4.0	5.0

Sources: Bank of Mexico, *Indicadores Económicos*; and Ministry of Finance.

[1] Gross fixed investment plus changes in inventories.

[2] Defined here as the difference between domestic savings (investment-external savings) and public savings.

[3] Government deficit minus public sector investment.

Note: Table 2.22 shows ratios of investment to saving. Mexico maintains a significant level of domestic savings, which has enabled it to generate a high rate of investment, even though it achieved only low per capita growth.

Table 2.23. Effective Real Exchange Rate

(Index, 1970 = 100)

Year	Rate
1982	124.2
1983	135.2
1984	110.9
1985	106.8
1986	155.9
1987	169.4
1988	139.2
1989	128.2
1990	128.0
1991	116.4

Note: In Table 2.23, the real effective exchange rate shows a considerable decline over the mid-1980s. Unlike in Argentina, however, the rate remains high in comparison with 1970.

Table 2.24. Balance of Payments

(In millions of U.S. dollars)

Year	Current Account	Capital Account	Errors and Omissions	Change in Reserves	Export Volume	Import Volume	Terms of Trade
1980	−10,740	11,442	98	1,018	100	100	100
1981	−16,052	26,357	−9,030	1,012	—	—	—
1982	−6,221	9,753	−6,832	−3,185	—	—	—
1983	5,418	−1,416	−884	3,101	—	—	—
1984	4,238	39	−924	3,201	199	65	85
1985	714	−1,809	−1,327	−2,328	180	79	86
1986	−1,644	1,837	410	985	184	70	64
1987	3,752	−576	2,924	6,924	206	73	72
1988	−2,521	−1,448	−2,764	−7,127	220	105	62
1989	−6,051	3,037	3,409	271	224	137	66
1990	−7,114	8,164	2,184	3,414	233	160	70
1991	−13,283	20,179	1,241	7,821	255	186	62

Sources: Bank of Mexico, *Indicadores Económicos*; Aspe Armella (1993).

Note: Table 2.24 shows the balance of payments, as well as indicators of export and import volumes and the trade ratio. Noteworthy here are the dramatic increase in capital inflows, occurring without fiscal imbalance, and the extremely sharp deterioration in the terms of trade.

Table 2.25. Evolution of the Parastatal Sector

Years	Net Increase in the Number of Firms Incorporated in the Public Sector	Cumulative Number of Parastatal Firms at the End of the Period
1920–34	15	15
1935–40	21	36
1941–54	108	144
1955–62	62	206
1963–70	66	272
1971–75	232	504
1976–82	651	1,155

Note: Table 2.25 shows trends in Mexico's parastatal sector, particularly the spectacular growth in the 1970s in the area of state agencies.

Table 2.26. Divestiture of the Parastatal Sector

Status	Dec. 1, 1982– Nov. 30, 1988	Dec. 1, 1988– Nov. 1, 1991	Total
Concluded	595	310	905
Liquidated or closed	294	137	431
Merged	72	10	82
Transferred	25	7	32
Sold	204	156	360
In process	—	—	37
Parastatal sector in 1982	—	—	1,155
Parastatal sector in 1991[1]	—	—	239

Source: Mexico, Ministry of Finance, Office for Privatization.

[1]The figure on the size of the parastatal sector in 1991 includes the effect of the creation of new entities.

Note: Table 2.26 shows the results of privatization, which reached levels higher than 5 percent of GDP.

Uruguay

Table 2.27. Inflation, Real GDP Growth, and Public Sector Balances

Year	Real GDP Growth (percent change from previous year)	Inflation Rate[1]	Public Sector Balance (percent of GDP)
1985	1.5	83.0	−7.2
1986	8.9	70.6	−5.5
1987	7.9	57.3	−4.2
1988	0.0	69.0	−4.8
1989	1.3	89.2	−7.0
1990	0.9	129.9	−3.0
1991	1.9	81.5	−0.7
1992	7.7[2]	58.9	−0.2[2]

Source: Central Bank of Uruguay.
[1]Calculated from December to December.
[2]Preliminary data.
Note: Table 2.27 gives an overview of Uruguay's aggregate accounts. It is interesting to note the high rate of inflation, in spite of a minimal fiscal imbalance.

Table 2.28. Operations of the Combined Public Sector

(In percent of GDP)

Category	1988	1989	1990	1991
General government current account balance	0.5	−0.7	2.2	2.6
Current revenue	23.1	22.0	25.6	28.4
Current expenditure	22.6	22.7	23.4	25.8
Public enterprise current account balance	1.8	1.0	2.4	3.0
Capital expenditure	4.2	3.8	4.1	4.3
Nonfinancial public sector overall balance	−1.9	−3.5	0.5	1.3
Operating losses of the financial public sector (−)	−4.1	−4.3	−4.5	−2.8
Central Bank	−3.1	−3.4	−3.6	−2.3
Mortgage Bank	−0.5	−0.4	−0.6	−0.3
Intervention banks	−0.5	−0.5	−0.3	−0.2
Combined overall balance	−6.0	−7.8	−4.0	−1.5
Memorandum item:				
Nonfinancial public sector savings	2.3	0.3	4.6	5.6

Source: Uruguay, Ministry of Economy and Finance; and Central Bank of Uruguay.
Note: Table 2.28 provides a detailed analysis of the fiscal accounts. It is noteworthy that these accounts are not corrected for the inflation in nominal interest. If this had been done, there would have been surpluses in 1991 and 1992.

Table 2.29. Net External Debt by Borrower
(In millions of U.S. dollars at end of period, unless otherwise indicated)

	1987	1988	1989	1990	1991	1992[1]
Total[2]	2,788	3,166	3,245	2,933	2,438	2,195
Public sector	1,927	2,197	2,778	2,169	1,940	1,820
(percent of GDP)	26	27	29	27	22	16
Private sector	860	969	967	765	498	375
(percent of GDP)	11	12	12	11	6	3

Source: Central Bank of Uruguay.
[1]Preliminary data.
[2]Total external debt minus gross international reserves. Gold valued at London market prices.
Note: Table 2.29 partially explains what happened with the public sector's net indebtedness. It was reduced, and the improvement in net wealth linked to the inflation tax was basically used in its reduction.

Table 2.30. Savings and Investment
(In percent of GDP at current market prices)

	1987	1988	1989	1990	1991
Gross domestic investment	14.3	13.2	11.3	11.5	13.0
Fixed capital formation	11.4	11.9	11.6	11.2	11.9
Public sector	4.0	4.0	4.3	3.6	4.2
Private sector	7.4	7.9	7.2	7.7	7.8
Changes in stocks	2.9	1.3	−0.3	0.2	1.0
Gross national savings	12.5	13.6	12.8	13.8	14.1
Public sector[1]	−0.7	−0.8	−4.0	0.1	2.8
Private sector	13.2	14.3	16.8	13.8	11.3
External savings-current account balance					
of payments deficit	1.8	−0.4	−1.5	−2.4	−1.1
Net capital flows	2.3	0.6	−0.3	−1.4	−3.6
Public	4.0	3.5	2.0	0.3	−5.9
Private	−1.7	−2.9	−2.3	−1.7	2.3
Changes in reserves before devaluation					
adjustment (increase −)	−0.6	−1.0	−1.2	−1.0	2.5

[1]Includes losses of the Central Bank. Since 1989, also includes operational losses of the intervention banks and the Mortgage Bank.
Note: Table 2.30 describes Uruguay's national accounts, the inflation tax being expressed as a surplus in external savings. The low investment rate is linked to the fact that the population grows at 0.5 percent a year, and the share of social security is extremely high. In the early 1980s, Uruguay was investing 23 percent of GDP.

Table 2.31. Composition of Private Sector Financial Assets[1]
(In percent of total)

Item	1987	1988	1989	1990	1991
Total financial assets	100.0	100.0	100.0	100.0	100.0
Banking system	70.6	69.8	72.1	72.4	73.8
Money	9.4	8.1	6.3	6.1	6.8
Currency	6.1	5.3	4.2	3.7	4.3
Demand deposits	3.3	2.8	2.2	2.3	2.4
Quasi money	61.2	61.7	65.8	66.3	67.0
Local currency deposits	11.3	9.2	6.6	5.0	4.8
Foreign currency deposits	49.2	51.2	57.9	60.2	61.3
Held by residents	30.6	29.5	30.9	30.9	33.1
Held by nonresidents	18.5	21.7	27.0	29.4	28.3
Other	0.7	1.3	1.3	1.0	0.9
Treasury bills and bonds	19.8	21.0	19.3	19.0	17.5
Letras de Regulación Monetaria	1.4	1.8	1.2	0.8	0.5
Other financial system	8.1	7.4	7.4	7.8	8.2
Deposits in BHU	6.1	6.8	6.9	7.3	8.1
Mortgage bonds	2.0	0.6	0.5	0.5	0.1

Source: Central Bank of Uruguay.
[1]Foreign currency assets valued at end-of-period exchange rate.
Note: Table 2.31 shows the composition of private sector financial assets. Money and local currency deposits account for only 12 percent of total financial assets.

Comment

Felipe Larraín

This is an interesting paper on the topic of stabilization from a policy-maker's perspective. One of its major points is that successful stabilization packages increasingly include supply-side policies along with the more traditional demand-management policies. I agree with this. In fact, one could say that demand policies are necessary, but not sufficient, for successful stabilization.

In a classic paper, Thomas Sargent (1982) pointed out that a change in the regime of fiscal policy (for example, severing links with the printing presses) was essential to stop inflation in all the episodes of hyperinflation that followed World War I. In his words, "the changes that ended the hyperinflations were not isolated restrictive actions within a given set of rules of the game of general policy. Earlier attempts to stabilize . . . failed precisely because they did not change the rules of the game under which fiscal policy had to be conducted."[1] One could, however, go further than fiscal policy to other fundamental reforms.

Stabilization and Structural Reforms

In many cases, especially in the recent Latin American experience, stabilization would not have worked if traditional demand-management policies had not been complemented by structural adjustment measures. Thus, successful stabilization packages in Bolivia, Mexico, and, more recently, in Argentina have gone together with fundamental reforms of the public sector (including privatization and an overhaul of the tax structure and tax administration) and trade liberalization.

Many of these structural adjustment policies, however, bear fruit only in the medium to long term. This leaves open the question of whether they help stabilization in the short term. A tax reform, for example, is often preceded by heated discussion and takes time to pass in Congress; tax administration cannot be changed overnight.

However, some structural measures, for example, privatization, do help in the short term. Divesting loss-making enterprises helps the budget as privatization proceeds, long before efficiency gains can be factored in. The help comes in two forms: elimination of the fiscal drain incurred in covering the losses, and a significant source of revenue to the government.

---

[1]Thomas Sargent, "The Ends of Four Big Inflations," in *Inflation Causes and Effects*, ed. by R. Hall (Chicago: University of Chicago Press, 1982).

Authorities must be careful, though, not to use onetime resources to cover current expenditures. Rather, revenues from privatization should be used to reduce public liabilities and—in limited amounts—to improve the public infrastructure. Trade liberalization also helps stabilization in the short term by providing a benchmark for the prices of tradable goods that become subject to increased competition.

Successful stabilization programs in Argentina, Bolivia, and Mexico have all moved in parallel with trade liberalization. Of these three countries, only Bolivia did not undertake privatization at the time of the stabilization effort, but it did include substantial state reform, including the closing of several state-owned, loss-making mines in the government mining company COMIBOL.

Probably the most crucial aspect of structural measures in supporting stabilization is their effect on expectations, because they signal a change in regime. Credibility is a key element in the success of a stabilization program, and success normally does not come on the first try.[2] Why should agents accept that the government is serious, especially after several failed attempts? Economic authorities have an easier task of convincing people if they implement a major, coherent reform package along with the usual stabilization policies.

One major area where structural reform is crucial for sustained stabilization is—broadly defined—fiscal policy. Merely closing a fiscal deficit through some combination of emergency taxes, cuts in public investment, and the reversal of the Oliveira-Tanzi effect may not be enough. In many cases, only an in-depth reform of the state can guarantee that fiscal deficits will not recur.[3]

Role of Institutions

The paper mentions one interesting institutional element that has been essential in some stabilizations: the fiscal organization in countries with federal systems. No doubt, the author is influenced by the case of his own country, where quasi-fiscal deficits of more than 20 percent of GDP in the last two decades were largely explained by central bank credits to provincial banks, which, in turn, financed provincial governments.

Today, fiscal federalism is an important topic, not only in Argentina and Brazil, but also in such countries as Russia. In Argentina, tax co-sharing used to imply that the national treasury received only about 42 percent of

---

[2]In fact, many attempts to stabilize failed in Argentina and Bolivia before a successful program was launched.

[3]An analysis of this issue in the Latin American context is provided by Felipe Larraín and Marcelo Selowsky, *The Public Sector and the Latin American Crisis* (San Francisco: ICS Press, 1991).

increased collections. Because export taxes and government fees were exempted from co-sharing, stabilization programs relied especially on these instruments. This was not the most efficient mix, but rather one that responded to the institutional realities of the country.

This link has gradually eroded in Argentina over the past few years and has been a crucial aspect in Argentina's current stability. Brazil, also a federal country, has yet to succeed in stabilizing its economy. There are some important lessons for Brazil to learn from Argentina's reform of the co-sharing scheme and the severance of links between the provinces and the central bank.

A second institutional area that the paper mentions is the organization of social security. The basic issue is the accumulation of huge liabilities in state-run social security systems, which ultimately cannot be covered from the assets of the system, so that the government is called upon to finance the flow deficit. The problem is not with social security itself but rather with pay-as-you-go systems, which are hostage to two types of pressure. One is the lobbying from special interest groups that normally obtain increased benefits without commensurate increases in contributions. The other is demographic: the reduction of birthrates and the increase in life expectancy of the population, which—given retirement ages—increase the burden on the current workers. In contrast, a social security scheme based on capitalization and individual accounts avoids both of these pressures and partially explains why several countries in Latin America are switching to this scheme. The difficult part, of course, is to finance the transition period.

A third major institutional area—one not mentioned by the paper—is the move to independent central banks. International evidence indicates a clear inverse relationship between central bank autonomy and inflation. A widely quoted study by Alberto Alesina shows a clear negative correlation between the two variables for industrial countries.[4] Alesina built an index of independence and showed that countries with more autonomous central banks had lowered average inflation during 1973–86.

Many countries in Latin America are granting increased independence to their monetary authorities. In the context of stabilization, one needs to answer the question of why the central bank will deny financing to the public sector the next time it is requested. In such a situation, autonomy is important. In some countries with a long history of inflation, such as Argentina, the law prohibits monetary financing of fiscal deficits.

---

[4]Alberto Alesina, "Politics and Business Cycles in Industrial Democracies," *Economic Policy: A European Forum*, Vol. 4 (April 1989), pp. 57–98.

Stopping High Versus Moderate Inflation

One issue that the paper does not discuss is the important difference between stabilization of very high inflation and hyperinflation and stopping moderate inflation.[5] This is a central issue in Latin America today because—unlike a few years ago—most countries are fighting moderate inflation. A crucial distinction is indexation. Very high inflation and hyperinflation tend to destroy indexation (with the notable exception of Brazil). Reducing moderate inflation is harder, however, in the presence of indexation, which adds inertia to the inflation process.

The most damaging aspect of indexation is backward-looking wage adjustments in labor contracts. In Chile, indexation was established by law in 1979 (for workers under collective bargaining) and abolished in 1982. But the practice remained, and workers still look at past inflation when bargaining with their employers. The situation is more complicated in Uruguay, where the requirement to adjust pensions for past inflation has constitutional status and applies with a two-and-a-half month lag. This fact, together with widespread dollarization, helps explain why Uruguay's inflation is stuck at about 50 percent when the fiscal budget is balanced. It is important, then, to eliminate legal and constitutional mandates for indexation.

Stabilization and Currency Appreciation

An interesting aspect of the 1990s is that countries are trying to reduce inflation in the midst of strong capital inflows that put downward pressure on the exchange rate. This is a double-edged sword. Exchange rate appreciation helps reduce inflation, but at the cost of reducing the competitiveness of a country's tradables sector. In recent years, Argentina and Mexico have faced this trade-off most vividly.

Past experience suggests, however, that one should avoid the temptation of leaning too heavily on the exchange rate as a stabilization device. Countries in the Southern Cone of Latin America learned a painful lesson in the late 1970s and early 1980s, when the use of active crawls to stop inflation was popular.[6]

---

[5]See the paper by Rudiger Dornbusch and Stanley Fischer, "Moderate Inflation," *World Bank Economic Review*, Vol. 7 (January 1993), pp. 1–44.

[6]For an account of the Argentinean experience at the time, see Guillermo Calvo, "Fractured Liberalism: Argentina Under Martinez de Hoz," Columbia University, International Economics Research Center Paper No. 58 (February 1985).

3

Distributive and Welfare Effects of Inflation and Stabilization

Edward J. Amadeo

Orthodox stabilization plans in the member countries of the Organization for Economic Cooperation and Development (OECD)—such as the Reagan and Thatcher plans in the early 1980s—have had significant negative distributive and welfare effects. Unemployment and real wage reductions caused by the Phillips curve trade-off between inflation and the level of activity result from stabilization attempts that were based on contractionary monetary policies. The long stabilization in Chile, for example, although mixed with some incomes policy ingredients, had a strong orthodox flavor and was also associated with significant distributive and welfare consequences.

Heterodox experiments in Argentina, Brazil, and Peru during the 1980s, in contrast, had positive distributive consequences: real wages and employment grew during the initial phases of the plans. However, these plans failed to stabilize the economies in which they were applied. The conventional view is that they failed because policymakers neglected to deal with the "fiscal fundamentals" of the inflationary process, but they may have failed because they were associated with distributive shifts that were socially unsustainable. Recent plans in Argentina, Israel, and Mexico seem to combine the best of both types of previous experience: they have been successful in bringing down inflation and at the same time have had either nonnegative or positive consequences on the level of activity and real wages.

This paper examines the extent to which these plans did not have negative distributive and welfare consequences in the context of public finance issues.

Its objective is to explore the relationship between high and chronic inflation, successful and unsuccessful stabilization attempts, and distributive and welfare issues. The last mentioned are discussed in a broad

Note: I am very thankful to João Carlos Scandiuzzi for his excellent work as research assistant.

sense, taking into account the behavior of real wages, poverty, and employment as well as the role of the level and structure of tax revenues and of government expenditures.

Unsuccessful stabilization attempts contribute to an inflationary crisis. Successful stabilization plans mark the end of such a crisis. That is why the analysis of distributive and welfare issues in this paper is separated into two basic contexts: that of an inflationary environment, which includes periods of accelerating inflation and of unsuccessful stabilization attempts, and that of successful stabilization. However, it is not true that the stabilization of an economy begins only when the final and successful plan is launched. Fiscal adjustments take time, and a few stabilization attempts may fail while the adjustment is in process. Therefore, the discussion of distributive issues associated with the stabilization period cannot overlook the distributive consequences of the inflationary period in which part of the required adjustments might have taken place. The extent to which distributive shifts should be associated with the inflationary crisis or with the stabilization process is a matter of interpretation.

Background

The origins and dynamics of high and chronic inflation have been analyzed in detail in the literature (see, for example, Bruno, 1993; Kiguel and Liviatan, 1992; and Calvo and Végh, 1992). However, in view of the specific objectives of this paper, a brief *reconte*, with minor variations, may be of some use.

In the recent Latin American experiences—in Argentina, Brazil, Mexico, and Peru, for example—the external debt crisis of the early 1980s had an important impact on the macroeconomics of those countries and can be seen as the original cause of the ensuing inflationary crises.

Compared with the facts, a textbook response to the external shock would have led to a different, and certainly less tortuous, story. A real devaluation of the domestic currency would have shifted relative prices in favor of tradables, thus improving the balance of payments; a reduction in absorption would, at the same time, have reduced imports and inflationary pressures; and a more efficient government could have reduced the impact of the external debt on the internal debt where the so-called transference problem was relevant. However, textbook solutions are hard to reproduce because the social, political, and institutional constraints might prove hard to overcome. History is shaped by such constraints, and to disregard them, blaming inefficient, populist, or weak governments, is naive.

In Argentina and Brazil, for example, devaluations were attempted in the context of the redemocratization of national policies—a context in which unions were recovering their bargaining power and in which some degree of wage rigidity was inescapable. To blame the unions is to forget the political history of both countries.[1] The dynamics of the exchange rate and wages, with the formation of prices in between, were at the core of the inflationary and distributive processes in those countries. Struggles over wage indexation rules and the institutional context in which wage bargaining takes place, and attempts to introduce concerted income policies and make wage policies more effective are all behind the vicissitudes of the real exchange rate, the real wage, and the path of inflation itself.

The link between the external and domestic debts has also had an important influence on the dynamics of the fiscal debt. Changes in the exchange rate and the interest rate have an immediate impact on government finances, reducing considerably the positive effects of the huge effort to produce primary surpluses. Through the connection between a government's external and domestic accounts, the lack of capital inflows and the increase in international interest rates over the 1980s greatly diminished the results of fiscal efforts.

This is not to say that the accounts of governments are not affected by political factors. In democratic regimes, and in the processes of democratization in particular, the adjustment needed to reduce fiscal deficits requires complex political struggles. Social demands for public resources increase during periods of democratization, and if the governments in power do not have strong political support, they will find it difficult to increase taxes, reduce expenditures, and implement changes in priorities. Changes in priorities are opposed by conservative forces that supported the government during military periods in Latin America. The conflict between more universal and social demands, on the one hand, and corporatist demands, on the other, makes it very difficult to implement deficit reductions.

The failure to reduce inflation through wage and price freezes creates new dynamics for the inflationary process, with unions and firms trying to anticipate new policy initiatives. Uncertainty and expectations start to play a role. In this new environment, the dynamics of inflation and relative prices become relatively independent of so-called fundamentals. This is when institutions become important: the degree of centralization and synchronization of wage bargaining, the existence of wage and price setters, the role of business associations and central unions in supporting stabilization plans, and the efficacy of government agencies in providing

---

[1] See Amadeo and Banuri (1991) for an analysis of labor market institutions and their role in the adjustment process in Latin America and Southeast Asia.

price guidelines and implementing price controls all play an important role in making the stabilization effort work.

When nothing else works, the government is left with the interest rate as the only instrument to prevent price explosions. If, on the one hand, the policy prevents capital flight into real assets, on the other, it leads to very significant changes in the size of the domestic debt as well as in transfers of wealth from the government to holders of the treasury debt. In recent periods, high interest rates have attracted capital inflows that increase the stock of reserves and help prevent speculative attacks but at the same time fuel the increase in government debt because the central bank, to avoid monetizing the inflow of capital, issues treasury bonds.

Distributive Effects of Inflation

The distributive effects of the inflationary process are associated, in part, with the reduction in real wages as inflation accelerates.[2] The degree of wage indexation to past inflation and the time between adjustments help explain the path of wages. It is easy to show that the average real wage over a year (W_t) depends on the peak real wage ($w_{-1}{}^p$), the degree of wages of indexation to past inflation (m), the rate of inflation over the year (P_t), and the length of the indexation period (d) (see Ros, 1989 and Amadeo, 1994):

$$w_t = w^{p-1} \left(\frac{1 + mp_{-1}}{1 + p_{-1}} \right) \left(\frac{1}{(1 + P_t)\, d} \right).$$

Given the rate of inflation, the shorter the indexation period and the greater the degree of indexation, the greater the real wage. An acceleration of inflation, all other things being equal, leads to a reduction in the real wage. That is why in economies with accelerating inflation, it is usual to see unions demanding a shortening of the indexation period. In these circumstances, if firms are able to keep their markup constant, the result will be a further acceleration of the rate of inflation. Vicious circles involving the rate of inflation, the degree of wage indexation, and the length of the adjustment period are part of the inflationary history of many Latin American countries and of Israel in the 1980s.

There are two instances in which wage indexation becomes a cornerstone of adjustment or stabilization efforts. In countries hit by external shocks, wage indexation eventually makes real devaluations difficult. Attempts to devalue in a situation involving wage indexation give rise to

---

[2]Cardoso (1992) estimates an equation using data from seven Latin American countries to show that annual "real wages fall by 14 percent when inflation doubles." She also argues that in many countries the decline in real wages can be associated with the increase in poverty.

accelerated inflation. The other instance has to do with the rigidity imposed on the rate of inflation by backward-looking indexation in stabilization plans.

The distributive conflict between the exchange rate and the real wage is part of the perennial inflation story of some Latin American countries. As argued in the section on the distribution and demand for stabilization (pp. 69-70), resolving this conflict or alleviating it through trade deficits is at the core of many examples of successful and unsuccessful stabilization experiences.

Except for Israel, where real wages grew almost continuously before and after the successful stabilization plan of 1985, in all other economies with recent episodes of high inflation, indexation has never been able to protect wages against creeping inflation. Notwithstanding the natural tendency toward greater indexation and a shortening of the adjustment period, real wages in the industrial sector fell over the 1980s in Argentina (after 1984), Brazil (after 1986), Chile (until 1987), Mexico (until 1989), and Peru.

Devaluations, coupled with recession or restrictive wage policies, were instrumental in reducing wages in Argentina (1981-82), Brazil (1981-84 and 1990-93), Chile (1982-87), and Peru (1983-86). The political control over unions explains the continual reduction in wages in Brazil (1964-74), Chile (1970s), and Mexico (1980s). Hyperinflation explains the reduction in wages in Argentina in 1989 and 1990.

The trajectory of the minimum wage, which serves as a standard for the wages of the less organized workers and is usually determined unilaterally by the government, is even more dramatic. Over the 1980s, the real minimum wage fell by 30 percent in Argentina, 40 percent in Brazil, 30 percent until 1987 in Chile, 58 percent in Mexico, and more than 80 percent in Peru (Table 3.1).

Two questions should be addressed in the context of the relationship between the path of real wages and inflation. First, to what extent should factors such as sluggish growth or external shocks, rather than inflation itself, be responsible for the reduction in wages? Second, to what extent does the reduction in wages necessarily improve macroeconomic performance?

It should be clear that it is almost impossible to separate the macroeconomic crisis of the 1980s from the inflationary process in most Latin American countries. The reduction in real wages was a deliberate policy measure to reduce absorption and increase the profitability of exports, thereby reducing the trade deficit in most Latin American countries in the early 1980s. It was relatively successful in this respect, but, at the same time, devaluations induced greater indexation of wages, thereby fueling inflation and creating the vicious circle mentioned above.

Table 3.1. Selected Latin American Countries: Real Minimum Wages
(1980 = 100)

Country/Wage Category	1981	1982	1983	1984	1985	1986	1987	1988	1989	1990	1991[1]
Argentina											
I. Real average industrial wage	89.4	80.1	101.1	129.5	107.2	108.1	99.6	95.7	79.7	76.2	76.6
II. Urban real minimum wage	97.8	97.8	136.9	167.7	117.1	111.1	122.3	95.6	69.9	—	—
Relative wage (I ÷ II)	91.4	81.9	73.8	77.2	91.5	97.3	81.4	100.1	114.0	—	—
Brazil											
I. Real average industrial wage	96.1	97.7	81.9	80.3	90.6	105.3	112.2	92.2	99.5	89.4	—
II. Urban real minimum wage	98.7	99.2	87.9	81.3	83.9	82.3	64.8	63.3	68.5	50.8	58.9
Relative wage (I ÷ II)	97.3	98.4	93.1	98.7	107.9	127.9	173.1	145.6	145.2	175.9	—
Chile											
I. Real average industrial wage	108.9	109.1	97.2	97.4	93.5	95.0	94.7	100.9	102.9	104.8	109.7
II. Urban real minimum wage	115.7	117.2	94.2	80.7	76.4	73.6	69.1	73.9	79.8	87.5	95.5
Relative wage (I ÷ II)	94.1	93.0	103.1	120.6	122.3	129.0	137.0	136.5	128.9	119.7	114.8
Peru											
I. Real average industrial wage	101.8	110.2	93.4	87.2	77.6	97.5	101.3	76.1	41.3	42.7	38.7
II. Urban real minimum wage	85.0	79.6	80.6	62.3	54.4	56.4	59.7	52.0	25.1	23.4	16.8
Relative wage (I ÷ II)	119.7	138.4	115.8	139.9	142.6	172.8	169.6	146.3	164.5	182.4	230.3
Mexico											
I. Real average industrial wage	103.5	102.2	80.7	74.8	75.9	71.5	71.3	71.7	75.2	77.9	77.2
II. Urban real minimum wage	101.9	92.7	76.5	72.3	71.1	64.9	61.5	54.2	50.8	45.5	42.5
Relative wage (I ÷ II)	101.5	110.2	105.3	103.4	106.7	110.1	115.9	132.2	148.0	171.2	181.6

Source: Marinakis (1993).
[1]Preliminary figures.

In stabilization plans, depending on the balance of political power and the degree of consensus about the appropriateness of the policy, it is possible to have wages carrying part of the adjustment burden. Consensual, or negotiated, wage restraint did not play a role in Latin America, although in Israel in 1985, it was an important element of the stabilization plan. In Latin America, there were situations under authoritarian governments in which the wage policy was deliberately used to curb inflation.

In a significant number of circumstances, however, the reduction in real wages is no more than an accommodation to the socioeconomic crisis. It is not a response to policy impulses; nor does it necessarily lead to macroeconomic improvement. The reduction in wages may be associated with a distributive shift owing to changes in the bargaining power of the agents in labor and goods markets. Episodes of overindexation of prices in anticipation of policy actions were common after a series of unsuccessful stabilization attempts in Argentina and Brazil. When inflation accelerates in this way, the reduction in wages does not improve macroeconomic performance. The effect may even be negative, to the extent that the wage bill is a major component of aggregate demand and thus has an important effect on the level of activity.

The prolonged inflationary crisis in some Latin American countries is at the root of the almost continual reduction in real wages. Such a crisis is characterized by repeated, unsuccessful attempts to adjust to external shocks and reduce inflation and by episodes of pre-emptive or anticipated inflationary hikes, all of which lead to the erosion of real wages in a sluggish economy. In sum, reductions in real wages make a strong redistributive dent. They may help economies adjust to external shocks or they may result in sluggish economic conditions. A policy-induced underindexation of wages helps curb inflation. Finally, reductions in real wages with distributive effects may result from endogenous inflationary spurs, and in such cases are either without purpose from the standpoint of macroeconomic performance or have negative effects.

The distributive effects of inflation also depend on the extent to which the poor pay the inflation tax on idle cash balances, and the rich benefit from high interest rates on government bonds. Cardoso (1992, p. 5) argues that middle-class families usually have their savings wiped out by the inflation tax. This, of course, is true only if savings are not indexed to inflation and if the real interest rate on savings is negative. If interest rates are positive, the inflation tax does not apply to savings. High interest rates are not an exception in countries with chronic inflation. On the contrary, to avoid capital flight into real assets, interest rates are usually kept very high. High interest rates not only have a negative effect on the effort to reduce the domestic deficit, but also have an important distributive effect to the extent that the holders of government bonds are banks, large firms, and rich families.

Table 3.2. Stabilization Plans

Outcome	Orthodox[1]	Incomes Policy[2]
Successful	Chile (1973–83) Bolivia (1985)	Brazil (1964–67) Israel (1985–89) Argentina (1991–) Mexico (1988–)
Unsuccessful	Argentina (1976–78) Uruguay (1974–78)	Chile (1979–82) Argentina (1981–82) Uruguay (1981–82) Argentina (1985–86) Brazil (1986,1987,1989,1990)

[1]Based on money anchors.
[2]Based on different nominal anchors.

High interest rates reduce the demand of durables, establish a floor for profit margins and inhibit production, thus creating the conditions for stagflation. For firms, the higher the short-run rate of interest, the greater the profit margin required to induce production. In contrast, because inventories are kept very low, any time demand increases, excess demand develops, creating inflationary pressures. Hence, if, on the one hand, tight monetary policy avoids speculative attacks and hyperinflationary episodes, then, on the other hand, it has stagflationary side effects. Although government creditors obviously benefit from high interest rates, wage earners suffer the effects of the tight monetary policy on aggregate demand, employment, and real wages.

Welfare Effects of Successful Stabilizations

The main subject of this section is the successful stabilization programs implemented in Argentina (1991), Israel (1985), and Mexico (1988). However, before the welfare effects of these recent successful plans are analyzed, a few general observations based on Table 3.2 are presented.

First, there are cases of successful stabilizations both in the orthodox and in the incomes policy columns. The role of incomes policy ingredients is relevant, particularly in cases of chronic inflation, in which the dynamics of prices become relatively independent of "fundamentals." Second, although the recent plans in Argentina, Israel, and Mexico had important incomes policy elements, substantial fiscal and monetary restrictions preceded and followed the plans. Finally, when generally successful orthodox and incomes policy plans are compared, the former usually had worse distributive and welfare ratings than the latter. The same is true of unsuccessful orthodox and incomes policy attempts to stabilize, although the differences are not relevant to this discussion. The immediate distributive and welfare effects of the successful plans in

Table 3.3. Argentina: Macroeconomic Indicators
(In percent)

Year	Total GDP Growth	Growth of Manufacturing Output	Real Wages in Manufacturing
1985	−6.6	−9.9	−9.3
1986	7.3	11.4	−3.9
1987	2.6	1.8	−8.3
1988	−1.9	−4.9	−1.0
1989	−6.2	−7.1	−8.8
1990	0.1	2.0	−5.1
1991	8.9	11.9	−5.1
1992	8.7	7.3	−0.6

Source: Inter-American Development Bank (1993).

Argentina, Israel, and Mexico were far from negative, considering the behavior of real wages, unemployment, and per capita consumption.

In Argentina, after almost a decade of negative rates of growth in total GDP and manufacturing GDP, both grew strongly after the convertibility plan of 1991 was implemented. Real wages in manufacturing fell continuously after 1985 and did not begin to recover until 1992 (Table 3.3).

In Israel, real wages, GDP, and employment grew faster, on average, in the years following the implementation of the stabilization plan (1986-91) than in the years characterized by high inflation that preceded the plan (1981-85) (Table 3.4). The average rate of unemployment was higher in the post-plan period, but this is, at least in part, the result of the massive immigration of Russians. Per capita consumption rose by about 20 percent between the first half of 1985 and the first half of 1987. The average annual rate of increase in consumption was 11.8 percent in 1986-87, 2.1 percent in 1988-89, 5.3 percent in 1990, and 7.6 percent in 1991.

Table 3.4. Israel: Macroeconomic Indicators
(In percent)

Year	Growth of Real Wages	Unemployment	GDP Growth	Employment Growth
1981–85	1.6	5.4	3.4	1.6
1986–91	2.9	7.2	5.2	2.6
1986	9.0	7.1	5.7	1.6
1987	8.0	6.1	7.8	4.5
1988	5.0	6.4	2.5	3.0
1989	−1.0	8.9	2.0	−0.4
1990	−1.0	9.6	6.6	2.1
1991	−2.0	10.6	7.0	4.7

Source: Bruno (1993, p. 110).

Table 3.5. Mexico: Macroeconomic Indicators
(In percent)

Year	GDP Growth	Investment Growth	Real Wage Index (1978 = 100)
1983–86	0.5	–7.7	73
1987	1.7	–0.1	69
1988	1.4	5.8	66
1989	3.1	6.5	70
1990	3.9	13.4	72
1991	3.6	8.5	75

Source: Bruno (1993, p. 193).

In Mexico, the debt crisis and the period of fiscal adjustment were characterized by a reduction in GDP and investments, and a 27 percent reduction in real wages, compared with the golden years of 1977-80. After 1988, with the solidarity pact between government, trade unions, and businesses, investment and GDP recovered, and, after falling by 35 percent between 1978 and 1988, real wages grew by 14 percent between 1988 and 1991 (Table 3.5).

Exchange-rate-based stabilization plans in Argentina, Israel, and Mexico were accompanied by an increase in the level of activity and real wages. In open economies, the real wage depends on the price of both tradables and nontradables. If, in an extreme case, only the exchange rate is under-indexed in relation to inflation, the appreciation of the real exchange rate will imply a reduction in the relative price of imported tradables and an increase in the real income of wage earners. As a result, there will be an increase in consumption, demand, and imports, leading to a deterioration of the trade balance. On the supply side, the reduction in the cost of production resulting from the fall in the domestic price of imported inputs will also induce an expansion of output, thus reinforcing the expansion of aggregate demand. The expansion in the level of activity will lead to an increase in the demand for labor, reducing unemployment and putting pressure on the real wage. In the experiences of Argentina, Israel, and Mexico, this account seems to be a plausible explanation of macroeconomic developments during the exchange-rate-based programs.[3]

In sum, comparing the behavior of GDP, employment, and real wages in the periods immediately preceding and following the stabilization effort in all three countries, stabilization had neutral or positive effects. The figures for real wages in Argentina are still very modest, but, in comparison with previous years, the situation did not worsen. Therefore, these

---

[3]Calvo and Végh (1992) and Kiguel and Liviatan (1992) raise another hypothesis—usually based on the behavior of the interest rate—for the behavior of the level of activity in the course of exchange-rate-based stabilization plans.

three experiences did not duplicate the negative distributive and welfare performance of the "classical" orthodox stabilization programs.

However, the analysis of the distributive effects of stabilization efforts cannot be restricted to the movement of real wages and the level of activity, although this is certainly an important factor. The other factor is public finances, that is, the tax structure as it affects government receipts, the distribution of the tax burden through progressive forms of taxation, and the apportionment of government expenses among different programs. Because stabilization efforts are associated with the capacity to produce fiscal surpluses, the distribution of the tax burden and expenditure reduction have obvious welfare and distributive effects.

In this connection, perhaps the design of a "social welfare function" to study the distributive and welfare effects of stabilization should not give equal weight to government expenses accruing to the rich and those devolving to the poor. In an environment in which the incidence of poverty is high and the poor suffer from severe credit constraints, the impact of government expenses on the living standards of the poor is far from negligible. In such a context, uniformly distributed budget cuts, or cuts that reduce the share of social expenditures, will certainly have significant negative welfare, and even efficiency, consequences.

The increase in international interest rates in the early 1980s doubled the external debt of highly indebted Latin American countries. The inflation crisis that ensued further deteriorated public finances. The Oliveira-Tanzi effect reduces tax revenues. The internal transfer problem indicates that the size of the domestic deficit is linked to movements of the exchange rate and to the balance of payments, with devaluations and trade surpluses having a positive effect on the domestic debt.

Successful stabilization plans have been associated with major fiscal restrictions. As seen in Table 3.6, the significant increase in the interest rates on the domestic and external debts after 1981 resulted in an enormous effort by all countries to reduce the level of the public sector borrowing requirement. Current expenditures suffered major cuts in order to increase public sector saving, which, in Chile and Mexico, reached 10 percent of GNP in certain years. Public investments had to be reduced to diminish borrowing requirements.

The budget cuts associated with the fiscal effort led to significant reductions in the share of social expenditures in shrinking GNPs. Table 3.7 shows heavy cuts in social budgets for all countries except Brazil, where the per capita share of social expenditures in relation to GNP increased between 1979-85 and 1986-88. Figures reported by the UN Economic Commission for Latin America and the Caribbean show that the share of social expenditures in relation to GNP fell 14 percent in Argentina, 25 percent in Bolivia, and more than 30 percent in Mexico between 1979-81 and 1986-88. Per capita expenditures in education fell by 26

Table 3.6. Public Sector

(In percent of GNP)

Country	1978	1979	1981	1983	1984	1985	1986	1987	1988	1989
Argentina										
Saving before interest on debt	10.17	6.88	3.56	0.26	0.63	6.26	6.40	4.35	2.17	—
Real interest on debt	2.02	3.12	7.40	5.96	4.96	5.45	3.86	3.62	2.82	—
Saving after interest	8.15	3.76	-3.84	-5.70	-4.33	0.81	2.54	0.73	-0.65	—
Public sector borrowing requirement (operational)	4.72	6.49	13.24	15.15	11.91	6.01	4.74	7.21	2.56	—
Brazil										
Saving before interest on debt	5.72	4.31	5.65	3.57	4.10	3.59	5.32	5.15	5.10	2.16
Real interest on debt	0.67	0.84	1.37	2.95	3.76	3.81	2.42	2.28	3.01	2.68
Saving after interest	5.05	3.47	4.28	0.62	0.34	-0.22	2.90	2.87	2.09	-0.52
Public sector borrowing requirement (operational)	1.91	3.47	2.89	5.07	4.35	5.07	2.43	3.25	3.94	5.86
Chile										
Saving before interest on debt	10.93	10.79	6.62	3.86	5.27	9.60	—	—	—	—
Nominal interest on debt	2.37	1.94	1.51	4.26	4.84	6.04	—	—	—	—
Saving after interest	8.56	8.85	5.11	-0.46	0.43	3.56	—	—	—	—
Public sector borrowing requirement (operational)	-1.44	-4.61	-0.39	3.44	4.51	2.87	—	—	—	—
Mexico										
Saving before interest on debt	—	—	1.13	9.57	9.79	8.12	6.71	9.66	11.29	10.88
Nominal interest on debt	—	—	2.52	3.03	3.59	2.75	1.91	-2.01	8.23	9.15
Saving after interest	—	—	-1.39	6.54	6.20	5.37	4.86	11.60	3.06	1.73
Public sector borrowing requirement (operational)	—	—	10.54	-1.20	-1.16	-0.72	-0.17	-7.39	0.71	1.53

Sources: Argentina (Chisari and others, 1993), Brazil (Carneiro and Werneck, 1993), and Chile and Mexico (Amadeo, 1993).

Table 3.7. Social and Education Expenditures per Capita
(In percent of GNP; 1979–81 = 100)

Country	Social		Education	
	1982–85	1986–88	1982–85	1986–88
Argentina	85.5	86.3	80.68	73.86
Bolivia	75.5	76.5	73.93	52.39
Brazil	97.2	113.5	96.60	57.93
Chile	108.8	95.5	94.69	84.11
Costa Rica	83.1	98.3	67.51	84.92
Mexico	88.2	69.2	94.59	72.78
Uruguay	97.5	100.5	76.59	88.89
Venezuela	90.6	85.5	90.48	87.99

Source: United Nations, Economic Commission for Latin America and the Caribbean (1992).

percent in Argentina, 47 percent in Bolivia, and 27 percent in Mexico in the same period.

The distributive and welfare effects of such budget cuts cannot be over-emphasized. Poor families are the main recipients of social services. It is a mistake to assume that budget cuts are uniformly distributed across programs and subprograms. The extent of the cuts is determined by the political leverage of the groups affected, and, again, the ability of the poor to resist budget cuts that have a direct effect on their welfare is negligible.

When the tax structures in Latin America, Southeast Asia, and OECD member countries are compared, it can be seen that, first, the tax burden in Latin America and Southeast Asia is around one-half that of the OECD countries and, second, that the share of direct taxes in GNP in Latin America is half that of Southeast Asia and about one-fourth of the share in OECD countries (Table 3.8). A "progressive" increase in the tax burden in Latin America would clearly mean an increase in direct taxes on income and wealth. Had such a tax reform been introduced together with the stabilization effort, the negative distributive and welfare effects of the fiscal effort would have been considerably smaller. Again, as in the case of budget cuts, the political aspect of tax reform is complex.

Budget cuts with significant distributive effects may have an influence on the long-run efficiency of the economy. It can be argued that the decrease in the education, health, and other social budgets reduces the overall productivity of a country in the long run, not just the productivity of those workers directly affected. To the extent that educated and less educated workers perform complementary tasks in the economy, a reduction in the productivity of the latter will eventually hinder the productivity of the former and, by extension, will affect the economy and society as a whole. If this argument makes sense, budgetary cuts aimed at reducing deficits should be accompanied by redistributive measures both in the tax

Table 3.8. Tax Burden in Selected Regions

(Ratio of taxes to GNP in percent; average 1987–89)

Country	Tax Burden Excluding Social Security	Direct Taxes
OECD		
France	25	8
Former Fed. Rep. of Germany	24	13
Italy	25	13
Sweden	42	24
United Kingdom	30	14
United States	21	13
Southeast Asia		
Malaysia	17	8
Singapore	15	8
South Korea	16	6
Thailand	15	10
Latin America		
Argentina	17	3
Brazil	14	4
Chile	20	3
Colombia	13	4
Costa Rica	16	3
Mexico	18	3
Uruguay	16	3

Source: United Nations, Economic Commission for Latin America and the Caribbean (1992).

structure and in the structure of government expenditures in order to enhance equity and long-run efficiency.

Distributive Conflict and Exchange-Rate-Based Stabilizations

Successful and unsuccessful stabilization plans are usually associated with significant distributive shifts. In the case of chronic inflation, in which the formulation of prices and wages is relatively independent of fiscal fundamentals, the coordination of disinflation is difficult. Repeated, unsuccessful attempts to stabilize or the fear of firms or unions concerning price or wage losses lead to important price and wage rigidities. Such rigidities translate into "inflationary residuals" when a stabilization plan is in place. When coordination difficulties arise in promoting a "uniform deindexation," policymakers are tempted to choose one (or more) key prices to "lead the way." The already-mentioned Brazilian plan of 1964–67 is known for underindexing wages in order to promote stabilization. The exchange rate has also been used in many countries to guide the stabilization process. The fact is that the underindexation of one or more major prices in an environment of pervasive indexation helps promote stabilization.

Changes in relative prices affect economic agents in different ways. If only wages are underindexed, real wages fall and wage earners are hurt. If only the exchange rate is underindexed, the real exchange appreciates and exporters are hurt. In stabilization plans based on underindexation, the distributive conflict involving relative prices is a decisive element in the success of stabilization attempts.

It is a mistake to think that the only factor behind the failure of the Cruzado Plan in Brazil (1986) was the lack of a fiscal adjustment. The increase in real wages fueled by the expansion of the level of activity gradually began to squeeze profit margins in sectors where the price freeze was effective. These were precisely the oligopolistic sectors that, before the stabilization plan, were free to mark up costs but that, during the plan, were unable to raise prices. Hence, in the Cruzado Plan, the prices of the 18 oligopolistic sectors (and the exchange rate) were underindexed and, indeed, played the role of the main anchors of the plan. The change in relative prices implied by the dynamics of the Cruzado Plan was unacceptable to the large industrial and commercial firms, which demanded the relaxation of the price freeze.

The distributive conflict under stabilization plans based on indexation can be "suppressed" depending on the bargaining power of the agents involved. In democratic systems, a hegemonic political coalition may legitimize the underindexation of certain prices. Exporters may have to carry the burden of the stabilization in exchange-rate-based stabilizations if the majority favors such a plan. In authoritarian systems, the government can enforce the underindexation of certain prices and blue-collar workers may carry the burden.

Distributive conflicts can also be avoided, as they can under exchange-rate-based stabilization plans where capital inflows play the role of adjustment variables. The distributive shifts in the Southern Cone exchange-rate-based stabilization attempts in the late 1970s and early 1980s were not sustainable because the trade deficits resulting from the appreciation of the exchange rate were intolerable. Major distributive shifts and trade deficits—especially in Mexico (see Table 3.9)—are at the core of the success of recent stabilization plans based on exchange rate anchors. Huge capital inflows are required to equilibrate the balance of payments.

Capital inflows in Argentina increased from an average of less than US$2 billion between 1985 and 1990 to US$5.8 billion in 1991 and US$13 billion in 1992. In Mexico, they rose from an average of negative US$0.2 billion between 1985 and 1989 to US$20.4 billion in 1991 and US$26 billion in 1992.

It is likely that inflationary residuals in the recent exchange-rate-based plans were smaller than in the earlier Southern Cone plans—because wages and prices were not completely free in the former—and this obviously helped strengthen the program. But it is also true that the possibil-

Table 3.9. Argentina and Mexico: Selected Economic Indicators

Indicator	1985	1986	1987	1988	1989	1990	1991	1992
Argentina								
GDP (annual growth, in percent)	−6.6	7.3	2.6	−1.9	−6.2	0.1	8.9	8.7
Real effective exchange rate	100	112	123	135	154	104	76	65
Trade balance (in billions of U.S. dollars)	4.9	2.4	1.0	4.2	5.7	8.6	4.6	−1.6
Capital account (in billions of U.S. dollars)	2.5	1.7	2.4	3.6	0.2	0.8	5.8	13
Mexico								
GDP (annual growth, in percent)	2.6	−3.8	1.7	1.2	3.5	4.4	3.6	2.6
Real effective exchange rate	100	144	156	130	119	119	108	102
Trade balance (in billions of U.S. dollars)	8.5	4.6	8.4	1.7	−0.6	−4.4	−11.1	−20.7
Capital account (in billions of U.S. dollars)	−2.1	1.1	−1.0	−1.4	1.3	8.5	20.4	26.0

Source: Inter-American Development Bank (1993).

ity of bypassing the distributive conflict between real wages and the real exchange rate through a massive inflow of capital helps sustain the plan. In this context, the long-run effects on the competitiveness of Argentine and Mexican industries, on the one hand, and the sustainability of capital flows into the two economies, on the other, are two important issues to keep in mind.

Distribution and the Demand for Stabilization

The recent literature on the political economy of inflation and stabilization (for example, Alesina and Drazen, 1991) emphasizes the distributive conflict between different social groups before and after stabilization programs are launched. Stabilization is delayed as long as the costs of inflation (associated with the existence of fiscal deficits and "distortionary finance") to each group are perceived to be greater (owing to tax increases or budget cuts) than the costs associated with the stabilization plan.

Alesina and Drazen argue that there may be an "agreement on the need for a fiscal change but a *political* stalemate over how the burden of higher taxes or expenditure cuts should be allocated" (p. 1172); and that "when stabilization occurs, it coincides with a political consolidation." Furthermore, they maintain, one side becomes politically dominant. The burden of stabilization is sometimes quite unequal, with the politically weaker group bearing a larger burden. Often this means the lower classes, with the burden of a successful stabilization being regressive" (p. 1173). The stalemate to which Alesina and Drazen refer makes sense in relatively homogeneous societies in which the level of information and bargaining power of the groups involved in the "war of attrition" are not unevenly distributed. Political representation in OECD countries is accorded to all citizens, which makes the distributive conflict more transparent and balanced. In Latin American countries, in contrast, the upper and middle classes have considerably more access to information and political leverage than the lower classes. Hence, the distributive battle involves a relatively smaller segment of society, and a disproportionate share of the burden of the adjustment falls on the least organized members of society.

Stabilization has been delayed in Latin America, in part, because there are internal conflicts among the most elite members of society. Stabilization is also delayed because the demand for it is weak. As seen above, the hardship of inflationary and stabilization processes falls disproportionally on the poor, who are less well organized and cannot voice their dissatisfaction. The agents who can protect their income and wealth against inflation do not have the incentives to demand stabilization actions or to act to sustain stabilization attempts. The technologies that permit an economy to function in spite of inflation and the ability of certain groups to protect themselves against adjustment costs therefore give rise to prolonged periods of inflation.

Conclusion

Distributive issues are at the core of inflationary and stabilization processes. They are associated not only with the path of real wages and other key relative prices, but also with the structure of taxes and government expenses. It has been shown that the "politically weak" tend to lose before successful stabilizations programs begin because (1) backward-looking wage indexation protects wages imperfectly, (2) the poor do not have access to indexed financial assets, (3) the poor do not have the political leverage to make their interests represented in budgetary disputes, and (4) high interest rates imply a major redistribution of wealth from the government to its creditors.

In Latin America, it has been shown that the politically weak lose under stabilization programs because of the major budget cuts in social expenses. Finally, the tax structure in these countries has not changed in recent years to alleviate and compensate for the burden of the stabilization effort that has primarily affected the poor. That recent stabilization plans based on exchange rate and other nominal anchors did not lead to real wage repression or unemployment hides the fact that the period preceding stabilization was associated with major distributive shifts against the poor. In other words, it can be argued that the effects of the adjustment are felt before the stabilization plan is fully implemented. Perhaps the stabilization effort would have failed if such adjustments had not taken place.

Hence, to argue that recent exchange-rate-based stabilizations in Latin America have been socially harmless is to forget that a redistribution of income and wealth took place before all elements of the stabilization program were in place. Moreover, the welfare consequences of budget cuts were not uniformly distributed between the rich and the poor. This is not to deny the importance of political conflicts over the distribution of income and government resources. Institutional and political factors, the history of relations between the state and society, and the conflict between the elite members of society and the newly empowered social groups in the wave of recent democratization processes in many Latin American countries complicate the solution to macroeconomic problems. To say that stabilization plans fail because they lack credibility or because of the populist attitude of governments oversimplifies the complexities associated with these factors and therefore cannot account for economic developments in the region.

References

Alesina, Alberto, and Allan Drazen "Why Are Stabilizations Delayed?" *American Economic Review*, Vol. 81 (December 1991), pp. 1170-88.

Amadeo, Edward, "Adjustment, Stabilization, and Investment Performance: Chile, Mexico and Bolivia," in *Savings and Investment Requirements for the Resumption of Growth in Latin America*, ed. by E. Bacha (Washington: Inter-American Development Bank; Baltimore, Maryland: Distributed by Johns Hopkins University Press, 1993), pp. 161-207.

———, *Institutions, Inflation, and Unemployment* (Aldershot, Hants, England; Brookfield, Vermont: E. Elgar, 1994).

———, and Tariq Banuri, "Policy, Governance, and the Management of Conflict," in *Economic Liberalization: No Panacea: The Experiences of Latin America and Asia*, ed. by T. Banuri (Oxford: Clarendon Press, 1991), pp. 29-55.

Bruno, Michael, *Crisis, Stabilization, and Economic Reform: Therapy by Consensus* (Oxford: Clarendon Press, 1993).

Calvo, Guillermo, and Carlos Végh, "Inflation Stabilization and Nominal Anchors," IMF Paper on Policy Analysis and Assessment 92/4 (Washington: International Monetary Fund, 1992).

Cardoso, Eliana, "Inflation and Poverty," NBER Working Paper No. 4006 (Cambridge, Massachusetts: National Bureau of Economic Research, 1992).

Carneiro, Dionísio, and Rogério Werneck, "Obstacles to Investment Resumption in Brazil," in *Savings and Investment Requirements for the Resumption of Growth in Latin America*, ed. by E. Bacha (Washington: Inter-American Development Bank; Baltimore, Maryland: Distributed by Johns Hopkins University Press, 1993), pp. 57-102.

Chisari, Omar, José M. Fanelli, Roberto Frenkel, and Guillermo Rozenwurcel, "Argentina and the Role of Fiscal Accounts," in *Savings and Investment Requirements for the Resumption of Growth in Latin America*, ed. by E. Bacha (Washington: Inter-American Development Bank; Baltimore, Maryland: Distributed by Johns Hopkins University Press, 1993), pp. 1–56.

Inter-American Development Bank, *Situación Económica y Perspectivas de los Países de América Latina y El Caribe* (Unpublished; Washington: Inter-American Development Bank, 1993).

Kiguel, Miguel, and Nissan Liviatan, "The Business Cycle Associated with Exchange-Rate-Based Stabilization," *World Bank Economic Review*, Vol. 6 (May 1992), pp. 279–305.

Marinakis, Andrés E., "Wage Indexation, Flexibility and Inflation: Some Latin American Experiences During the 1980s," ILO Occasional Paper No. 6 (Geneva, Switzerland: International Labor Office, 1993).

Ros, Jaime, "A Review of Literature on Inflation and Stabilization" (Unpublished; Helsinki: World Institute for Development Economics Research, 1989).

United Nations, Economic Commission for Latin America and the Caribbean, *Equidad y Transformación Productiva: Un Enfoque Integrado* (Santiago, 1992).

Comment

Ricardo Ffrench-Davis

In his paper, Edward Amadeo provides a perceptive look at a broad range of relevant issues concerning the relationship between price stabilization programs and social welfare and income distribution.

The usefulness of his analysis lies from the outset in the fact that the choice discussed is not whether or not to stabilize, but rather when and how. Amadeo illustrates his article with many examples of the various "whens" and "hows" of stabilization. His study shows that the effectiveness and equity of the adjustment can be significantly affected by the whens and hows.

I will focus in this comment on a few aspects that, in my view, require greater attention.

Measuring the Effects

It is clear that measuring the effects cannot be limited to a comparison of situations with and without stabilization because to do so ignores the two essential questions: when and how. Furthermore, measuring the effects should not be limited to a comparison of situations before stabilization has begun and after it has been completed because this ignores both the characteristics of the initial economic situation and the evolution during the adjustment.

The results depend on the characteristics of the initial economic situation: it is essential to control for variables such as actual versus "equilibrium" wages (W) and exchange rates (ER), fiscal institutionality, and the relationship between productive capacity (PC) and effective GDP. For example, if there is a significant gap between PC and GDP, it is easier to harmonize stabilization with growth and an improvement in the standard of living, given that production, employment, and consumption can be increased without more investment. It is the ex post efficiency or productivity that increases as the economy moves toward the production frontier. This was the situation in Chile in 1975–80 and 1983–88, as Chart 3.1 illustrates.

In addition, to measure welfare, it is important to examine what happens with, among other variables, employment, W, and GDP paths during the transition. The present value of the integral of the process of adjustment indicates what has happened to the welfare and wealth of the various agents until a new equilibrium is reached. The evolution of investment in human and physical capital also indicates how productive capacity

73

Chart 3.1. Chile: Effective and Potential GDP, 1950–89

(In billions of 1977 U.S. dollars)

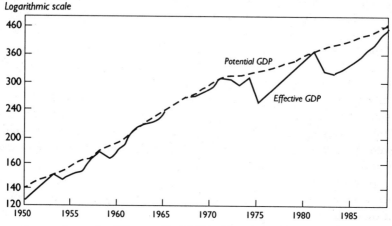

Sources: International Monetary Fund (1992, 1993). (Information for 1989 is unavailable.)

may develop once the stabilization program has ended. It has a strong impact on the future level of employment and its productivity, and, consequently, on the ability of the economy to sustain rising wages. In reality, the hysteresis of the adjustment process affects both the interpretation of the past as well as projections for the future.

Removal or Creation of Obstacles to Growth with Equity

The mix of policies can lead to the removal of obstacles to sustainable development but can also create new distortions or obstacles. The latter outcome is not unusual, particularly when price stability as such is given absolute priority or is assumed to be the principal ingredient for spontaneous economic growth. If, as a result of this kind of approach, stabilization is achieved at whatever cost, the result may be stabilization with stagnation or short-term stabilization followed by instability.

For stabilization programs to be lasting and to contribute to development (as they undoubtedly do when they are well designed), the hysteresis of the adjustment process must be closely monitored: How are the basic ingredients of growth (for example, investment, training, innovation, and technology) being managed? And how do they affect capacity and the opportunities available to the various social sectors? Stabilization programs can have progressive or regressive results, depending on their quality.

Single Anchors

The results of programs that depend on a single variable to lead the stabilization process are generally not very satisfactory: they tend to be short lived and contribute little to economic growth. The two single anchors most often used are the fixing of the exchange rate and isolated control of the money supply.

Fixing the nominal exchange rate helps slow down inflation in the short term but tends to do so more strongly and rapidly for tradables, while the prices of nontradables react more slowly. The typical result is a significant exchange rate appreciation, as was the case in Argentina and Chile in 1978-81. Both countries were successful in reducing inflation, even achieving negative rates (Chile in 1982), but with an unsustainable distortion in the external sector.

For economic or political reasons, creating imbalances such as those described above may at times be unavoidable. The key then is to be aware of them and to provide an effective way out before the correction is too late and traumatic.

Something similar happens if the single anchor is the money supply. Except in cases of incipient inflation in economies with no indexation, total dependence on tight money tends to generate prolonged underutilization of productive capacity, even when such capacity is high initially. This was the case in Chile between 1974 and 1976. Inertial inflation operating in the aggregate supply pushed prices upward for a period of time although unemployment and underutilization of domestic productive capacity grew substantially.

Depending exclusively, or heavily, on a single monetary variable tends to lead to very high real interest rates (overshooting). It excessively rewards the financial side at the expense of the productive side and tends to place the economy below the production frontier. For both reasons, it discourages capital formation and the creation of productive jobs.

Multiple Anchors

To be successful, that is, to achieve sustainable stability with growth and equity, it is imperative to coordinate a series of variables or prices in order to avoid overlooking some or overemphasizing others: public and private wages, the exchange rate, utility rates, the money supply, interest rates, fiscal balance, and expectations of private price setters. Social cooperation efforts involving the more relevant economic sectors, such as those made in Mexico in 1987 and in Chile since 1990, while limited in scope, can be useful in achieving more sustainable balances with a higher effective productivity (associated with operating closer to the production frontier).

Macroeconomic Policies Designed to Place the Economy in the Production Frontier

One of the basic macroeconomic balances is the capacity utilization rate. Latin America was operating considerably below the production frontier during the 1980s, as a result of external restrictions. Chart 3.1, based on data for Chile, provides a perfect example.

A significant gap between utilization and capacity seriously discourages capital formation and the level of productive employment. In the 1990s, to a large extent because of the restoration of capital flows, there was a moderate economic recovery. In 1991-94, in fact, growth of per capita GDP once again exceeded population growth, with about one-third of GDP growth corresponding to use of capacity.

During the recovery stage in this decade, with the disappearance of the external restrictions that dominated in the 1980s, management of macroeconomic policy has been less demanding than it will be when the production frontier is reached. When this frontier is reached, any new aggregate demand and output to match it will require new investment to support it. Consequently, to sustain even the current moderate levels of growth (3.5 percent in 1991-94), investment must exceed the current level. To return to the average rate of growth of 5.3 percent experienced in Latin America from 1950 to 1981, tens of billions of additional dollars in capital formation would be required each year. It should be noted, underlining the intensity of that challenge, that the flow of foreign direct investment totaled some $15 billion in 1993 (approximately one-fourth of total capital flows).

The other important point is that when the production frontier is reached, more active policies will be required to regulate aggregate demand. If these are not applied, internal or external shocks (changes in interest rates, terms of trade, and availability of capital) will place inflationary or recessionary pressures on the economy. The result is a lower *average* net utilization of productive capacity, with the consequent negative impact on effective productivity (ex post) and discouragement of investment.

Both effects generate a decline in social welfare and lower productive employment (and/or lower domestic wages). This contrast is seen, in the industrial world, for example, between the automatic adjustments during parts of the nineteenth century and in the 1920s versus those of the years 1950-80. In the last period, the capacity utilization rate (or proximity to the frontier) was much higher, as was the rate of investment. The result was per capita GDP growth two to three times higher in 1950-80 than in the other periods (as well as a significantly greater improvement in social welfare). The shortcoming (not an input for growth but an undesirable side effect of increasing costs) was higher inflation, which culminated in the high levels of the 1970s (significantly higher in the United States than in Germany or Japan).

It is essential now to perfect the ability to design macroeconomic policies that harmonize the economy's proximity to the production frontier with price stability.

It is clear that the national macroeconomy does not regulate itself spontaneously. Until there is a world central bank, as well, I would emphasize, as world welfare and finance ministries, national policies must be perfected. Their ever-declining ambit, be it monetary, fiscal, or exchange rate policies, must be broadened, and cooperation between the public and private sectors (management and labor) must be strengthened.

Comment

Carlos Noriega

The 1980s and early 1990s have been rich in terms of stabilization experiences, and, as a result, a consensus has gradually emerged among economists on how to proceed to eradicate inflation. However, there has not been a parallel advance in the analysis of the welfare and distributive effects of stabilization processes. Therefore, Amadeo's paper, by focusing on these issues, enlightens us and advances our knowledge of inflationary episodes. Indeed, unless and until those issues are well understood, arguments favoring stabilization policies should be viewed with a certain degree of skepticism. This paper also serves as a stepping-stone for distributive and welfare studies by reviewing the impact in this context of the most common policy measures of a stabilization program.

The analysis in the paper, however, fails to take into account methodological considerations, thus weakening its conclusions. Let me refer first to some identification problems. At the outset, it must be acknowledged that the existence of inflation already denotes a previous macroeconomic disequilibrium. Therefore, the analysis should begin by measuring the impact of the original measures or shocks that led to the macroeconomic disequilibrium and that derive from inflation itself (already a difficult feat). Only then can one proceed to identify the effects stemming solely from the stabilization programs. Unless this point is addressed explicitly, it is difficult to give much weight to conclusions based only on the timing of the stabilization program and the ensuing evolution of distributive and welfare indicators.

A related issue is that the disinflation experiences analyzed by Amadeo were part of more comprehensive structural adjustment programs, and, therefore, the effects on distribution and welfare cannot be attributed only to the stabilization part of the programs. Furthermore, because the efficacy of stabilization depends on whether the program is supported by structural measures, disentangling their effects may be practically impossible without a more formal model.

Amadeo touches upon these issues tangentially when he states that "the discussion of distributive issues associated with the stabilization period cannot overlook the distributive consequences of the inflationary period in which part of the required adjustments might have taken place. The extent to which distributive shifts should be associated with the inflationary crisis or with the stabilization process is a matter of interpretation."

The identification problem is relevant not only for measuring the effects of stabilization programs but also for establishing the issues to be analyzed. In this respect, welfare costs of stabilization across countries were not independent of such issues as the previous existence of a debt overhang problem, over- or undervaluation of the exchange rate, and, very important, the extent to which real wages had deviated in both directions from their equilibrium paths. In this context, little can be said about the comparative failures or successes of the stabilization programs surveyed in the paper.

Another set of issues related to the methodology employed in the paper is associated with the measurement of the distributive and welfare effects. Because stabilization processes do not occur overnight, it is difficult to determine the lag structure of the impact. It is interesting to note that even in the "successful" stabilization experiences, such as those of Israel (1985-89) and Mexico (1988-), after an initial surge in the rate of growth of real GDP, a decline took place in later years. Real wages behave similarly. Thus, it might still be too early to assess the final impact of stabilization. The paper also lacks a discussion of the merits of the indicators used to measure the effects under study. Furthermore, the use of different indicators in the analysis prevents a coherent picture of these issues from emerging. Also, one could think of other potentially useful indicators that were not taken into account, such as the sources of income from national accounts statistics.

Turning now to a different topic, Amadeo raises a relevant question on the extent to which a reduction in wages necessarily improves macroeconomic performance. Although he responds that in a nonnegligible number of circumstances, reducing wages is not a response to policy impulses, nor does it necessarily lead to any macroeconomic improvements, the question deserves more in-depth consideration. Heterodox programs have attached great importance to nominal anchors, including nominal wages. Thus, besides reflecting shifts in bargaining power of the agents in the labor and goods markets, wage policy does, in the medium and longer term, seem to affect the final outcome of stabilization. In that context, real wage reductions may bear importantly on the speed of convergence to macroeconomic stability and ultimately on welfare gains.

The question could have been posed in the inverse. Is a reduction in real rents to capital necessary for improving macroeconomic performance? In answering the question from the perspective taken by Amadeo, it is worthwhile considering that the stabilization experiences under analysis generally took place together with significant trade liberalization. There is a presumption that in developing countries, trade protection generally served to increase the rate of return to capital at the expense of a reduction in the return to labor. Therefore, stabilization programs, in addition to profiting from the discipline that the international price level imposes on domestic prices, also play a critical role in reversing the bias in favor of returns to capital. In this context, one may hypothesize that price stabilization, by reducing in the longer run the average rate of return to capital without inhibiting productive investment, strongly contributes to a better distribution of income.

One final comment refers to the view of inflation as a tax. The theory of public finances would assert that, in the absence of other distortions, the inflationary tax entails a net welfare loss. It may thus be presumed that if that tax is eliminated, society as a whole will gain. In our imperfect world (which is the one Amadeo considers, for well-founded reasons), that result does not always hold, but this line of thought does set a guideline to measure welfare gains of disinflation.

Although my comments may be seen as highly critical of the paper, in fact, they only point to an obvious shortcoming of this type of analysis, which is the lack of a consistent model for measuring welfare and distribution effects. However, had Amadeo stopped in the face of this challenge, we would have been deprived of the opportunity to ponder these important issues.

Capital Inflows in Latin America
Causes, Consequences, and Policy Options

Roberto Steiner

During the past several years, many Latin American countries have faced an abundant foreign exchange supply. In some cases, this was the result of capital inflows in unprecedented amounts, at least since the advent of the debt crisis in 1982. The size, timing, and characteristics of the inflows have varied among countries, as have the initial conditions that these countries faced when the inflows began. Additionally, not all countries have had the same short-term policy objectives; while some were leaning heavily toward reducing inflation, others were engaged in consolidating exports.

This paper compares the experiences of five large Latin American economies[1] in regard to the nature and size of foreign exchange inflows, the policy response that was brought about, and the impact on investment and growth. The fact that inflows are said to be, at least partially, the response to sound macroeconomic policies and structural reforms makes it extremely difficult to isolate the effects of the inflows themselves.

Characteristics of the Flows

A correct assessment of the possible causes, and, needless to say, of the amount of the inflows, is necessary to understand the rationale behind the design of macroeconomic policy and to evaluate its impact. Preliminary data suggest that the foreign exchange inflows continue to be an important issue in Latin America (Table 4.1). In fact, in some countries, the assessment made by Calvo, Leiderman, and Reinhart (1994) that the current episode is smaller than the one that preceded the debt crisis may no longer hold true.

Note: Comments by Alberto Carrasquilla, Patricia Correa, Juan Carlos Jaramillo, and seminar participants were extremely helpful.

[1]Argentina, Brazil, Chile, Colombia, and Mexico. Together they account for about 80 percent of the region's GDP.

Table 4.1. Balance of Payments
(In percent of GDP)

Country	1980	1981	1982	1983	1984	1985	1986	1987	1988	1989	1990	1991	1992	1993
Argentina														
Current account	-2.3	-2.8	-2.8	-2.3	-2.1	-1.1	-2.7	-3.9	-1.2	-1.7	3.2	-0.3	-2.9	-2.9
Capital account	1.0	0.8	2.0	0.1	2.1	2.5	1.9	2.0	2.8	—	-0.8	1.7	4.9	3.9
Net FDI	0.4	0.6	0.3	0.2	0.2	1.0	0.5	—	0.9	1.3	1.3	1.3	1.8	2.5
Portfolio	0.1	0.7	0.4	0.6	0.3	-0.7	-0.5	-0.5	-0.6	-1.4	-1.0	—	-0.3	-3.5
Overall balance	-1.3	-1.9	-0.7	-2.2	—	1.4	-0.8	-1.9	1.5	-1.7	2.4	1.4	2.0	1.0
Brazil														
Current account	-5.4	-4.5	-5.9	-3.5	—	-0.1	-2.0	-0.4	1.3	0.3	-0.9	-0.4	1.6	-0.1
Capital account	3.9	4.7	3.4	3.2	2.4	0.1	0.6	1.0	-0.8	-0.1	1.1	0.6	2.5	2.3
Net FDI	0.7	0.9	0.9	0.7	0.8	0.6	0.1	0.4	0.8	0.2	0.1	—	0.4	-0.1
Portfolio	0.1	—	—	-0.1	-0.1	-0.1	-0.2	-0.1	-0.2	-0.1	0.1	1.0	2.0	2.9
Overall balance	-1.6	0.2	-2.5	-0.3	2.4	-0.1	-1.3	0.6	0.5	0.2	0.3	0.2	4.2	2.1
Chile														
Current account	-7.1	-14.5	-9.5	-5.7	-11.0	-8.6	-6.7	-3.9	-0.7	-2.5	-2.1	—	-1.7	-4.6
Capital account	11.7	14.7	4.7	2.9	11.1	8.0	5.4	4.2	3.7	4.1	9.9	3.6	7.5	5.9
Net FDI	0.8	1.2	1.6	0.7	0.3	0.9	1.8	4.5	4.2	4.5	1.9	1.2	0.8	0.9
Portfolio	-0.2	-0.1	-0.1	—	—	—	—	—	—	0.3	1.2	0.7	1.1	1.6
Overall balance	4.5	0.2	-4.8	-2.7	0.1	-0.6	-1.3	0.3	3.0	1.6	7.8	3.6	5.8	1.3
Colombia														
Current account	-0.6	-5.4	-7.8	-7.8	-3.7	-5.2	1.1	0.9	-0.6	-0.5	1.3	5.7	2.1	-4.6
Capital account	3.4	5.2	5.7	3.0	2.7	5.6	2.6	0.2	1.0	1.4	0.2	-1.3	0.7	4.9
Net FDI	0.2	0.6	0.9	1.3	1.5	2.9	1.8	0.8	0.4	1.4	1.2	1.0	1.7	1.6
Portfolio	—	—	—	—	—	—	0.1	0.1	—	0.5	—	0.2	0.1	n.a.
Overall balance	2.8	-0.2	-2.2	-4.8	-1.0	0.4	3.7	1.1	0.5	0.9	1.6	4.4	2.8	0.3
Mexico														
Current account	-5.4	-6.5	-3.4	3.9	2.4	0.4	-1.1	3.0	-1.4	-2.8	-3.1	-5.2	-7.5	-6.5
Capital account	5.8	7.0	0.6	-1.8	-1.2	-1.9	1.0	1.0	-2.5	2.9	4.0	8.0	8.1	8.5
Net FDI	1.1	1.2	1.1	1.5	0.9	1.1	1.6	0.8	1.2	1.4	1.0	1.7	1.3	1.4
Portfolio	—	0.5	0.5	-0.4	-0.4	-0.5	-0.9	-1.0	0.1	0.1	-1.6	4.2	5.8	7.7
Overall balance	0.4	0.5	-2.8	2.2	1.2	-1.5	-0.1	4.0	-3.9	0.1	0.9	2.8	0.5	2.0

Source: IMF, *International Financial Statistics.*

Timing and Size

In Argentina, the capital inflows issue began to be relevant in 1991. In 1992 and 1993, their amount was more significant than in the years prior to the debt crisis. Even though this time around a substantial amount of foreign reserves has been accumulated, the current account deficit reached 3 percent of GDP by 1992.[2] Foreign direct investment (FDI) has increased substantially; it accounted for one-third of the capital account surplus in 1992 and for more than one-half in 1993.

In Brazil, substantial capital inflows appeared in 1992, with portfolio investments playing an important role. The capital account surplus has not financed a current account deficit unlike the situation observed at the beginning of the 1980s, when capital inflows financed significant current account deficits.

Capital inflows to Chile have been important all along, although the amounts involved since 1990 are by no means as large as they were at the beginning of the 1980s, and have financed a significantly smaller current account deficit.[3] Foreign investment has been very important, particularly in the late 1980s.

Until 1992, the foreign exchange inflow in Colombia was basically a current account surplus, although a case has been made that private unrequited transfers, which show up in the current account, are actually capital movements. That being the case, capital inflows would have been an important issue since 1991–92. The current account deficit reached 4.6 percent of GDP in 1993. About one-third of the capital account surplus of 1993 can be attributed to FDI.

In the case of Mexico, huge capital inflows that finance significant current account deficits have been important at least since 1990, with portfolio investments playing a dominant role. It is the only country in which the size of the inflow and of the current account deficit now approach the levels that prevailed before the debt crisis.

A straightforward conclusion that can be drawn from this short description is that the typical picture of a significant capital account surplus that finances both a current account deficit and reserve accumulation[4] does not necessarily fit all the Latin American countries being reviewed. Though most of them have experienced an abundant supply of foreign exchange during the first years of this decade, the timing and size of the inflows have been quite diverse. A huge capital surplus has characterized the Mexican

---

[2]All ratios to GDP are influenced by the choice of the latter in U.S. dollars. The trends in these ratios are highlighted rather than their absolute level.

[3]Of course, the capital inflows of the mid-1980s were insufficient to finance the current account deficit that emerged, especially because of the heavy debt burden.

[4]A pattern that is also found in Spain (Galy, Pastor, and Pujol, 1993) and in some Asian countries (Reisen, 1993).

experience since 1990, a year in which a large and growing current account imbalance emerged. In Argentina, the inflows arrived later, are smaller, and finance a current account deficit that is not very large. In Brazil, the inflows have been even more recent, not very significant, and, at least until 1992, were manifested entirely in a buildup of reserves. In Chile, the capital inflow goes way back; it has not been as large as it was before the debt crisis and it has been accompanied by smaller current account deficits. In Colombia, the episode is more recent and probably less significant.

New forms of access to international financial markets have been developed in recent years, and most Latin American countries have made use of some or all of them. These will not be explored in this discussion. Even though part of the inflow is explained by FDI, in no single case is it the only relevant factor. In fact, with the exception of Chile during the late 1980s, and of Argentina and Colombia in 1993, in no other country is FDI the single most important item in the capital account.

Possible Causes

The events of the early 1990s have prompted an important body of literature in which different characterizations of the inflows have been suggested, although most analysts have emphasized that various elements were playing important roles simultaneously. Some recent case studies are a useful complement to the analysis that emerges from papers that have presented interesting assessments of events in the region as a whole.[5]

With regard to the causes of the capital inflows, some of the relevant questions that have been raised include the following: Are these inflows mainly the response to "push" factors in the member countries of the Organization for Economic Cooperation and Development (OECD), or are they explained by "pull" factors in Latin America? In the latter case, are those factors related to structural changes in domestic policy or are they more closely related to speculative motives? If "push" factors are the cause, do they mainly affect resources that represent, in essence, the capital flight of the 1980s?

In all interpretations offered, the main concerns have been related to the possibility of an abrupt and sizable currency appreciation and an eventual reversal, on short notice, of the recent inflows.[6] Let us look, in slightly more detail, at some of the interpretations that have been offered.

---

[5]A detailed explanation of particular events in Argentina, Chile, Colombia, and Mexico appears, respectively, in Fanelli and Damill (1994); Agosin, Fuentes, and Letelier (1994); Cárdenas and Barrera (1994); and Ros (1994). Details of the Brazilian case as well as another description of the Chilean experience are found, respectively, in Carneiro and García (1994) and in Budnevich and Cifuentes (1994).

[6]In what follows, an increase in the real exchange rate index (say, from 100 to 110) represents a depreciation.

Calvo, Leiderman, and Reinhart (1993, 1994) highlight the role played by a "common external shock" that has affected not only most of the countries in the region, but also several Asian countries.[7] This shock is identified with a deterioration in investment opportunities in some OECD countries. Support for this position is provided both by their "principal components analysis" and by many country case studies that have emphasized that external conditions are the only plausible explanation for the shifting of capital to countries in which macroeconomic imbalances were still significant, and market-oriented structural reforms incipient (as in Brazil and Peru until 1991 and as in Ecuador more recently).[8] According to this interpretation, an improvement in investment opportunities in industrial countries could eventually produce significant capital outflows.

Speculative factors have been singled out by Rodríguez (1993) as an explanation for capital inflows to economies that faced currency substitution and pursued stabilization programs after hyperinflationary episodes. A good number of studies on the Colombian experience also emphasize the role of speculative forces caused by attempts by the Central Bank to sterilize, with a policy of very high interest rates, a current account surplus that could have originated in a policy of maintaining an undervalued exchange rate.[9] Similar problems, though apparently not as significant, also appear to have emerged in Chile.[10] According to the interpretation offered by Carneiro and García (1994), the Brazilian experience is one in which speculative factors are the response to a monetary policy of high interest rates aimed at offering a good domestic substitute for the national money to avoid currency substitution.

Sound macroeconomic programs and market-oriented reforms have been identified by, among others, Blejer (1993) as the main cause of the inflows. With the exception of Brazil, a review of case studies indicates that these factors have been recognized as significant, particularly in Argentina, Chile, and Mexico. They include successful stabilization programs, ambitious trade reforms, significant privatization efforts, tax amnesties on previous capital outflows, and successful foreign debt negotiations.[11] According to this alternative interpretation, a subsequent

---

[7]On the Asian experience, see also Reisen (1993) and Frankel (1994). A detailed comparative analysis of experiences in various countries, including Chile, Colombia, and Mexico, appears in Schadler and others (1993).

[8]Capital inflows have also affected other economies. On the Bolivian case, see Morales (1994); on the Peruvian experience, Dancourt (1994).

[9]See, for example, Steiner, Suescún, and Melo (1992).

[10]See, for example, Bianchi (1994).

[11]From a different perspective, the hypothesis that the capital inflows to developing countries are the response to economic fundamentals, in the sense that they operate so as to smooth consumption in the event of temporary shocks to national cash flow (defined as output minus investment minus government expenditure), receives empirical support for an important group of countries in Ghosh and Ostry (1993).

outflow should be expected only if the reforms that attracted them turn out to be unsustainable. In this regard, an important question is related to the sustainability of stabilization programs that have relied heavily on the use of the exchange rate as a nominal anchor.

Evidence suggests that capital repatriation played a dominant role (Kuczynski, 1993). In certain aspects of policy design, this might turn out to be a relevant issue. In particular, capital controls might be less effective when it is a resident who is trying to take advantage of the perceived improvement in domestic investment opportunities.

Causality Between Foreign Exchange Inflows and Real Exchange Rate Changes

The causality between current and capital account deficits is another way of looking at the dominance of push and pull factors. Push factors refer to an exogenous inflow that appreciates the real exchange rate, prompting a current account deficit. Pull factors may result from a credible macroeconomic policy that boosts expenditure and temporarily creates a current account deficit that foreigners are willing to finance. The causality could also be the result of a policy of attempting to increase competitiveness through exchange rate policy; the undervalued currency will generate a current account surplus while at the same time prompting expectations of exchange rate appreciation that may in turn induce speculative inflows.

Because detailed balance of payments statistics are rarely available other than on a yearly basis, empirical approximations using higher-frequency data[12] have "proxied" capital movements through changes in international reserves. As in Morandé's (1988) study of Chile, Calvo, Leiderman, and Reinhart (1993, 1994) suggest that causality goes from reserves to the exchange rate, giving supporting evidence to the exogenous nature of the inflows and to the fact that the capital surplus causes the current deficit.

It is clear that if reserve accumulation is the counterpart of a current account surplus, such accumulation may well be the result of the previous exchange rate policy. This accumulation will then probably "cause" an appreciation. In that case, the issue is not one of an exogenous capital inflow prompting an appreciation but, instead, the inability to maintain, for prolonged periods, a significantly undervalued real exchange rate. The undervalued currency argument has been mentioned in explanations of the Colombian experience of the early 1990s. Using monthly data for Colombia from June 1989 to November 1993 (not reported here), we were

---

[12]As in Edwards (1991) in the case of Colombia.

unable to reject (Granger) causality also going from the real exchange rate to reserves.[13]

How Sustainable Are the Inflows?

Probably the most relevant question regarding foreign exchange inflows is: How likely is it that they will be reversed? After all, policymakers are unlikely to design macroeconomic policy as if the flows will be permanent; still, they might be tempted to believe that the capital that already came is here to stay.

The dominance of sound domestic policies, and even the lack of good investment opportunities in the OECD, is consistent with increases in FDI and in more medium- to long-term flows. Instead, by definition, the speculative motive emphasizes the possibility of reversibility on short notice. The perceived transitoriness of the inflows plays a significant role in determining macroeconomic policy in general and sterilization and the degree of real exchange rate appreciation that is to be tolerated in particular.[14]

From an expenditure point of view, one might expect that the higher the FDI component of the flows, the lower the real exchange rate appreciation.[15] The authorities in charge of exchange rate policy might hold the opposite view—that the higher the FDI component, the less probable a sudden reversal of flows, in which case the perception is that of a stronger currency. Of course, the opposite is also true: the higher the perceived "speculative" nature, the less likely a substantial real exchange rate appreciation is considered an acceptable policy option unless the capital flow affects a country engaged in an exchange-rate-based stabilization program. In such a case, inflation concerns are so dominant that real exchange appreciation is deemed a cost well worth paying.

From a practical point of view, it is impossible to determine how transitory a capital inflow is. Even if it were possible, changes in macroeconomic conditions could cause a short-run speculative flow to transform itself into a long-term investment, and vice versa. Addressing the issue about how sustainable the inflow might be is equivalent to pronouncing on the sustainability of the factors that attracted it. If the external shock is

---

[13]According to Schadler and others (1993), the "overshooting" of the exchange rate also explains part of the capital inflows to Egypt in 1991-92. For somewhat similar arguments in the cases of Argentina and Mexico, see, respectively, Fanelli and Damill (1994) and Ros (1994).

[14]The policy stance in Chile, shifting as a function of the changing perception of the authorities with regard to the durability of the inflow, is described in Bianchi (1994).

[15]Calvo, Leiderman, and Reinhart (1994) point out that real exchange rate appreciation has been less significant in East Asia than in Latin America because, in the latter, speculative flows have been more important than in the former, and the demand for nontradables increases more with speculative flows than with FDI.

indeed the dominant factor, then, from a policy viewpoint, one should probably be prudent enough to recognize that a reversal is likely. In contrast, if macroeconomic policies and structural reforms have been an important element in stimulating the inflow, then the flow is likely to endure as long as those policies and reforms are sustainable.

The latter point notwithstanding, one might argue that FDI implies capital flows that are longer lasting than other types of flows. By historical standards, the recent developments in terms of FDI have been impressive only in Chile, and, to a lesser extent, Argentina (Table 4.1).[16] The role of privatization and debt-conversion schemes in some of the countries that we are analyzing is shown in Table 4.2. Until 1992, FDI did not play a significant role in Colombia, the only country in which no debt conversion was implemented and in which privatization was nonexistent until 1993.

Even in countries in which the absolute amount of FDI is large, it generally represents only a small percentage of the overall capital surplus. This implies that those countries that implemented the most significant reforms, and therefore attracted the largest portion of FDI, are the same countries that relied more heavily on capital inflows that were probably less stable. This is especially true in the case of Mexico.

Without covering all possibilities regarding the nature of the inflow, a simple matrix will help summarize some of the ideas stated (Chart 4.1). The first column shows the inflows as being the response to pull factors, which can be a temporary event (option 1) if such factors are speculative, or permanent (option 3) if the attracting factors are credible and sustainable domestic policies. The second column characterizes the inflows as being determined by push factors, which can be temporary (option 2) or permanent (option 4). We rule the latter case as implausible.

Option 2, which is the characterization of Calvo, Leiderman, and Reinhart (1993), calls for macroeconomic management that avoids real exchange rate appreciation, current account deficits, and significant increases in the financial intermediation of the inflows. At the opposite extreme, option 3, which is emphasized by Blejer (1993) and most policymakers, should bring about an appreciation that is offset by productivity increases. It could also reasonably finance any excess in domestic aggregate demand and should be intermediated in the process. The biggest policy dilemma has less to do with identifying an event as conforming to option 2 or to option 3 than with recognizing the possibility that something that looked like option 3 is ultimately unsustainable, for example, because of the market's perception that the exchange rate is substantially overvalued.

---

[16]In spite of this, Rodríguez (1993) identifies the inflow to Argentina as being essentially speculative. This assessment is partially challenged by Ghosh and Ostry (1993).

Table 4.2. Debt Conversion and Privatization

Country	1985	1986	1987	1988	1989	1990	1991	1992
Argentina								
Foreign direct investment (FDI) (in millions of U.S. dollars)	919.0	574.0	−19.0	1,147.0	1,028.0	2,008.0	2,439.0	4,693.0
Through debt conversions (in percent)	—	38.2	—	29.6	15.5	40.6	—	—
Through privatizations (in percent)	—	—	—	—	—	20.7	80.9	39.2
Brazil								
FDI (in millions of U.S. dollars)	1,347.0	319.9	1,225.6	2,969.3	1,267.0	901.0	972.0	2,000.0
Through debt conversions (in percent)	43.1	64.4	28.0	70.3	74.6	31.4	7.0	4.8
Through privatizations (in percent)	—	—	—	—	—	—	—	—
Chile								
FDI (in millions of U.S. dollars)	144.3	315.5	930.3	1,026.7	1,505.6	660.6	539.1	573.5
Through debt conversions (in percent)	20.8	63.0	75.4	86.3	87.8	66.9	−6.8	−5.5
Through privatizations (in percent)	—	—	—	11.1	—	—	—	—
Mexico								
FDI (in millions of U.S. dollars)	491.0	1,523.2	3,245.6	2,594.6	3,036.9	2,633.2	4,761.5	5,366.0
Through debt conversions (in percent)	—	23.8	44.7	33.5	12.8	3.2	0.4	—
Through privatizations (in percent)	—	—	—	—	—	32.8	8.4	—

Source: Calderón (1993).

A review of case studies suggests that all countries have benefited from an external shock but that, in every case, other factors also played a role. It also seems to be the case that, at least until 1992, Brazil and Colombia conformed to option 1, in which domestic rates of return were much higher than foreign rates, not only because of high interest rates stemming from sterilization attempts, but also, in Colombia, as a result of a severely undervalued real exchange rate, which fostered expectations of a nominal appreciation. Although speculative factors seem to have played

Chart 4.1. Characterization of the Inflows

Main Determinants / Durability	"Pull" Factors	"Push" Factors
Temporary	1	2
Permanent	3	4

an important role in the Chilean experience, most authors suggest that having in place a sound, credible, and sustainable program was the most relevant factor (option 3).

Characterizing the Argentine and Mexican experiences is more complicated, even though, in both cases, as in the region as a whole, lack of good investment opportunities in the OECD probably played an important role. Both countries have implemented policy reforms across the board that should be credited with attracting a significant amount of foreign capital. However, both countries experienced a significant real exchange rate appreciation.[17] The sustainability of most reforms is probably not jeopardized; indeed, many are, for practical purposes, irreversible. However, the same assessment cannot be made of exchange rate policy. If indeed the exchange rate is perceived as being severely overvalued, a capital outflow could eventually occur.

The different elements involved can be integrated in one framework. Latin America has attracted capital because of expectations of high rates of return, which are determined by at least four elements: (1) rates of return increase when the currency is undervalued and an eventual appreciation is a reasonable possibility; (2) they increase when high real domestic interest rates are used in the fight against inflation; (3) they increase when OECD countries experience adverse developments; and (4) they increase when the country risk premium falls.

---

[17]Although, when corrected by productivity gains, the appreciation is obviously smaller and, according to some, probably not very significant.

The idea we would like to stress is that, at some point, the currency can become overvalued. Even if all the other elements that imply an increase in the expected rate of return remain in place, the capital losses that may result from a currency depreciation may be large enough to offset all positive forces. Of course, sound policies can appreciate the equilibrium real exchange rate, making matters much more difficult to assess, because the "observed" real exchange rate—which does not fully correct for all productivity changes—may no longer be a good barometer of macroeconomic consistency.

Another way to view the current episode is as one in which several elements combined so that the relative expected rates of return in the region increased. This increase should presumably subside, diminishing the inflow but not necessarily implying a subsequent outflow. The latter event could come about as a result of expectations of exchange rate depreciation if, notwithstanding the scope of recent reforms, market participants consider the recent real appreciations to be unsustainable.

In some countries, the current account deficit that has emerged is a reflection of a significant fall in private savings. In those cases, the medium-term sustainability of the whole process requires significant amounts of *additional* capital inflows. It may not be reassuring to recognize that the recent inflows will not be reversed because a continued flow will be necessary, at least while private savings remain at a low level.

Policy Response

The policy response to a foreign exchange inflow depends on whether it is perceived to be permanent, which, as was just mentioned, is a function of the stability of the conditions that were responsible for attracting the inflow. With regard to FDI, it is generally believed that the short-term costs (that is, the exertion of pressure on the exchange rate) are outweighed by long-term benefits (that is, FDI complements domestic savings and is a means of transferring technology). In addition, FDI may be import intensive, thereby implying fewer inflationary pressures to begin with.

Matters are quite different if the capital inflow consists of "hot money." In that case, as Kuczynski (1993) phrased it, "central banks in Latin America may say they dislike hot money, but they like the increase in international reserves and the anti-inflationary effects of higher exchange rates. So do finance ministries, because the fiscal cost of external debt service declines. Treasurers of large companies certainly like it, because their cost of funding declines and their possibilities of cheap equity financing improve. Then, who dislikes hot money? Presumably, import competing industrialists, exporters, and those making foreign direct investment" (p. 330).

Table 4.3. CPI Annual Inflation

(In percent)

Country	1985	1986	1987	1988	1989	1990	1991	1992	1993
Argentina	385.4	81.9	174.8	387.7	4,923.3	1,343.9	84.0	17.6	7.7
Brazil	239.1	58.6	394.6	993.3	1,863.6	1,584.6	475.8	1,149.1	2,489.1
Chile	26.4	17.4	21.4	12.7	21.4	27.3	18.7	12.7	12.2
Colombia	22.3	21.0	24.0	28.2	26.1	32.4	26.8	25.2	22.6
Mexico	63.7	105.7	159.2	51.7	19.7	29.9	18.9	11.9	8.0

Source: United Nations, Economic Commission for Latin America and the Caribbean.

If we disregard differences in "initial conditions" and/or in "policy objectives," the analysis of the characteristics of the inflows suggests that if one considers only their nature, a real appreciation would probably have been a reasonable response in Chile, where the inflow was responding to a sound macroeconomic policy apparently perceived as permanent. A real appreciation would not have been a reasonable response in Brazil and Colombia, where, presumably, short-term speculative movements were dominant.

On the nature of the inflow, one must superimpose both specific initial conditions and distinct policy objectives. The following characterizations of the five countries when the inflows became important present the information in an orderly fashion. By 1990 Chile had consolidated its structural reforms, its fiscal position was strong, and inflation was moderate. Reducing inflation was an important goal, but the highest priority was assigned to maintaining a competitive real exchange rate. In 1992, Colombia was involved in an ambitious reform program, its fiscal position was good, and inflation was at its usual moderate level. Policy priorities were aimed at consolidating the reforms, which called for the maintenance of a competitive exchange rate. In both Argentina and Mexico, substantial reforms were under way, and further, substantial inflation reduction was a cornerstone of the countries' macroeconomic policies. Brazil is different; reforms were at an early stage, inflation was very high, and the targeting of the real exchange rate remained an important feature of macroeconomic policy. Inflation and the fiscal balance appear in Tables 4.3 and 4.4.

We can think of a "loss function" in which one dislikes inflation and likes a competitive real exchange rate and it takes time for domestic inflation to converge to a reduction in the rate of nominal depreciation. In that case, countries must choose, temporarily, between maintaining a competitive real exchange rate with stable and moderate to high inflation or a decreasing rate of inflation with a less competitive exchange rate.[18] It

---

[18]In the long run, inflation reduction and a competitive real exchange rate are not competing objectives, and, in fact, if the economy is sufficiently open and indexation is not widespread, the convergence of inflation to the rate of nominal depreciation can be quite fast.

Table 4.4. Public Sector Balance, Excluding Privatizations
(In percent of GDP)

Country	1987	1988	1989	1990	1991	1992	1993
Argentina Nonfinancial public sector excluding local governments	–4.6	–6.0	–3.8	–3.8	–1.6	0.4	1.1
Brazil Nonfinancial public sector	–5.7	–4.8	–6.9	1.2	1.4	–2.1	0.3
Chile Nonfinancial public sector	2.6	3.5	5.0	3.1	2.2	2.9	2.0
Colombia Nonfinancial public sector	1.9	–2.5	–2.4	–0.3	0.1	–0.3	0.2
Mexico Consolidated public sector	–15.5	–12.5	–5.7	–4.0	–0.4	1.6	0.7

Source: United Nations, Economic Commission for Latin America and the Caribbean.

is quite clear that Brazil represents the first choice and Argentina and Mexico the second. Chile and Colombia fall between the two scenarios.

The actual evolution of the real exchange rate for the five countries is shown in Table 4.5. A comparison of the level at the end of 1993 with the level in the year prior to the inflows shows that real appreciation has been significant in Argentina and Mexico, and insignificant in Brazil and Chile. In Colombia, the 1993 level was not significantly lower than the average for 1987–89, although a significant appreciation took place from the high, unsustainable levels of 1991.

Foreign Exchange Intervention and Sterilization

Foreign exchange intervention took place in all of the countries considered, which made no attempt to appreciate the nominal exchange rate openly. In Chile, Colombia, and Mexico, however, episodes of small

Table 4.5. Real Exchange Rate
(1990 = 100)

Country	1986	1987	1988	1989	1990	1991	1992	1993
Argentina	100	122	130	143	100	83	78	74
Brazil	161	157	143	108	100	119	127	111
Chile	88	96	102	96	100	99	95	96
Colombia	77	85	87	89	100	101	90	83
Mexico	130	135	110	103	100	91	84	79

Note: Weights by destination of exports; CPI is the deflator.
Source: United Nations, Economic Commission for Latin America and the Caribbean.

nominal appreciations occurred when the authorities discretely reduced the central bank's effective intervention rate and/or widened the band within which the exchange rate was allowed to fluctuate. In most countries, as in Colombia in 1991, a substantial tariff reduction, equivalent to an appreciation of the nominal effective exchange rate for imports, occurred.

Once foreign exchange intervention is established, monetary sterilization becomes crucial. The benefits of sterilization are that it contains inflationary pressures and also reduces the chance of significant credit expansion by the financial system while, at the same time, providing the cushion that limits the country's vulnerability to a reversal of flows.[19] The costs stem from the possibility that high interest rates will further attract inflows, discourage investment, and generate fiscal losses for the central bank.

For analytical purposes, we will follow Frankel (1994) and make use of the simple *IS-LM* textbook model in the context of an open economy that faces less-than-perfect capital mobility (as reflected in a positively sloped *BP* curve).[20] The horizontal axis represents nominal income. Three cases are distinguished:

(1) A drop in foreign interest rates (Chart 4.2, panel A): initial equilibrium is at *s*. If the foreign exchange inflow is sterilized, it remains at *s*, at an interest rate that is above the international rate. If monetization is allowed, the economy will move to the right, reaching point *m*. If the exchange rate is allowed to appreciate, equilibrium will be somewhere around *a*. Note that both *a* and *m* lie south of *s*; the increased demand for domestic bonds will imply a drop in interest rates or unchanged interest rates in the extreme case of complete sterilization. The real exchange rate appreciates at *m* and at *a*; it is a matter of choice if this is achieved through a nominal appreciation or through higher inflation. If there is insufficient flexibility in the exchange rate system, increased inflation will be a very likely outcome.

(2) An increase in net exports (panel B): initial equilibrium is at *a*. A trade balance improvement, for example, because of an exchange rate depreciation, will shift the *IS* and *BP* curves to the right. Sterilization might temporarily imply high interest rates (at *s*) although increased reserve inflows will eventually move the economy toward *m*. However, if the exchange rate is allowed to adjust, equilibrium will again be at *a*,

---

[19]In certain countries, particularly in Argentina, the financial intermediation of the inflows has taken the form of significant increases in assets of the financial system that are denominated in foreign currency. In that case, it is very difficult to assess if the central bank's foreign reserve accumulation constitutes sufficient "backing" for an eventual capital outflow.

[20]Assuming perfect capital mobility will imply no significant changes with regard to the main conclusions. Reactions that take time under less-than-perfect mobility should occur instantaneously when mobility is perfect.

Chart 4.2. Domestic Interest Rates and
Foreign Reserve Inflows

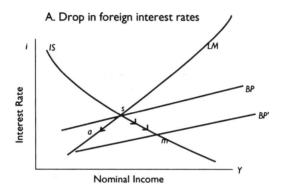

A. Drop in foreign interest rates

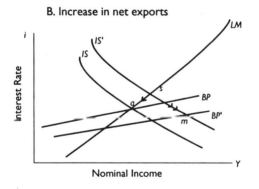

B. Increase in net exports

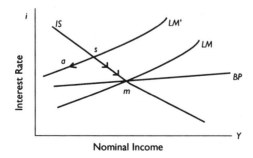

C. Increase in money demand

Source: Frankel (1994).

rendering the initial depreciation ineffective.[21] Again, the real appreciation can be obtained through a nominal appreciation or through higher inflation.

(3) A successful stabilization program that stimulates capital repatriation while simultaneously increasing money demand (panel C): from an initial equilibrium at *m*, we move to a point like *s*, in which interest rates are unnecessarily high. It is better not to attempt sterilization at all but to allow the money supply to adjust to what residents are demanding, with equilibrium at *m*. Residents' attempts to convert foreign currency into domestic currency might lead the central bank to allow an exchange rate appreciation; in that case, the *BP* and *IS* curves shift leftward, and equilibrium is reached at *a*, with a reduction in net exports. The higher the weight given to bringing down inflation, the more likely that an exchange rate appreciation will be allowed for.

Because of the common external shock, panel A applies across the board. However, the shock itself does not seem to be the only important factor in any specific case. Elements of panel B are relevant to all countries, either because they have made export promotion the cornerstone of their macroeconomic policy (particularly Brazil, Chile, and Colombia) or because they received significant FDI. Successful exchange-rate-based stabilization programs that significantly increase money demand make panel C relevant in explaining the Argentine and Mexican experiences.[22]

The framework discussed, although limited in a number of respects, suggests certain guidelines. On the one hand, sterilization is not necessarily called for. On the other, when sterilization is implemented, only under very particular conditions should one observe a (temporary) increase in domestic interest rates.

Countries that implemented, among other reforms, credible exchange-rate-based stabilization programs have faced a substantial increase in money demand (notice the significant decrease in M1 velocity in Argentina and Mexico, Table 4.6). They have not been involved in sterilization efforts. However, when money demand does not increase significantly, one could be tempted to avoid sterilization under the presumption that the money supply increase will reduce interest rates and foster a capital outflow. This approach is always risky; policymakers are afraid that the excess money supply will pass through to prices before

---

[21]An increase in net exports that produces a current account surplus is also an increase in net wealth; portfolio effects, including an increase in money demand, should take place. A similar pattern will emerge in the case of FDI that effectively increases domestic investment. In many cases, especially in those linked with privatizations, it is not clear if FDI increased overall investment or simply substituted one investing agent for another.

[22]Strictly speaking, money demand should also increase in the scenario described in panel B.

Table 4.6. Velocity of M1

(Annual percent change)

Country	1991	1992	1993
Argentina	5.60	−15.90	−16.00
Chile	−14.80	5.30	−6.60
Colombia	−2.00	−12.10	−0.10
Mexico	−43.70	2.50	−4.70

Source: Author's calculations based on IMF staff estimates.

having any significant effect on the net foreign asset position of the central bank.[23]

In the recent episode, countries that have targeted the real exchange rate did implement sterilization. Indeed, increases in interest rates, which at first glance are an "incorrect" answer to an exogenous capital inflow, were actually part of the policy mix in Brazil, Chile, and Colombia. With the exception of Brazil, the increase was temporary. Both the quasi-fiscal effects and the fact that speculative flows were being further attracted soon rendered sterilization inefficient.

Fiscal Policy

In many countries, fiscal policy is dependent, in part, on the exchange rate. By definition, the fiscal balance depends on that part of the capital inflow that stems from privatization programs, a crucial element in both Argentina and Mexico. Additionally, in most countries, prudent fiscal policy, more than a response to the inflows, was part of the policy mix that attracted foreign capital in the first place. This point is particularly true in the Mexican experience, where, even when one excludes the revenue from privatization, the improvement in the fiscal balance has been spectacular.

All the countries under review have improved their fiscal balance (Table 4.4) and in all countries public expenditure has, at least, not increased (Table 4.7). These developments are significant. It is easy to imagine the gruesome real exchange rate scenario that would have come about if fiscal policy had not been as prudent as it was. As Calvo, Leiderman, and Reinhart (1994) have pointed out, in countries with abundant foreign capital, private sector expenditure is quite independent of tax obligations. In that case, the best fiscal policy is one that reduces government expenditure but does not rely on heavily increasing the tax burden.

---

[23]Recent estimates by Budnevich and Cifuentes (1994) for Chile and Cárdenas and Barrera (1994) for Colombia suggest that the "offset coefficient" is low enough to give support to the policymakers' reluctance to monetize the reserve inflow.

Table 4.7. Nonfinancial Public Sector Revenue and Expenditure
(In percent of GDP)

Country	1987	1988	1989	1990	1991	1992
Argentina						
Total revenue	. . .	13.4	14.4	13.5	16.4	18.9
Expenditure	18.9	19.2	17.0	17.3	17.9	18.9
Brazil						
Current revenue[1]	. . .	26.9	27.3	33.5	28.9	26.5
Expenditure	37.9	43.3	51.5	43.3	31.1	25.5
Chile						
Total revenue	. . .	34.6	33.2	28.3	29.6	29.8
Expenditure	31.4	30.7	27.6	26.8	27.9	26.9
Colombia						
Total revenue	. . .	32.5	32.7	32.0	33.6	31.7
Expenditure	33.8	34.9	35.1	32.3	33.5	32.3
Mexico						
Total revenue	. . .	30.5	29.6	29.6	30.0	30.4
Expenditure	45.4	39.8	34.5	31.9	27.0	25.9

Source: United Nations, Economic Commission for Latin America and the Caribbean.
[1]In 1991 and 1992, it excludes financial accounts.

Other Policies

Another important policy option is to impose taxes on capital inflows. Countries that deemed it important to maintain a competitive real exchange rate—such as Chile and Colombia—did in fact establish explicit taxes and/or reserve requirements on foreign capital. Temporary restraints were also implemented in Mexico.

The policy, which seemed to fare rather well in Chile, was considered ineffective in Colombia.[24] Policy discussions in the latter case suggest that such an outcome is probably the result of the fact that capital repatriation was an important element, with residents being capable of eluding most restraints that the authorities imposed.

Most countries lifted restrictions on capital outflows as part of a policy package aimed at compensating for the inflationary pressures of the inflows. Again, results do not seem to be favorable; in fact, the lifting of such restrictions may have had the undesirable effect of further stimulating inflows.

---

[24] Most, if not all, assessments of the Chilean experience lend support to the belief that capital controls—in the form of differential reserve requirements—have been effective in curtailing the size of the capital inflow. A pessimistic view with respect to the effectiveness of controls, based on the experiences of Ireland, Portugal, and Spain, appears in Fieleke (1994).

Investment and Growth

The poor economic performance of Latin America during the 1980s has been blamed, in part, on the severely restricted access to foreign financing. It is reasonable to expect that bridging the foreign exchange gap would help boost growth, which has certainly picked up during the current episode, albeit for different reasons and to different degrees in the countries considered. Isolating the effects of the foreign exchange inflow is a difficult task, which will not be attempted here. Instead, some possible linkages between inflows and growth that might be relevant will be cited.

There is no clear answer to how foreign exchange inflows affect growth. It is sometimes believed that inflows, by appreciating the real exchange rate, hamper exports while boosting investment because imported capital goods become less expensive.[25] Additionally, inflows can relax savings and foreign exchange constraints if they are intermediated by the financial system. Furthermore, the stock market boom that has resulted from the foreign exchange inflows—a common occurrence in all the countries that we are considering—may also provide businesses with additional, inexpensive financing possibilities. Simultaneously, inflows could presumably hamper growth if fiscal and monetary policies designed to accommodate them are sufficiently restrictive, as could have happened in Colombia during the first half of 1992. Finally, capital inflows can substitute for domestic savings, thereby increasing consumption without affecting investment. In this case, inflows can have a positive, but short-lived effect on growth.

Although the rate of exchange rate appreciation has varied among countries, and although some have implemented—at least temporarily—contractionary monetary and fiscal policies, for the most part the results in terms of growth have been good, and in Argentina and Chile, quite remarkable (Table 4.8). Sustainability of growth depends critically on the factors that help explain the recent boost in aggregate demand.

Investment has rebounded in Argentina, Chile, and Colombia (Table 4.9), regardlesss of its absolute level and despite the fact that, if anything, public investment has been curtailed in most cases. The impact of FDI on this evolution is probably not important because, through debt conversion schemes, FDI might actually be substituting private domestic investment, while privatization implies the purchase of existing assets.[26]

---

[25]Depending on its sectoral destination, FDI can have a positive effect on export performance, notwithstanding the real exchange rate appreciation. A rather pessimistic assessment of this possibility in the cases of Argentina and Chile stems from the analysis of Fanelli and Damill (1994) and Agosin, Fuentes, and Letelier (1994), respectively. On the relationship between investment and the real exchange rate, see Serven and Solimano (1991).

[26]For a somewhat skeptical view of FDI in Chile through debt-conversion mechanisms, see Ffrench-Davis (1990).

Table 4.8. Growth of GDP

(Annual percent change)

Country	1987	1988	1989	1990	1991	1992	1993
Argentina	2.7	−2.1	−6.2	−0.1	8.9	8.7	6.0
Brazil	3.6	−0.1	3.2	−4.4	0.2	−0.8	4.1
Chile	5.7	7.0	9.6	2.8	5.7	9.8	5.6
Colombia	5.6	4.2	3.5	4.0	1.8	3.6	4.9
Mexico	1.9	1.2	3.3	4.4	3.6	2.8	0.6

Source: United Nations, Economic Commission for Latin America and the Caribbean.

The funding for the increase in investment has, of course, differed considerably between Chile on the one hand and Argentina and Mexico on the other. While in Chile the increase in investment has been coupled with a significant rise in domestic savings, thereby reflecting rather small current account deficits, in Argentina the resurgence of investment has basically been financed with foreign savings (Table 4.9). In Mexico, increased foreign savings have brought about increases in consumption, with no important effect on investment. In the latter case, the drop in domestic savings has been remarkable even though public sector savings have increased (Table 4.9). When analyzing the balance of payments, one might be skeptical about the sustainability of the capital inflow in countries that have experienced a significant real appreciation. A review of the national accounts leads to skepticism because it is unlikely that countries

Table 4.9. Gross Domestic Investment and Savings

(In percent of GDP)

Country	1980	1985	1991	1992	1993
Argentina					
Investment	25.3	17.6	14.6	16.7	18.4
Savings	23.8	23.1	16.2	15.1	16.5
Brazil					
Investment	23.3	19.2	18.9	17.5	18.2
Savings	21.1	24.4	20.9	20.8	20.2
Chile					
Investment	24.6	17.2	22.2	24.1	26.2
Savings	20.5	19.6	26.8	25.8	23.9
Colombia					
Investment	19.1	19.0	16.8	17.6	21.2
Savings	19.7	20.3	24.3	20.9	20.4
Mexico					
Investment	27.2	21.2	22.4	23.3	21.7
Savings	24.9	26.3	19.3	17.7	15.9

Source: World Bank, *Trends in Developing Economies* (Washington, 1994).

Table 4.10. Contributions to GDP Growth

(Annual averages)

	Demand				
	Consumption		Gross	Domestic	Exports of goods and
Country/Year	Government	Private[1]	investment	demand	services
Argentina					
1981–83	–0.2	–2.1	–2.6	–5.1	1.0
1984–87	0.4	1.0	0.2	1.6	–0.2
1988–90	0.7	–4.1	–2.0	–5.4	1.8
1991	1.6	–7.8	3.9	13.3	–1.5
1992	1.6	6.6	4.7	12.8	0.1
Brazil					
1981–83	0.2	–2.5	–2.5	–4.8	0.9
1984–87	0.4	4.1	1.4	5.7	0.7
1988–90	—	0.4	–0.7	–0.3	0.3
1991	0.4	2.1	–0.7	1.8	–0.1
1992	–0.1	–2.8	–0.8	–3.7	2.4
Chile					
1981–83	–0.3	–4.5	–2.2	–7.3	0.4
1984–87	–0.1	2.2	1.7	3.7	2.6
1988–90	0.3	4.0	2.1	6.2	2.9
1991	0.3	3.4	–0.2	3.5	4.3
1992	0.4	7.5	3.4	11.3	4.4
Colombia					
1981–83	0.3	2.5	0.6	3.3	–1.4
1984–87	0.4	1.5	0.2	2.1	2.9
1988–90	0.6	2.7	0.1	3.4	1.2
1991	0.2	1.7	–1.2	0.7	0.7
1992	1.3	2.3	2.2	5.8	1.4
Mexico					
1981–83	0.5	–1.6	–2.6	–3.7	2.5
1984–87	0.2	0.4	—	0.7	0.9
1988–90	0.1	3.6	1.4	5.0	0.8
1991	0.4	3.2	1.5	5.2	1.2
1992	0.2	3.6	2.7	6.5	0.1

Source: United Nations, Economic Commission for Latin America and the Caribbean.
[1]Includes changes in stocks.

will be able to sustain current account deficits if these imbalances reflect a decrease in savings rather than an increase in investment.

The contraction in the ratio of savings to GDP ratio obviously reflects increases in consumption. With the exception of Brazil, total consumption (both public and private) has been the most dynamic element of aggregate demand (Table 4.10). As is to be expected given the evolution of the real exchange rate, exports have played an important role in boosting aggregate demand in Brazil, Chile, and Colombia, but not in Argentina and Mexico. The trade balance results have been in line with real

Table 4.11. Exports of Goods
(In billions of U.S. dollars)

Year	Argentina	Brazil	Chile	Colombia	Mexico
1984	8.1	27.0	3.7	4.3	24.2
1985	8.4	25.6	3.8	3.7	21.7
1986	6.9	22.4	4.2	5.3	16.0
1987	6.4	26.2	5.2	5.7	20.7
1988	9.1	33.8	7.1	5.3	20.6
1989	9.6	34.4	8.1	6.0	22.8
1990	12.4	31.4	8.3	7.1	26.8
1991	12.0	31.6	8.9	7.6	27.1
1992	12.2	36.1	10.0	7.3	27.5
1993	13.1	38.8	9.2	7.4	30.0

Source: United Nations, Economic Commission for Latin America and the Caribbean.

exchange rate developments. Those countries in which appreciation has been significant have seen their trade balance worsen the most. The dominant factor in the trade balance deterioration has been a marked increase in imports, with purchases of capital goods playing a significant role (Tables 4.11 and 4.12). In most countries, this description has held true since 1991 or 1992; in Colombia it is evident only in 1993.

If one accepts that sound structural policies affect capital inflows, then the link between reforms and growth, regardless of the flows, is obvious. That link has to do with the increases in productivity that should emerge from a more outward-oriented economy, a smaller and more efficient public sector, and spillovers of increased FDI. All of these elements must play an important role in any explanation of changes in long-run growth paths; their short-term effects are probably not as significant and, in any event, are quite difficult to analyze at this stage.

Conclusions

The region as a whole has received significant inflows of foreign exchange, which, in most cases, are the result of a capital account surplus that has financed both current account deficits and foreign reserve accumulation. The inflows come at a time when most countries are engaged in reducing inflation and promoting exports. Because the foreign exchange inflows tend to appreciate the real exchange rate, those countries that have focused on export promotion have worked toward preventing such an appreciation. Success in that effort has, in most cases, implied only modest reductions in inflation.

In countries in which inflation reduction has been considered the premier goal, real appreciation has been marked, trade balance deterioration significant, and achievements in price stabilization remarkable. Even

Table 4.12. Imports of Goods

Year	Argentina Total imports[1]	Argentina Capital goods[2]	Brazil Total imports[1]	Brazil Capital goods[2]	Chile Total imports[1]	Chile Capital goods[2]	Colombia Total imports[1]	Colombia Capital goods[2]	Mexico Total imports[1]	Mexico Capital goods[2]
1984	4.1	20.6	13.9	10.5	3.3	19.1	4.0	28.0	11.3	27.2
1985	3.5	23.3	13.2	12.1	2.9	22.6	3.7	21.5	13.2	28.5
1986	4.4	21.3	14.0	15.5	3.1	25.5	3.4	28.2	11.4	39.0
1987	5.3	27.5	15.1	17.5	4.0	27.8	3.8	29.0	12.2	25.3
1988	4.9	25.8	14.6	19.3	4.8	29.6	4.5	27.2	18.9	23.5
1989	3.9	24.1	18.3	17.0	6.5	31.8	4.6	27.2	23.4	22.6
1990	3.7	21.4	20.7	19.1	7.0	33.5	5.1	29.4	31.3	22.8
1991	7.6	23.7	21.0	20.0	7.4	27.5	4.5	27.3	38.2	22.2
1992	13.9	28.4	20.5	30.6	9.2	27.5	6.0	32.2	48.2	24.0
1993	15.5	—	25.5	32.2	10.2	31.4	9.1	39.8	48.9	—

Source: United Nations, Economic Commission for Latin America and the Caribbean.
[1] In billions of U.S. dollars.
[2] In percent of total.

though capital inflows exacerbate pressures on the exchange rate, they are necessary to the sustainability of the exchange rate system.

It seems to be the case that most countries have been successful because either inflation came down, exports increased, or overall growth picked up. In only a few cases is inflation still a major concern; those countries that used the exchange rate as a nominal anchor and that maintained a strong fiscal stance are now experiencing inflation that is rapidly converging to international levels. Generally, exports have increased, although not at the same pace as imports, which have consisted, in an important proportion, of capital goods.

If developments in investment have not been as good as expected, it is in part because overall macroeconomic management has been quite cautious. The data presented suggest that, if anything, the positive assessments of 1992 and 1993 are still valid. Capital has continued to flow into the region, while exchange rate appreciation has subsided markedly. It seems appropriate to conclude that it is a distant possibility that a crisis will occur as a result of the capital that flowed into Latin America in the early 1980s, particularly if the policies that attracted the inflows are not reversed.

References

Agosin, Manuel R., J. Rodrigo Fuentes, and Leonardo Letelier, "Chile: The Origins and Consequences of External Capital," in *Foreign Capital in Latin America*, ed. by J.A. Ocampo and R. Steiner (Washington: Inter-American Development Bank, 1994).

Bianchi, Andrés, "Política Cambiaria, Desarrollo Exportador y Estabilización: La Experiencia Chilena, 1990-92," *Monetaria*, Centro de Estudios Monetarios Latinoamericanos, Vol.17 (July-September 1994), pp. 209-61.

Blejer, Mario, "Comment on Kuczynski," *Proceedings of the World Bank Annual Conference on Development Economics* (Washington: World Bank, 1993), pp. 341-43.

Budnevich, Carlos, and Rodrigo Cifuentes, "Manejo Macroeconómico de los Flujos de Capitales de Corto Plazo: La Experiencia en Chile," in *Afluencia de Capitales y Estabilización en América Latina*, ed. by R. Steiner (Bogota: Fedesarrollo, 1994).

Calderón, Alvaro, *Tendencias Recientes de la Inversión Extranjera Directa en América Latina* (Santiago, Chile: UN Commission for Latin America and the Caribbean, 1993).

Calvo, Guillermo A., Leonardo Leiderman, and Carmen Reinhart, "Capital Inflows and Real Exchange Rate Appreciation in Latin America: The Role of External Factors," *Staff Papers*, International Monetary Fund, Vol. 40 (March 1993), pp. 108-51.

———, "The Capital Inflows Problem: Concepts and Issues," *Contemporary Economic Policy*, Vol. 12 (July 1994), pp. 54-66.

Cárdenas, Mauricio, and Felipe Barrera, "The Macroeconomic Effects of External Capital: Colombia," in *Foreign Capital in Latin America*, ed. by J.A. Ocampo and R. Steiner (Washington: Inter-American Development Bank, 1994).

Carneiro, Dionisio D., and Marcio P.G. García, "Flujos de Capital y Control Monetario bajo Sustitución Doméstica de Dinero: La Reciente Experiencia Brasilera," in *Afluencia de Capitales y Estabilización en América Latina*, ed. by R. Steiner (Bogota: Fedesarrollo, 1994).

Dancourt, Oscar, "Sobre el Retrase Cambiario y la Repatriación de Capitales en una Economía Dolarizada," in *Afluencia de Capitales y Estabilización en América Latina*, ed. by R. Steiner (Bogota: Fedesarrollo, 1994).

Edwards, Sebastián, "Flujos de Capitales, Tasas de Interés y Tipo de Cambio en Colombia" (Unpublished; Washington: World Bank, 1991).

Fanelli, José María, and Mario Damill, "External Capital Flows to Argentina," in *Foreign Capital in Latin America*, ed. by J.A. Ocampo and R. Steiner (Washington: Inter-American Development Bank, 1994).

Ffrench-Davis, Ricardo, "Debt-Equity Swaps in Chile," *Cambridge Journal of Economics*, Vol. 14 (March 1990), pp. 109–26.

Fieleke, Norman, "International Capital Transactions: Should They Be Restricted?," *New England Economic Review*, Federal Reserve Bank of Boston (March–April 1994), pp. 27-39.

Frankel, Jeffrey, "Sterilization of Money Inflows: Difficult (Calvo) or Easy (Reisen)?," in *Afluencia de Capitales y Estabilización en América Latina*, ed. by R. Steiner (Bogota: Fedesarrollo, 1994).

Galy, Michel, Gonzalo Pastor, and Thierry Pujol, *Spain: Converging with the European Community*, IMF Occasional Paper No. 101 (Washington: International Monetary Fund, 1993).

Ghosh, Atish, and Jonathan D. Ostry, "Do Capital Flows Reflect Economic Fundamentals in Developing Countries?," IMF Working Paper 93/34 (Washington: International Monetary Fund, 1993).

Kuczynski, Pedro Pablo, "International Capital Flows to Latin America: What Is the Promise?," *Proceedings of the World Bank Annual Conference on Development Economics* (Washington: World Bank, 1993), pp. 323-36.

Morales, Juan Antonio, "Los Efectos en la Economía Boliviana de los Flujos Recientes de Capital Externo Privado," in *Afluencia de Capitales y Estabilización en América Latina*, ed. by R. Steiner (Bogota: Fedesarrollo, 1994).

Morandé, Felipe, "Domestic Currency Appreciation and Foreign Capital Inflows: What Comes First? (Chile, 1977–82)," *Journal of International Money and Finance*, Vol. 7 (December 1988), pp. 447-66.

Reisen, Helmut, "Southeast Asia and the 'Impossible Trinity,'" *International Economic Insights*, Vol. 4 (May–June 1993), pp. 21-23.

Rodríguez, Carlos A., "Money and Credit Under Currency Substitution," *Staff Papers*, International Monetary Fund, Vol. 40 (June 1993), pp. 414-26.

Ros, Jaime, "Financial Markets and Capital Flows in Mexico," in *Foreign Capital in Latin America*, ed. by J.A. Ocampo and R. Steiner (Washington: Inter-American Development Bank, 1994).

Schadler, Susan, Maria Carkovic, Adam Bennett, and Robert Kahn, *Recent Experiences with Surges in Capital Inflows*, IMF Occasional Paper No. 108 (Washington: International Monetary Fund, 1993).

Serven, Luis, and Andrés Solimano, *Adjustment Policies and Investment Performance in Developing Countries* (Washington: World Bank, 1991).

Steiner, Roberto, Rodrigo Suescún, and Fernando Melo, "Flujos de Capital y Expectativas de Devaluación," *Coyuntura Económica*, Vol. 22 (June 1992), pp. 93–110.

Comment

Guillermo A. Calvo

The paper by Steiner is a welcome addition to the literature on one of the most pressing macroeconomic issues for Latin America. While earlier papers have focused on the region as a whole or on specific countries, the present one offers a more balanced view of regionwide and country-specific factors that may be lying behind the remarkable surge of capital inflows in Latin America.

I will start my comments with a clarification that addresses a common misunderstanding about the central message in Calvo, Leiderman, and Reinhart (1993). (I should hasten to say, though, that Steiner's paper is not guilty of that.) These authors show evidence suggesting that the recent capital inflows in Latin America may be strongly affected by factors lying outside the region—like U.S. interest rates. However, even though our paper's emphasis is on external factors, the evidence presented there suggests that only 50 percent of the flows may be explained by those factors, the remaining 50 percent probably being due to factors internal to each country. Therefore, there is no contradiction between Steiner's findings that the timing of the flows is not the same across countries—possibly reflecting policies being undertaken in each country—and those in Calvo, Leiderman, and Reinhart. It should be noted, incidentally, that Steiner's paper does not utilize statistical methods and, therefore, is unable to provide us with estimates about the explanatory power of country-specific factors. This is a subject that deserves further study.

Capital inflows are in principle a good thing. They relieve the tight financial constraints under which Latin American countries had to operate during the 1980s, helping to replenish badly needed international reserves and to increase capital accumulation from alarmingly low levels. One central concern, however, is that domestic financial institutions may not have the know-how to handle these flows properly, increasing financial vulnerability. The latter may be the result of (1) an inability of the financial system to assess risk—particularly when funds are channeled to new customers or new activities—and/or (2) a pronounced maturity mismatch between deposits and loans—the latter normally being of longer maturity than the former. This type of concern is heightened by the prevalence of explicit or implicit bank insurance given by the central bank, a fact that weakens the incentives of financial institutions to mind loan risk and maturity mismatch.

Under those circumstances, capital inflows may cause serious disruptions even though, otherwise, monetary and fiscal policies follow strict canons. Unfortunately, the "black holes" that may be created by financial vulnerability can be seen only when they happen, which is too late.

Consequently, I believe that we should pay special attention to policies that contribute to lowering financial vulnerability. From that perspective, for example, sterilized intervention (by means of open market operations) is attractive because it lowers the impact of capital flows on the expansion of domestic bank credit to the private sector. Unfortunately, such policy has proven to be fiscally expensive, prompting Colombia to rely much less on it from 1991, and Argentina to abandon it altogether after the start of the Convertibility Plan.

An alternative is sterilized intervention through different procedures, for example, by increasing banks' (nonremunerated) reserve requirements. To avoid causing serious banking illiquidity, the higher reserve requirements could apply only to deposits in excess of those prevailing in any given base period. This policy is highly effective in the short run and—unlike sterilization through open market operations—brings about no direct fiscal cost. However, in the medium run, high reserve requirements will cause disintermediation, heavier reliance on offshore banking, and the growth of a parallel financial system.

Consequently, in a protracted episode of capital inflows, like the current one, there seem to be two major realistic monetary policy alternatives: (1) floating exchange rates, and (2) strengthening the domestic financial industry through external support.

One major advantage of floating exchange rates is that the central bank recovers some of its powers of "lender of last resort." However, in heavily dollarized systems like those in Argentina, Peru, and Uruguay, this advantage could be limited. Furthermore, countries are reluctant to allow wide fluctuations of the nominal exchange rate. Under normal circumstances, changes in nominal exchange rates are closely mirrored by changes in the *real* exchange rate. Therefore, wide fluctuations in the nominal exchange rate also entail wide fluctuations in key relative prices that, as a general rule, are not seen as welcome developments. Consequently, exchange rate flexibility—although, on occasion, useful—is unlikely to provide a full solution to the capital inflows problem.

Now we come to the last realistic monetary policy alternative, namely, international support. Let me first make it very clear that international support is of no use if domestic policies are unsound. For the present discussion, this means, in particular, that domestic regulations must ensure the soundness of the asset side of banks' balance sheets. Loans must, on the whole, be fully performing. To ensure this, the central bank may have to set high reserve requirements at the beginning of the capital inflows episode given that, as noted above, the banking industry may initially be ill prepared to intermediate the new flows effectively. Again, for reasons mentioned above, this draconian policy may have to be relaxed over time;

however, it is to be hoped that such a policy will be accompanied by much-improved banking supervision.

The existence of performing loans does not necessarily prevent a banking crisis. Bank runs could take place and, unless there is a "lender of last resort," financial institutions may be forced into bankruptcy. Thus, if the central bank did not receive external assistance, it would have to hold very large international reserves—a requirement that may be infeasible in the short or medium run or exceedingly costly.

External assistance can take several forms. It may take the form of a stabilization fund like the one set up by Poland's donors in 1990, or automatic swap arrangements like those presently available for Mexico from its NAFTA partners. External assistance could also take more subtle forms. For example, the central bank's role as "lender of last resort" may be less critical if banks get *direct* financial support from external sources. This may be the case for a branch of a well-known international bank, because the bank may be reluctant to let its subsidiary file for bankruptcy and, therefore, may be more willing to provide the necessary short-run liquid funds to avoid it. Another, more basic reason for greater expeditiousness in obtaining funds from the parent company is that the latter may have better information than the market about the soundness of its subsidiary's portfolio.

Latin America appears to be marching into an era of progress and stability: the capital inflows phenomenon may well be seen in the future as the harbinger of such an era, and much of this discussion as excessive "wringing of the hands." This will be a much better mistake, I believe, than the one made at the turn of the 1980s, when the flows were considered a panacea until the region was plunged into its longest, and arguably most painful, twentieth-century recession.

5

Central Bank Independence and Coordination of Monetary Policy and Public Debt Management

Tomás J.T. Baliño

Monetary and public debt management are closely linked aspects of economic policy: actions in one area heavily influence the other. At the same time, however, there is a trend toward making the monetary authority—the central bank—more independent of the government, which is the issuer of public debt. This paper discusses the key links between these policies and suggests possible arrangements to reconcile central bank independence with coordination of monetary and public debt management.

Effects of Public Debt Management on Monetary Policy

The volume and characteristics of public debt must be taken into consideration in the formulation of monetary policy. They influence the behavior of the public with respect to money holdings as well as the actions of the central bank.

Public debt can influence the demand for money in at least two ways. First, in the absence of Ricardian equivalence, an increase in the amount of public debt held by residents will have a positive wealth effect, which will tend to increase the volume of real balances demanded.[1] Second, liquid government securities can be a substitute for money balances, tending to reduce the demand for such balances. In addition, large outstanding

Note: The views expressed in this paper are those of the author and do not necessarily reflect the views of the International Monetary Fund. Comments received from Messrs. Carlo Cottarelli, Ernesto Feldman, David Hoelscher, from the two discussants (Messrs. Roberto Junguito and Sérgio Ribeiro da Costa Werlang), and from other participants of the seminar are gratefully acknowledged.
    [1]For a discussion of this issue see Tanner and Devereux (1993). They suggest the possibility that a positive correlation between public debt and real money balances might reflect a supply rather than a demand effect. They argue that if public debt is monetized but the public adjusts its money holdings with a lag, then such a correlation might be observed. For the United States, however, they find evidence of a demand but not of a supply effect.

amounts of public debt may create expectations of future inflation, which would also lower the demand for money.

A large amount of public debt will also affect the behavior of the central bank. It can lead to a multiplicity of objectives for the central bank, some of which may be inconsistent with one another. This is particularly the case if the central bank is obliged to ensure that the government debt is financed at a certain cost. Several financing possibilities exist. First, the central bank directly purchases the government debt, thereby expanding base money as the government spends the proceeds of the sale. Second, the debt is placed in the market, but the central bank adjusts its monetary policy stance so as to reduce the cost of market borrowing to the government. Third, the government or the central bank establishes portfolio restrictions that force various economic agents to hold government debt that pays below-market rates.

In the first case, the central bank may try to sterilize the excess supply of reserve money by selling securities in its portfolio or by issuing its own paper. However, this can entail losses for the central bank and consequently cause another expansion of base money when interest payments become due. That will be the case if the sterilization is done through the issuance of central bank liabilities at market rates while the government debt acquired by the central bank carries a below-market rate. The same result obtains if the central bank has to sell at a discount government debt that it purchased at par.

In the second case, the objective of allowing the government to finance the deficit cheaply will often conflict with the anti-inflation objectives of the central bank. The U.S. Federal Reserve pursued such an objective until 1951, when it came to an agreement with the Treasury to stop supporting the price of government bonds. This agreement, called the "Accord" in the literature, was reached so that the high government deficit caused by the Korean War would not lead to a surge in inflation.[2]

In the third case, the government places restrictions on the composition of the portfolios of certain economic agents—typically pension funds, insurance companies, or financial intermediaries. Pension funds and insurance companies are often required to hold government securities as part of their technical reserves. Liquidity requirements are a common instrument that central banks use to induce banks and other deposit-taking institutions to finance the government.[3] Countries as different as Brazil, Cyprus, and India have used this type of instrument extensively.

---

[2]For an excellent discussion of this episode, see Friedman and Schwartz (1963).

[3]This instrument has also been viewed as a prudential tool, to ensure that those institutions are able to meet their obligations. However, modern prudential criteria focus on the overall liquidity position of an institution (that is, including all assets and liabilities as well as off-balance-sheet items) and do not rely on mandatory minimum ratios.

Insofar as liquidity ratios induce commercial banks to hold government debt, such lending does not appear on the books of the central bank. However, the economic result is equivalent to what obtains when the central bank lends directly to the government but sterilizes the monetary expansion by forcing commercial banks to hold base money (for instance, by raising reserve requirements) or any other central bank liability (for example, central bank securities).[4]

Both liquidity ratios and reserve requirements are implicit taxes on financial intermediation. Banks obtain a lower yield on their assets than in the absence of such restrictions, which drives a wedge between deposit and lending rates. This creates incentives for disintermediation, as economic agents shift their business to financial transactions that are not subject to those requirements. Domestically, this may involve transferring deposits to nonbank financial intermediaries if these intermediaries are not subject to portfolio restrictions,[5] investing the funds in nonintermediated financial assets, increasing currency holdings, or buying nonfinancial assets. Thus, changes in liquidity ratios or reserve requirements will affect relative asset prices. The central bank can make liquidity ratios and reserve requirements more or less burdensome by determining the assets that banks can use to fulfill them. For instance, it can allow a broader set of assets (including, for example, commercial paper) to be counted in fulfillment of the liquidity ratio or it can remunerate deposits held to meet the reserve requirement.

Depending on how burdensome portfolio restrictions are, banks will try to circumvent them. They may package their deposits differently, use off-balance-sheet financing (for example, banker's acceptances), or set up affiliates—at home or abroad—that can offer financial products that are exempt from such restrictions. Economic agents can also avoid the costs of portfolio restrictions by buying foreign assets. To prevent this, financially repressed economies usually impose restrictions on international transactions. These restrictions always comprise capital account transactions but often also current transactions—since the latter can also serve to facilitate evasion of capital account restrictions.

Portfolio restrictions and interest rate controls are common forms of financial repression. This repression can generate sizable revenue for the government, which largely explains why they have been so prevalent.[6] In

---

[4]Which instrument the central bank chooses is not trivial, owing to differences in the remuneration among them.

[5]For instance, in Cyprus deposits with credit cooperatives as a share of total deposits rose from less than 25 percent to about 33 percent between 1983 and 1992. At least in part, this shift was due to the imposition of a liquidity ratio on banks but not on those cooperatives. This allowed the latter to gain market share gradually, as they could offer better rates to their clients; this process tapered off as the fall in international interest rates began to be felt in Cyprus.

[6]In addition to misguided efforts to provide cheap finance to certain sectors.

Table 5.1. Size of Revenue from Financial Repression

| Country | Sample Period | Revenue from Financial Repression | |
		Percentage of GDP	Percentage of tax revenue
Algeria	1974–87	4.30	11.42
Brazil	1983–87	0.48	1.57
Colombia	1980–84	0.24	2.11
Costa Rica	1972–84	2.33	12.76
Greece	1974–85	2.53	7.76
India	1980–85	2.86	22.38
Indonesia	1976–86	—	—
Jamaica	1980, 1982	1.38	4.74
Jordan	1978–87	0.60	2.40
Korea	1975–87	0.25	1.36
Malaysia	1974–81	0.12	0.31
Mexico	1984–87	5.77	39.65
Morocco	1977–85	2.31	8.89
Pakistan	1982–83	3.23	20.50
Panama	1977–87	0.69	2.49
Papua New Guinea	1981–87	0.40	1.90
Philippines	1975–86	0.45	3.88
Portugal	1978–86	2.22	6.93
Sri Lanka	1981–83	3.40	19.24
Thailand	1976–86	0.38	2.57
Tunisia	1978–87	1.49	4.79
Turkey	1980–87	2.20	10.89
Zaïre	1974–86[1]	0.46	2.48
Zimbabwe	1981–86	5.50	19.13

Source: Giovannini and De Melo (1993).
[1]The sample for Zaïre does not include the years 1981, 1982, and 1983.

a recent study, Giovannini and De Melo (1993) compute such revenue for 24 countries. They measure it as the differential between the cost of foreign borrowing and the cost of domestic borrowing, multiplied by the annual average stock of domestic debt. Their estimates exclude central bank holdings of government debt on the grounds that those holdings are financed by issuing reserve money—and therefore are not directly related to financial repression—and that interest paid to the central bank is reflected in the bank's profits, which typically are transferred back to the government. As shown in Table 5.1, these revenues ranged from zero (in the case of Indonesia) to almost 6 percent for Mexico.[7] That paper also suggests a positive correlation between the revenue from financial repression and seigniorage.

---

[7]Owing to differences in data availability, the sample periods differ and their length is not uniform.

Moore (1993) presents evidence on the linkages between portfolio restrictions on banks and fiscal deficits in Mexico. He notes that "as the deficit was approaching its highest levels, the banking system was subject to numerous restrictions that may have been intended to reduce the government's borrowing cost but that had the unintended effect of crippling bank lending to the private sector" (p. 35). He also finds that elimination of the deficit made it possible to lift restrictions on bank portfolios.

Moore's results and those of Giovannini and De Melo, discussed above, illustrate an important linkage between central bank policy and fiscal developments. In a country that is heavily dependent on the revenue from fiscal repression, the central bank would have serious difficulties in attempting a financial liberalization unless the government has found a way to make up for the loss of revenue. Moreover, since the revenue from financial repression and seigniorage tends to be correlated, a large fiscal effort will likely be required to compensate for the loss of those two sources of revenue.

Changes in government deposits with the central bank are another important channel through which government operations can have a monetary impact. In many countries, the government keeps its accounts with the central bank. As a result, shifts of funds between the public and the government entail changes in reserve money. Thus, regular government operations, like tax collections and salary payments, result in a sizable sterilization or creation of reserve money that the central bank must include in its monetary programming and offset as appropriate. As discussed later in this paper, in some countries (Canada, Germany, and Malaysia), the central bank manages those balances on behalf of the treasury and can use them as an instrument to attain its monetary objectives. It does so by placing those deposits with commercial banks or with the central bank, depending on whether it wishes to expand or contract the monetary base. In other countries (for example, the United States), special arrangements are in place to minimize the effect of government deposit variations on monetary conditions.

The above discussion focused on the management of domestic public debt. However, the public debt manager also decides how much to borrow domestically and abroad. Other things being equal, borrowing abroad will increase the supply of base money to the extent that government converts the proceeds from the loan into local currency to finance its domestic expenditures. If foreign and domestic bonds are perfect substitutes, this monetary effect will be offset by a corresponding private capital flow. However, this perfect substitutability need not obtain—or its effects may take time—and therefore borrowing abroad will have at least a short-run effect on the supply of reserve money. Moreover, if the institutional arrangements result in the central bank's assuming the exchange rate risk for foreign borrowing, the central bank may incur heavy losses in case of a sharp depreciation of the currency. If these losses are monetized, a monetary expansion will follow.

Effect of Monetary Policy and Other Central Bank Actions on Debt Management

The above discussion suggests that government financing can have a major effect on monetary policy. In fact, in many countries both in the industrial world (for example, Italy) and in the developing world (for example, Argentina and Brazil), it has been the key influence.[8] In turn, monetary policy and other central bank actions affect debt management. These effects may not be easy to predict. For instance, an expansionary monetary policy will normally facilitate the placement of government debt. However, if it leads to inflation, different results may obtain. The government will have to adjust the yield on its paper to take inflation into account, either through indexation or through a nominal interest rate that compensates investors for expected inflation. Sometimes, the government may be unable to adjust the yield on government debt because of legal caps on interest rates—assuming of course that the cap also prevents the government from selling its paper below par.

In addition to the stance of monetary policy, the central bank's choice of instruments for its monetary operations can affect the government's debt management. Government securities not only serve to finance the budget but also often serve as a monetary policy instrument. Central bank participation in the market will make that paper more liquid and hence will reduce the government's borrowing cost. The coordination issues raised by the use of securities both to finance the government and for monetary operations are discussed later in this paper.

The design of a central bank rediscount facility can affect the demand for government debt. Often, a central bank will be prepared to rediscount government paper or to accept it as collateral for its loans. In particular, if it accepts government paper under better conditions than private paper (and even more if the latter is not accepted at all), it lowers the borrowing cost of the treasury with respect to that of the private sector (beyond what could be justified owing to the lower risk of government securities). Moreover, government paper that meets the requirements set by the central bank to accept it in its operations—for example, the paper's maturity—will tend to bear a lower yield than government paper that is ineligible for those operations. This will influence the choice of security characteristics that a cost-minimizing government debt manager makes.

---

[8]The same can be said of most transforming centrally planned economies in Eastern Europe and in the former Soviet Union.

Many central banks have issued their own securities to implement monetary policy. Those papers will typically compete with those issued by the government to finance itself and will tend to raise government borrowing costs.

The design of other central bank instruments also influences the demand for government debt management. For instance, reserve requirements will have different effects, depending on whether reserve balances must be maintained as an average or on a daily basis. In the former case, if the requirement is high, the stock of reserves is likely to suffice to meet a bank's liquidity needs as they may result, for instance, from the interbank settlement. Therefore, banks have less need for other liquid assets, such as government bonds that they can easily liquidate or use as collateral to obtain reserve money, than would be the case if the requirement had to be met on a daily basis. In the latter case, a bank cannot use its reserve balances to cushion changes in its liquidity needs.

Whether the reserve system is contemporaneous or lagged also has a strong influence on the demand for liquid paper. Under a contemporaneous system, commercial banks must adjust their reserve balances during the same reserve-maintenance period in which their deposit liabilities changed. Under a lagged system, banks have some scope to postpone adjustment or to adjust more gradually—depending on their expectations and when during the reserve-maintenance period the change occurred. Whether the reserve system is contemporaneous or lagged will also affect banks' preferences regarding holdings of liquid government debt. Other things being equal, banks will wish to hold a more liquid portfolio under a contemporaneous reserve requirement system than under a lagged one, and, therefore, will tend to hold a larger share in liquid government securities.

The central bank also affects the functioning of the money market, a major influence on the market for government debt. For instance, it may have established special arrangements, such as having designated a group of dealers as primary dealers, setting obligations for them, and giving them certain privileges. A typical obligation for these dealers is to quote buy and sell prices constantly for government securities, which enhances the liquidity of those securities.

In addition, the central bank either operates or regulates payments systems, whose arrangements also have a bearing on the demand for government debt and on the terms and conditions of government paper. A reliable, low-cost, and fast payments system for large-value transactions will facilitate the growth of the money market, including the market for government securities. Such large-value systems usually include mechanisms for the transfer of the securities that often are the counterpart of a transfer of reserve money.

In countries having capital controls, it is often the central bank that sets them. These controls (for example, special deposits established to equalize domestic and foreign borrowing costs) will also affect the borrowing costs of the government and will influence the debt manager's decision regarding where to borrow.

Finally, some central banks also manage or regulate deposit insurance schemes. These schemes can affect the demand for government debt. First, by making deposits safer, deposit insurance can make them closer substitutes of government securities for investors seeking safe assets. Second, if the scheme is funded and contributions are invested in government bonds, the demand for those bonds will tend to increase.

Case for Central Bank Independence

Recently, interest in central bank independence has increased. Papers and books dealing with the subject have been appearing at a fast rate. Many countries are adopting or revising legislation aimed at increasing central bank independence.

Central Bank Independence in the Economic Literature

What is central bank independence? How can it be measured? What can it achieve? These are the key questions that the literature has tried to answer. The empirical and the theoretical literature have followed different approaches in dealing with these issues.[9]

Empirical studies have focused on identifying certain attributes of independence, designing indicators to measure them, choosing a policy objective—such as inflation, growth, or the government deficit—and then comparing how countries whose central banks have different degrees of independence compare with one another in terms of attaining the chosen policy objective.

Those studies have considered various attributes of central bank independence, such as financial independence and political independence. The former has been measured by indicators such as the central bank's ability to set salaries for its staff, to control its budget, and its degree of discretion regarding distribution of its profits. Financial independence, particularly in many developing countries, should also include the freedom for the central bank not to undertake operations that will lead to central bank losses. For instance, in the 1980s in several Latin American countries (such as Argentina, Chile, and Uruguay), central banks had to bail out commercial banks and provide exchange rate guarantees that proved to be costly.[10]

---

[9]For a good survey of this literature, see Pollard (1993).

[10]These cases and some other financial crises are discussed in Sundararajan and Baliño (1991).

Political independence indicators have included such features as whether the government appoints the members of the bank's council, government representation in that council, and who has final authority—the government or the bank—in policy matters in the central bank's jurisdiction. To pass judgment on the degree of central bank independence, some authors have devised composite indices, which incorporate several of the above attributes.[11] The provisions of the central bank law have been a key criterion for gauging those attributes; other factors, such as the turnover of central bank governors, have also been considered.

Price stability has been the policy objective that most economic studies have considered. This stance reflects the view that inflation is a monetary phenomenon. Thus, the test aims to determine whether an independent central bank is better able to keep inflation low than a central bank that is not independent. Several studies fall in this category: Bade and Parkin (1985); Alesina (1988); Grilli, Masciandaro and Tabellini (1991); Cukierman (1992); and Cukierman, Webb, and Neyapti (1992). The first three cover member countries of the Organization for Economic Cooperation and Development (OECD) only; the last two cover 72 countries throughout the world. All these studies find evidence of a negative correlation between inflation and the degree of independence—one of them also found a negative correlation between the variance of inflation and central bank independence (Alesina and Summers, 1993).

Studies on the relationship between economic growth and central bank independence have yielded less conclusive results. Grilli, Masciandaro, and Tabellini (1991) and Alesina and Summers (1993) found no correlation between central bank independence and economic growth. The results in these papers are somewhat puzzling, as evidence for essentially the same set of countries suggests a negative correlation between inflation and growth (Grimes, 1991), and as discussed above inflation has exhibited a negative correlation with central bank independence. However, De Long and Summers (1992) observed a positive correlation between the growth rate of real GDP per worker and central bank independence.

An interesting insight regarding industrial and developing countries comes from the analysis of Cukierman and others (1993), who found no correlation between central bank independence and economic growth for industrial countries but a negative correlation for developing countries. This may be related to the fact that independence has been higher

---

[11]Bade and Parkin (1985); Alesina (1988); Grilli, Masciandaro, and Tabellini (1991); and Cukierman, Webb, and Neyapti (1992) constructed such indices. Alesina and Summers (1993) used the average of the indices of Bade and Parkin, and Grilli, Masciandaro, and Tabellini as their measure of central bank independence. For a good summary of their results, as well as for a discussion of the general issue of central bank independence and economic performance, see Pollard (1993).

for industrial countries as a group than for developing countries. Thus, beyond a certain (high) degree of independence, more independence seems to make little difference for economic growth.

Finally, a few studies have addressed the relationship between central bank independence and fiscal deficits. Parkin (1986) found a negative correlation between the two. Masciandaro and Tabellini (1988) had inconclusive results: despite the high degree of independence of the Federal Reserve, the United States showed fiscal deficits of the same order of magnitude as countries whose central banks are much less independent.[12] Grilli, Masciandaro, and Tabellini (1991) analyzed 18 OECD countries during 1950–89. They observed a negative correlation between central bank independence and fiscal deficits. However, that correlation disappeared once political factors—related to government stability— were taken into account.

Pollard (1994) finds a negative, but statistically not significant, correlation between central bank independence and fiscal deficits. Furthermore, she reports a negative correlation between the former variable and the variability of fiscal deficits.

The theoretical literature has defined independence using a criterion somewhat different from those used by the empirical literature, as discussed above. Rather than focusing on issues such as the governance and the financial autonomy of the central bank, it has defined independence as a lack of cooperation between the fiscal and the monetary authorities. Thus, an autonomous central bank is one that sets monetary policy without regard for the fiscal authority's objectives. Moreover, this literature assumes that the behavior of the fiscal and the monetary authorities results from the minimization of different loss functions, including growth and inflation. The assumption is that, in their loss functions, the fiscal authority will tend to give more weight to growth than the monetary authority and that the opposite holds for inflation.

The papers of Pyndick (1976), Andersen and Schneider (1986), Alesina and Tabellini (1987), Petit (1989), and Hughes Hallet and Petit (1990) follow the lines discussed above. These studies conclude that noncooperation is suboptimal. Policy conflicts between the central bank and the fiscal authority result in lower growth and higher inflation than what would obtain under cooperation.

Of particular interest for this paper are some theoretical studies that focus on the effect of central bank independence on government debt.[13] The argument starts with the assumption that the government cannot

---

[12]The first of these studies covered all OECD countries during 1955–83. The second covered only Australia, Canada, Japan, New Zealand, and the United States during 1970–85.

[13]See for instance Sargent and Wallace (1985), Tabellini (1986, 1987), and Blackburn and Christensen (1989).

indefinitely accumulate debt to finance itself. Thus, the issue is whether a policy of high deficits will eventually force the central bank to monetize part of that debt, causing inflation and reducing the outstanding value of the debt. These studies also show that cooperation yields better results in terms of lowering the value of the debt.

From the above, it appears that the empirical literature and the theoretical literature have reached different conclusions on the benefits of central bank independence. The former finds independence advantageous, and the latter disadvantageous. This need not entail a contradiction. The empirical literature defines independence differently from the theoretical literature. The former focuses on the ability of the central bank to be outside the direct influence of the government. The latter equates independence with lack of coordination. Thus, the contradiction between these two strands of the literature disappears, for instance, if a central bank is independent of the government politically and financially but its objectives agree with those of the government.[14]

Central Bank Independence Experiences

As noted earlier, many countries have endeavored to grant more independence to their central banks. Such independence has been interpreted as the ability of the central bank to design and implement monetary policy without interference from other government bodies. The argument behind these efforts rests on two premises. First, monetary policy can be effective in achieving price stability. Second, such a policy can be better implemented by an institution that is not subject to the daily political pressures that the government faces.

The member countries of the European Union have undertaken to give their central banks a high degree of independence. Under the Maastricht Treaty, central banks cannot receive instructions from the government, and their governors have a minimum term of five years, which can be extended. Moreover, the treaty has strict provisions regarding credit to the government. In particular, its Article 104, which discusses credit to the government from the European Central Bank (ECB) and the member countries' central banks, specifically states:

---

[14]The cases of New Zealand and Argentina, discussed below, are examples of countries that have independent central banks, but the policies that these banks can follow are constrained. In the case of New Zealand, the constraints arise from the explicit agreement between the Ministry of Finance and the Governor of the Reserve Bank on the inflation target. In the case of Argentina, they are embodied in the Convertibility Law, which requires the central bank to follow policies and use instruments that are consistent with the goal of preserving the peso-dollar parity set by the law.

1. Overdraft facilities or any other type of credit facility with the ECB or with the central banks of the Member States (hereinafter referred to as "national central banks") in favor of Community institutions or bodies, central governments, regional, local or other public authorities, other bodies governed by public law, or public undertakings of Member States shall be prohibited, as shall the purchase directly from them by the ECB or national central banks of debt instruments.

However, the treaty still allows central banks to purchase government debt instruments in the secondary market. The treaty has prompted a revision of central bank legislation in Europe to comply with the treaty's provisions.

Countries in other parts of the world have also adapted their legislation to make their central banks more independent. New Zealand and several countries in Latin America are examples of this movement. New Zealand's legislation, which took effect in February 1990, is often cited as a model in this regard. The old legislation it replaced was typical of central bank laws passed until the 1980s. It provided for the central bank to maintain and promote social welfare; to promote trade, production, and full employment; and to maintain a stable internal price level. The relative importance of these objectives changed over time, depending on circumstances and the views of the government in power.[15]

The multiplicity of objectives that the law gave to the Reserve Bank of New Zealand prevented it from focusing on any of the objectives. Moreover, government policies up to 1984 led to large fiscal deficits and a rapidly growing public debt (Charts 5.1 and 5.2). Domestic public debt was placed with the Reserve Bank and, compulsorily, with the rest of the financial system. Interest rates and the lending of financial institutions were strictly controlled. Pervasive exchange controls had little effect on large external deficits, and foreign debt was growing rapidly. An interesting feature of the change in the Reserve Bank's Act was that it came *after* the government had embarked on liberalization and had, in practice, granted more autonomy to the Bank.[16]

The reform of the law focused on giving a clear, single objective to the Bank's policy—price stability—and on ensuring transparency and accountability. Transparency is ensured by the Policy Targets Agreement, signed by the Minister of Finance and the Governor of the Reserve Bank, which establishes performance criteria for the Governor to meet under his or her contract. This agreement sets forth the inflation target that the Bank must pursue and indicates when it must be attained. It also includes

---

[15]For a description of the motivation and contents of the new central bank law for New Zealand, see Knight (1991).

[16]As will be discussed below, this has also been the case in other countries that have recently reformed their central banking legislation.

Chart 5.1. New Zealand: Domestic Public Debt

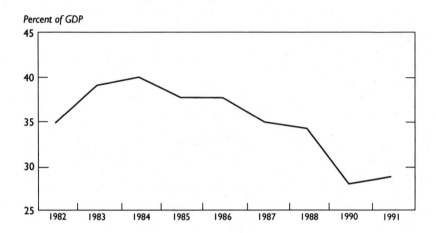

Sources: International Monetary Fund (1992, 1993). (Information for 1989 is unavailable.)

certain caveats, such as changes in indirect taxes or in the terms of trade, which would provide for a renegotiation of the terms of the agreement.

The terms of the policy targets are made public, and the Bank is also required to issue a public statement every six months, outlining its policy and discussing past monetary developments.. While the law makes price stability the sole focus of central bank policy, as an exception it allows the

Chart 5.2. New Zealand: Fiscal Balance

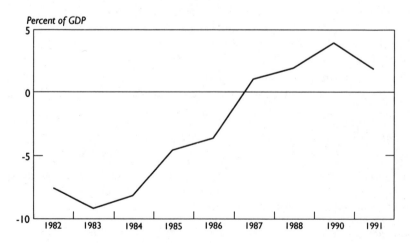

Sources: International Monetary Fund (1992, 1993). (Information for 1989 is unavailable.)

government to direct the Reserve Bank to pursue a different economic objective for a maximum period of 12 months, which can be extended

Other provisions of the Reserve Bank's law aim at providing accountability. For instance, the Minister of Finance and the Governor also sign a funding agreement, which establishes the maximum amount that the Bank can spend over the five-year duration of that agreement. The Governor is personally responsible for the achievement of the targets set forth in the Policy Targets Agreement. A board of directors exists but has no power to set policies; its main role is to monitor the Governor's performance under the Policy Targets Agreement. Unjustified failure to fulfill the agreement provides grounds for dismissing the Governor.

Thus, New Zealand's law affords great independence to the central bank but only to pursue a specific objective, which, in addition must be set in agreement with the government.[17] Also, the government has the power—which it has not yet exercised—to direct the Bank to follow a different objective. However, it must make such a directive explicit and public, which is likely to make it politically costly.

A final point about the reform of the Reserve Bank legislation is that it did not occur in a vacuum: the government had already granted de facto independence to the central bank, and a stabilization and liberalization program had been implemented. Thus, the legislative changes were meant not to increase such independence but to make it more permanent by including it in the law.

As noted earlier, several countries in Latin America have reformed their central bank legislation or are planning to do so.[18] The following countries recently introduced changes in their central bank legislation: Argentina (1992), Bolivia (1993), Chile (1989), Colombia (1992), Ecuador (1992), El Salvador (1991), Mexico (1993), Nicaragua (1992), and Venezuela (1992). Others are in the process of changing legislation: these include Costa Rica, the Dominican Republic, Guyana, Paraguay, and Uruguay.[19]

These legislative reforms aim at minimizing the potential for central banks to be pressured to adopt policies that undermine price stability, as was often the case in the past. Central banks in Latin America financed public sector deficits and undertook various quasi-fiscal activities, which in the end fueled inflation. Those activities have included, among others, financing the government at below-market interest rates, directing credit

---

[17]This represents an interesting way to reconcile the different views on independence espoused by the empirical and the theoretical literature on the subject. The central bank has full political and financial independence and also decides how to pursue its objectives. The objectives, however, are the result of an agreement with the government.

[18]The following discussion on central banking reform in Latin America relies heavily on Dueñas (1994).

[19]Bolivia and Ecuador are studying further amendments to their central bank legislation.

and granting interest subsidies to specific sectors, extending exchange rate guarantees—which entailed significant losses for the central bank when they had to be honored—assuming responsibility for exchange risk on external borrowing, administering multiple exchange rate arrangements, and funding poorly designed deposit insurance schemes.

As was the case in New Zealand, the legislative reform in Latin America was most often part of a package of measures aimed at attaining monetary stability. Furthermore, again as in New Zealand, the idea was not to reform the law so that a stronger central bank could *attain* stability but rather to protect the central bank from political interference in the future, so that stability could be better *preserved*. This protection against future mismanagement yielded the immediate benefit of greater credibility in the policies that were being implemented. The experiences of Chile and Argentina illustrate this general point.

In Chile, the 1980 constitution already included the principle of central bank autonomy. The objective was to prevent a recurrence of the old practice of monetization of fiscal deficits. A new draft central bank law was prepared in 1981, but the 1982–83 crisis caused the project to be shelved until 1986.

The law finally came into effect in October 1989, after the economy had recovered from the crisis and resumed rapid growth in a context of abated inflation. Moreover, the nonfinancial public sector balance had turned to surplus in 1988 and has remained in surplus since then.

In Argentina, discussions about reforming the central bank law began in 1989, when inflation had reached an annual rate of almost 5,000 percent and the nonfinancial public sector deficit was equivalent to about 12 percent of GDP. However, the reform project languished as the government tried to cope with an extremely difficult economic situation. It was put back on the agenda only after a successful stabilization program—which had started with a strong fiscal adjustment in 1990 and continued with the passage of the convertibility law in April 1991—was firmly in place.

The convertibility law committed the central bank to buying and selling foreign currency at the exchange rate of ARG$1 = US$1 and to maintaining at all times an amount of freely usable international reserves[20] equivalent, as a minimum, to 100 percent of base money. Thus, even before reforming central bank legislation, Congress limited the powers of the central bank through the convertibility law to increase domestic credit by lending to the public sector or to banks.

---

[20]This concept is similar to gross international reserves. However, it includes foreign-currency-denominated securities issued by the treasury and excludes the foreign currency deposits that commercial banks must hold with the central bank in fulfillment of the reserve requirements on foreign currency deposits.

The central bank law was finally adopted in October 1992 and incorporated the changes required to make it fully consistent with the convertibility law.

Swinburne and Castello-Branco (1991) review the experience of eight countries in addressing central bank independence. They reach several important conclusions.

> First, for both practical reasons and reasons of constitutional principle, it is not helpful to think of the ultimate responsibility for monetary policy lying anywhere else than with the political leadership. . . . Second, . . . central bank autonomy needs to be accompanied by effective monetary policy accountability. . . . Third, clear, nonconflicting objectives and a structure of incentives and sanctions that align the motivations of the central bank, as monetary policy agent, with what is considered to be welfare-maximizing monetary policy, are important requirements. . . . Fourth, for similar reasons, the respective roles of the central bank and the political authorities need to be clearly set out, and the relationships between the two need to be transparent and consistent. . . . Fifth, if there are conflicts and trade-offs inherent in a central bank's functions, monetary policy independence and credibility might, in the extreme, require reconsideration of the mix of functions allocated to the central bank. . . . Finally, it is worth noting that central bank independence by itself cannot guarantee monetary policy credibility (1991, pp. 443-44).

Central Bank Independence and Coordination

The discussion in the first two sections of this paper suggests that monetary policy and debt management are closely linked and that some other activities typically carried out by central banks, such as the operation of the payments system, have a heavy influence on debt management. Moreover, government debt instruments play a major role in the implementation of both fiscal and monetary policy. These factors argue for coordination between the central bank and the institution in charge of debt management.

At the same time, the discussion in the next two sections summarizes the growing trend to make central banks independent, in order to allow them to focus on achieving price stability, which is perceived as the main objective of monetary policy. How can these seemingly conflicting aspects be reconciled? What degree of coordination is appropriate for an independent central bank? Can some lessons be drawn from recent experiences?

Policy Coordination Issues

Subordinating monetary policy to the financing of the budget in the face of high fiscal deficits will lead to high inflation. The experience of the

United States before the 1951 accord and the experiences of countries in Latin America, among others, support this view. At the same time, as a practical matter, success in bringing down inflation and focusing the central bank on stabilization cannot rely solely on legislation that makes the central bank independent. Rather, support for stabilization must be broadly based to maintain such independence and preserve macroeconomic stability. It is no coincidence that initiatives to make central banks independent were often preceded by episodes of high inflation.

Limiting government access to central bank credit can help in avoiding inflationary financing.[21] Leone (1991) finds a close positive correlation between lending to the government and growth in reserve money. An important issue is determining what types of central bank credit to the government should be constrained. Cottarelli (1993) argues that overdrafts should be prohibited in countries with developed financial markets, as they make base money creation dependent on the government cash flow and provide the central bank with an unmarketable instrument. He also suggests that "purchases of government paper on the primary market may also be banned to strengthen the formal separation between the government and the central bank."[22] However, he argues that purchases of government securities in the secondary market need not be constrained. For cases in which markets are less developed, he suggests that some limited automatic access to central bank credit may be appropriate. He also notes that indirect credit may have to be constrained if there is a danger of its being used to circumvent limitations on direct lending. Table 5.2 below shows the way in which limits have been set in a sample of 57 countries.[23]

Leone (1991) introduces a note of caution on the effectiveness of legal limitations on central bank lending to the central bank. After analyzing data for 22 developing countries and 22 industrial countries, he concludes that in the presence of large deficits, ways are likely to be found to circumvent such limitations.

Coordination on Debt Issuance

The fiscal and monetary authorities should agree on certain objectives regarding debt issuance. *First,* a program of debt sales must be based on a sound fiscal strategy. If the public believes that the burden of public debt will cause the debt to be repudiated or monetized, the perceived risk and inflationary expectations will rise and, at a minimum, raise borrowing costs to the government. *Second,* the primary issuance of government

---

[21]For a detailed discussion of the rationale for this limitation, see Cottarelli (1993).

[22]*Ibid.*, p. 26.

[23]Detailed information on individual country arrangements is presented in Cottarelli (1993), Appendix III.

Table 5.2. Regulation of Central Bank Credit to the Government by Type of Credit

(Percentage composition)

Type of Credit	Industrial Countries	Developing Countries	Total
Overdraft facility			
Prohibited	43.8	56.1	52.6
Constrained	43.8	36.6	38.6
Unconstrained	12.4	7.3	8.8
Total	100.0	100.0	100.0
Fixed-term loans and advances			
Prohibited	43.8	22.0	28.1
Constrained (discretionary)	25.0	70.7	57.9
Constrained (mandatory)	—	2.4	1.8
Unconstrained (discretionary)	18.8	4.9	8.8
Unconstrained (mandatory)	12.4	—	3.4
Total	100.0	100.0	100.0
Purchase of government paper (primary market)			
Prohibited	25.0	19.5	21.1
Constrained (discretionary)	6.2	58.6	43.9
Constrained (mandatory)	6.2	2.4	3.5
Unconstrained (discretionary)	56.4	19.5	29.8
Unconstrained (mandatory)	6.2	—	1.7
Total	100.0	100.0	100.0
Purchase of government paper (secondary market)			
Prohibited	—	19.5	14.0
Constrained (discretionary)	—	26.8	19.3
Unconstrained (discretionary)	100.0	53.7	66.7
Total	100.0	100.0	100.0

Source: Cottarelli (1993, p. 33).

debt should be voluntary—that is, market placements with flexible and competitive interest rate determination—rather than based on captive markets using statutory reserve and liquid asset requirements and interest rate restrictions.

Third, the central bank and the ministry of finance should decide whether to use the treasury bill sales program only to finance part of the fiscal deficit and smooth out short-term fluctuations in treasury cash flows (a debt-management objective) or to also use it for monetary management. In either case, a joint committee (or working group) of central bank and finance ministry officials can serve to discuss the features of primary issues. If primary issues are mainly intended for deficit financing, the central bank should serve as an advisor, especially in the planning process, but final authority should rest with the ministry. If primary issues are also used for monetary policy purposes, the central bank must have much greater discretion in choosing the volume of securities to issue.[24] If the central bank uses primary issues of government securities for monetary operations, topics such as the remuneration of government balances held with the central bank require special consideration. The ministry of finance will generally be reluctant to issue securities—and pay interest on them—simply to have the proceeds held in unremunerated accounts with the central bank.[25] It may insist on having those balances remunerated at a market rate of interest (for example, at the same rate that it pays on the securities it issues).

Often, the central bank and the treasury will have different preferences regarding the types of paper they wish to use. Central banks tend to use only short-term paper in their operations, while treasuries, taking into account the expected pattern of their cash flows and expected movements in interest rates, use a mixture of debt maturities.

Some central banks have resorted to issuing their own securities to carry out monetary operations. Table 5.3 presents some examples.

The issuance of central bank paper for monetary operations has the advantage of giving the central bank more flexibility in deciding the volume of sales and in tailoring the characteristics of the paper to the preferences of the market. It has the disadvantage of introducing yet another security in the market, which competes with the treasury issues. Moreover, a proliferation of different securities will make the market for each one of them thinner and, therefore, less attractive to the public.

Although the central bank needs to have flexibility in determining the volume of its open market operations, it is important for the issuer of government debt to know the central bank's broad plans in this area—for instance, expected monetary developments and the likely size of central bank intervention. This would give the government debt manager a better idea of the market's capacity to absorb additional government debt.

Management of Government Deposits

As noted earlier, movements in government balances with the central bank can have a powerful monetary effect, sterilizing or expanding reserve money. Sales of government paper in the primary market are just one cause of such movements. Tax payments, payments for government purchases, and government salaries are other forms. These factors can introduce large variability in reserve money balances if payments into and out of government accounts are lumpy. They can disrupt money markets

---

[24]If there is a developed secondary market, central banks usually prefer to use it for their monetary operations. However, many central banks have used sales in the primary market as a substitute in the absence of sufficiently developed secondary markets.

[25]Sales of government securities serve a monetary purpose only to the extent that the sales proceeds are not spent.

Table 5.3. Debt Securities Issued by the Central Bank— Practices in Selected Countries

Country	Instrument	Purpose
Brazil (Central Bank of Brazil (CBB))	• Central bank bonds (28 days and above) and bills (no pre-established maturity: 180 days most common) issued by the CBB through auction to financial institutions.	Central bank bills introduced in 1986 and central bank bonds in 1991, for monetary management purposes.
Ghana (Bank of Ghana)	• Short-term central bank bills introduced in late 1988. The underdeveloped state of financial markets at the time, combined with the ineffectiveness of treasury bills in absorbing the required amount of liquidity, prompted the Bank of Ghana to issue its own debt instruments. • In late 1989, medium-term Bank of Ghana bonds were issued (180 days, 1 year, and 2 years) in an effort to address the persistent situation of liquidity overhang. Medium-term securities were not found to be attractive to holders, and the Bank of Ghana has relied more on short-term central bank bills. • Short-term central bank bills have been effective in the conduct of monetary management.	Introduced to absorb excess domestic liquidity, owing to the prolonged use of credit ceilings. Central bank bills became the main intervention instrument for monetary policy, with decreasing policy intervention through primary markets for government securities.
Korea (Bank of Korea)	• The Bank of Korea began issuing its own debt instruments, Monetary Stabilization Bonds (MSBs), as early as 1961. MSBs carry maturities of one year or less. Under the Monetary Stabilization Act (1961), the Bank of Korea is authorized to issue them in its own name. However, the terms are set by the Monetary Board. • Rigidities in the market for MSBs, as well as their narrow purpose, have limited the use of MSBs as the main instrument for monetary control.	For monetary management to deal with the liquidity absorption requirements at the time.
Nepal (Nepal Rastra Bank (NRB))	• Short-term NRB bonds (three-month and one-year central bank bills) introduced in February 1992 and issued through competitive auction simultaneously with auctions of three-month treasury bills; at the discretion of the central bank. • Have been effective in sterilization operations.	For monetary management purposes—primarily the sterilization of foreign exchange transactions by NRB.
New Zealand (Reserve Bank of New Zealand)	• Short-term Reserve Bank bills (63 days— changed from 91 days in February 1991) issued twice weekly through auction, nontraded and discountable with 28 days remaining to maturity. Because of the discount feature, the Reserve Bank bills yield slightly less than treasury bills. • Have been effective in separating debt and monetary management operations.	For monetary management purposes, used in conjunction with the discount margin (penalty) and open market operations (OMOs).

Table 5.3 (concluded)

Country	Instrument	Purpose
Poland (National Bank of Poland (NBP))	• Short-term NBP bills (one month), issued through auction, were introduced in July 1991. With the introduction of one-month treasury bills, NPB bills of three-month and six-month maturities were introduced. • Issuance of NBP bills was suspended in January 1992, in part because of lack of buying interest at the longer terms.	Introduced as a monetary instrument and replaced by OMO repurchase and reverse repurchase auctions in January 1993.
Philippines	• Medium-term securities (three–five years), issued through auction, introduced in 1970 and phased out in 1981. • Short-term bills introduced in 1984 and phased out in 1986. • Phased out in part owing to central bank losses.	To absorb excess liquidity in the banking system and increase central bank operational autonomy.
Germany (Bundesbank)	• Short-term treasury bills (three, six, and nine months) issued by the Bundesbank through auction to banks with operational accounts at the Bundesbank in accordance with section 42 of the Bundesbank Act and up to a maximum amount of DM 25 billion.	Introduced in February 1993, to stimulate short-term secondary markets.

Source: Sundararajan and others (1993).

and also make the exchange rate volatile under a regime of flexible exchange rates.

At a minimum, the central bank needs to have advance information on expected government cash flows to be able to manage their monetary effects. Some countries have gone further and established specific arrangements to deal with those effects and events to use them as a tool of monetary management. Table 5.4 presents examples of such arrangements.

Information and Operational Issues

To implement monetary policy properly, the central bank needs information on the timing and intended amount of government debt issues and, in general, on the cash flow of the government—particularly if the flow involves sterilization or creation of reserve money. Practical arrangements for coordination vary: they might involve participation of both treasury and central bank representatives in special committees that meet periodically to discuss the policy intentions of these two institutions and informal daily consultations to discuss expected changes in government balances with the central bank. The former allows the two institutions to set out their broad policy objectives and to review plans for debt issuance and medium-term perspectives. The informal consultations help the central bank plan its daily money market activities.

Table 5.4. Arrangements for Dealing with Variations in Government Cash Balances in Selected Countries

United Kingdom	The government maintains its cash balances primarily in an account with the Bank of England (BOE). Net disbursements of the government are a major determinant of changes in bank reserves. The BOE forecasts changes in the government's position and announces at 9:45 a.m. each day its projection of net reserves for the system, while clearing banks give the BOE their target reserve balances. Intra-day open market operations are then conducted to "neutralize" or sterilize the effect of government operations on bank liquidity. In addition, credit facilities are available to discount houses for end-of-day extension of liquidity when required.
United States	The Federal Reserve is the clearing agent for the government. However, the Treasury maintains cash balances with the Federal Reserve and the commercial banks (treasury tax and loan accounts). Each day, the Treasury shifts balances between these two accounts in sufficient amounts to cover any expected net debit/credit changes in the account at the Federal Reserve while aiming to maintain a low balance at the Federal Reserve as it does not pay interest, while the commercial banks do. Hence, the "expected" change in reserves due to government transactions is neutralized by the Treasury. Nonetheless, variability in reserves from government transactions is significant due to "unexpected" changes in government transactions.
Canada	As in the United States, the government maintains accounts in both the central bank and the commercial banks. Unlike the U.S. system, the central bank exercises discretion over how much is placed in the account of the central bank and the commercial banks through the drawdown and redeposit mechanism, and the bank actively uses this mechanism to "neutralize" the effect of government transactions and other central bank transactions. In addition, the payment system and the timing of the drawdown and redeposit permits the Bank of Canada to achieve a precise target change in the level of reserves. The drawdown/redeposit mechanism is the main instrument used to induce "dynamic," or policy-induced changes, in bank reserves. The discretion granted to the Bank of Canada (as fiscal agent to the government of Canada) to alter the distribution of government deposits between the central bank and the commercial banks is an example of a supporting operational arrangement for monetary management.
Malaysia	In 1981, a Money Market Operation (MMO) account was created, enabling Bank Negara Malaysia to shift government deposits to and from the commercial banks and to and from the government's current account at the central bank. Since then, the instrument has been refined, and coordination between the central bank and the fiscal authority has intensified. The central bank is given the authority to recycle the funds in the MMO account by placing them directly with the market or through principal dealers, consistent with monetary policy objectives. Thus, the central bank enjoys full control over the use of this policy instrument for short-term liquidity management.
New Zealand	Neutralization of the impact of government cash flows by the Reserve Bank of New Zealand is done through the issuance of seasonal treasury bills. Although these bills are a government debt instrument, the central bank decides autonomously on their maturities, taking into account the forecast of liquidity flows.

Source: Sundararajan and others (1993).

The central bank needs to work closely with other market participants and with the treasury in organizing a system for the transfer and payment of securities. Appropriate design can make government securities more liquid and reduce the risks of security transactions. This will make them more attractive assets and thus lower the costs for the government. In countries in which the central bank manages the issue of treasury paper, it also operates the debt registry. The efficiency of this registry is a key element for debt-management operations. It must suit the needs of the borrower (the government), the lenders (the holders of government debt), and the market operators.

The Central Bank as Fiscal Agent

In many countries, including most of Latin America, the central bank, in its role as fiscal agent, has a great deal of influence on public debt management. This helps coordination but may sometimes lead to a conflict of interest between the bank's duties as monetary authority and its duties as fiscal agent; in case of conflict, the central bank is likely to give priority to its duties as monetary policy authority. The arrangements discussed above, in fact, allow for coordination to proceed without necessarily having the central bank vested with the responsibility of managing public debt on behalf of the treasury.

The arrangements that are appropriate for a particular country are likely to change over time. For instance, the Bank of Canada, acting as fiscal agent, used to exercise a lot of influence on debt-management policy. However, the Ministry of Finance took a much more forceful role in debt management after the mid-1980s so as to concentrate more on cost minimization in the management of the public debt.

Conclusions

Monetary policy and public debt management are closely linked components of economic policy. Sales of public debt have important monetary effects and can be a key instrument in the implementation of monetary policy. Also, the monetary policy stance, the set of instruments used by the central bank, and other central bank operations have a direct bearing on the cost of government borrowing. These facts argue for close coordination of monetary policy implementation and debt management.

At the same time, there are important reasons for granting the central bank independence in its pursuit of monetary policy. Although there are difficulties in quantifying the advantages of having an independent central bank, evidence suggests that an independent central bank has a better chance of implementing a monetary policy conducive to price stability. Moreover, a number of countries have reformed their legislation to enhance the independence of their central banks, giving them a clear objective—price stability—and ensuring that they are accountable.

Therefore, the issue of how to coordinate monetary policy with public debt management arises in a context in which responsibility for these two aspects of economic policy implementation is vested in two different institutions, the central bank and the ministry of finance. Coordination requires, first, that the objectives of the fiscal and the monetary authorities be compatible. An independent central bank will be hard pressed to achieve its price stabilization objective without the support of the ministry of finance. Second, the two parties should have a clear understanding of the objectives of debt issuance. This requires deciding how large a fiscal deficit can be financed through this mechanism, what fraction of the debt will be placed abroad, and whether domestic primary issues will be used to implement monetary policy or whether the central bank should issue its own securities for that purpose. Ideally, they would also agree on a strategy for developing the market for public debt securities and the money market.

The central bank law will typically include restrictions or a strict prohibition on central bank direct lending to the government that provides a framework for the financial relationships between the bank and the government. Other issues that need to be addressed include the distribution of central bank profits as well as mechanisms to provide for central bank recapitalization in case of losses. Table 5.5 presents information on arrangements on the treatment of central bank profits and losses for a sample of countries. Finally, there will be a need for a frequent exchange of information between the two institutions, particularly to ensure that fiscal operations do not have unintended monetary consequences.

Various institutional arrangements, either formal or informal, can be designed to achieve those purposes. The agreement signed between the Minister of Finance and the Governor of the Reserve Bank of New Zealand is an example of a formal arrangement. A coordination committee comprising high officials of the ministry of finance and the central bank is an example of an informal arrangement used in many countries. In addition to a coordination committee, there should be frequent informal contacts between working-level staff of central banks and ministries of finance to stay abreast of day-to-day developments. Finally, specific arrangements to deal with the monetary effects of shifts of government deposits can be helpful.

In sum, central bank independence need not jeopardize appropriate coordination between the institutions responsible for monetary policy and debt management. On the contrary, by keeping these institutions well focused on their responsibilities, such coordination can be enhanced if appropriate arrangements are put in place to make the goals of both institutions consistent and to exchange information.

Table 5.5. Treatment of Profits and Losses in a Sample of Countries

Argentina	After replenishment of reserve funds, profits are transferred to the treasury. Losses are provisioned and charged to the treasury, to be repaid during the following fiscal year.
Brazil[1]	Central bank profits are distributed twice a year and, owing to inflation, are generally large. Profits are immediately credited against the central bank's holdings of treasury securities. Losses are charged to a provision account and treated as an interest-bearing claim against the treasury to be repaid during the following fiscal year, before any distribution funds are set aside to maintain the real value of capital and reserves.
Germany	Twenty percent of profits, or DM 20 million, whichever is higher, is transferred to the legal reserves until reserves reach 5 percent of the total amount of banknotes in circulation; the legal reserves may be used only to offset a decline in value and to cover other losses. Up to 10 percent of the remaining net profit may be used to form other reserves. These reserves cannot exceed the bank's capital. DM 30 million is transferred to a special fund for the purchase of equalization claims (to carry out open market operations). The balance is transferred to the federal government.
Japan	One-twentieth of profits are appropriated for a reserve fund to cover losses and for dividends. Special reserve funds may be opened with the permission of the Minister of Finance. Dividends cannot exceed 5 percent a year of paid-in capital. After deducting from the surplus the reserve funds and dividends, the Bank of Japan must transfer the remainder to the government within two months of the end of the fiscal year.
United States	Stockholders of the Federal Reserve Fund are entitled to receive an annual dividend of 6 percent on the paid-in capital stock. After these dividends have been met, net earnings are paid to the surplus fund of each Federal Reserve Bank. At the discretion of the Secretary of the Treasury, the earnings can be used to supplement the gold reserves or can be applied to the reduction of the outstanding bonded indebtedness of the United States.

Source: Sundararajan and others (1993).
[1]Brazil's central bank has assumed, however, a large foreign debt portfolio that reduces its profits substantially, as foreign exchange valuation adjustments are charged against profits.

References

Alesina, Alberto, "Macroeconomics and Politics," in *NBER Macroeconomics Annual,* ed. by Stanley Fischer (Cambridge, Massachusetts: MIT Press, 1988), pp. 13–52.

———, and Lawrence H. Summers, "Central Bank Independence and Macroeconomic Performance: Some Comparative Evidence," *Journal of Money, Credit, and Banking,* Vol. 25 (May 1993), pp. 151–62.

Alesina, Alberto, and Guido Tabellini, "Rules and Discretion with Noncoordinated Monetary and Fiscal Policies," *Economic Inquiry,* Vol. 25 (October 1987), pp. 619–30.

Andersen, Torben M., and Friedrich Schneider, "Coordination of Fiscal and Monetary Policy Under Different Institutional Arrangements," *European Journal of Political Economy* (February 1986), pp. 169–91.

Bade, Robert, and Michael Parkin, "Central Bank Laws and Monetary Policy" (Unpublished; University of Western Ontario, 1985).

Blackburn, Keith, and Michael Christensen, "Monetary Policy and Policy Credibility: Theories and Evidence," *Journal of Economic Literature*, Vol. 27 (March 1989), pp. 1-45.

Cottarelli, Carlo, *Limiting Central Bank Credit to the Government: Theory and Practice*, IMF Occasional Paper No. 110 (Washington: International Monetary Fund, 1993).

Cukierman, Alex, *Central Bank Strategy, Credibility, and Independence: Theory and Evidence* (Cambridge, Massachusetts: MIT Press, 1992).

———, Pantelis Kalaitzidakis, Lawrence H. Summers, and Steven B. Webb, "Central Bank Independence, Growth, Investment, and Real Rates," *Carnegie-Rochester Conference Series on Public Policy*, Vol. 39 (December 1993), pp. 95-140.

Cukierman, Alex, Steven B. Webb, and Bilin Neyapti, "Measuring the Independence of Central Banks and Its Effect on Policy Outcomes," *World Bank Economic Review*, Vol. 6 (September 1992), pp. 353-98.

De Long, Bradford J., and Lawrence H. Summers, "Macroeconomic Policy and Long-Run Growth," *Economic Review*, Federal Reserve Bank of Kansas City, Vol. 77 (1992), pp. 5-29.

Dueñas, Daniel, "Strengthening Central Bank Independence in Latin America: Recent Experiences in Argentina, Chile and Venezuela" (Unpublished; Washington: International Monetary Fund, 1993).

Friedman, Milton, and Anna Jacobson Schwartz, *A Monetary History of the United States, 1867-1960* (Princeton: Princeton University Press, 1963).

Giovannini, Alberto, and Martha De Melo, "Government Revenue from Financial Repression," *American Economic Review*, Vol. 83 (September 1993), pp. 953-63.

Grilli, Vittorio, Donato Masciandaro, and Guido Tabellini, "Political and Monetary Institutions and Public Financial Policies in the Industrial Countries," *Economic Policy: A European Forum* (October 1991), pp. 342-92.

Grimes, Arthur, "The Effects of Inflation on Growth: Some International Evidence," *Weltwirtschaftliches Archiv*, Vol. 127 (1991), pp. 631-44.

Hughes Hallett, Andrew, and Maria Luisa Petit, "Cohabitation or Forced Marriage? A Study of the Costs of Failing to Coordinate Fiscal and Monetary Policies," *Weltwirtschaftliches Archiv*, Vol. 126 (1990), pp. 662-90.

International Monetary Fund, *Government Finance Statistics Yearbook* (Washington, 1992).

———, *International Financial Statistics*, Vol. 46 (Washington, 1993).

Knight, R. Lindsay, "Central Bank Independence in New Zealand," in *The Evolving Role of Central Banks*, ed. by P. Downes, and R. Vaez-Zadeh (Washington: International Monetary Fund, 1991), pp. 140-46.

Leone, Alfredo, "Effectiveness and Implications of Limits on Central Bank Credit to the Government," in *The Evolving Role of Central Banks*, ed. by P. Downes and R. Vaez-Zadeh (Washington: International Monetary Fund, 1991), pp. 363-413.

Masciandaro, Donato, and Guido Tabellini, "Monetary Regimes and Fiscal Deficits: A Comparative Analysis," in *Monetary Policy in Pacific Basin Countries*, ed. by H. Cheng (Norwell, Massachusetts: Kluwer Academic Publishers, 1988), pp. 125-52.

Moore, Robert R., "The Government Budget Deficit and the Banking System: The Case of Mexico," *Studies*, Federal Reserve Bank of Dallas (October 1993), pp. 27-36.

Parkin, Michael, "Domestic Monetary Institutions and Deficits," in *Deficits*, ed. by J.M. Buchanan, C. Rowley, and R.D. Tollison (Oxford, England; New York: Blackwell, 1986).

Petit, Maria Luisa, "Fiscal and Monetary Policy Coordination: A Differential Game Approach," *Journal of Applied Econometrics* (April-June 1989), pp. 161-79.

Pindyck, Robert S., "The Cost of Conflicting Objectives in Policy Formulation," *Annals of Economic and Social Measurement*, Vol. 5 (Spring 1976), pp. 239-48.

Pollard, Patricia S., "Central Bank Independence and Economic Performance," *Review*, Federal Reserve Bank of St. Louis, Vol. 75 (July-August 1993), pp. 21-36.

Sargent, Thomas J., and Neil Wallace, "Some Unpleasant Monetarist Arithmetic," *Quarterly Review*, Federal Reserve Bank of Minneapolis, Vol. 9 (1985), pp. 15-31.

Sundararajan, V., and Tomás J.T. Baliño, *Banking Crises: Cases and Consequences* (Washington: International Monetary Fund, 1991).

Sundararajan, V., Peter Dattels, I.S. McCarthy, and Marta Castello-Branco, "Coordination of Debt and Monetary Management in Economies in Transition—Issues and Lessons of Experience" (Unpublished; Washington: International Monetary Fund, 1993).

Swinburne, Mark, and Marta Castello-Branco, "Central Bank Independence and Central Bank Functions," in *The Evolving Role of Central Banks*, ed. by P. Downes and R. Vaez-Zadeh (Washington: International Monetary Fund, 1991), pp. 414-44.

Tabellini, Guido, "Money, Debt, and Deficits in a Dynamic Game," *Journal of Economic Dynamics and Control*, Vol. 10 (December 1986), pp. 427-42.

———, "Central Bank Reputation and the Monetization of Deficits: The 1981 Italian Monetary Reform," *Economic Inquiry*, Vol. 25 (April 1987), pp. 185-200.

Tanner, Evan, and John Devereux, "Deficits and the Demand for Money," *Southern Economic Journal*, Vol. 60 (October 1993), pp. 316-26.

Comment

Roberto Junguito

In the first section of his paper, which deals with the effects of public debt management on monetary policy, Baliño analyzes the forms through which public debt can influence the demand for money, as well as the monetary impact of central bank behavior as manifested in its reactions to a large amount of public debt.

His discussion, however, deals exclusively with domestic public debt. My major comment, in this regard, is that the author does not analyze the monetary impact of sovereign external debt, given alternative exchange rate policies and sterilization efforts on the part of central banks. If the government or the central bank had any kind of real exchange rate targeting, it would be found that a higher external public debt would lead to an increase in base money owing to the additional flow of international resources. The central bank's most probable reaction would be to attempt to sterilize base money through higher interest rates in its open market operations. As the Colombian experience of 1991 showed, this exercise may be frustrating to the extent that it stimulates capital inflows and has severe quasi-fiscal losses.

By the same token, if the government places its debt domestically, it can do it only by increasing interest rates or at the cost of lowering the holdings of the central banks' papers in its open market operations. In both cases, there may also be a monetary impact. If interest rates rise, they could provoke the monetization of increased capital inflows owing to the differential interest rate. In the second case, the central bank would be forced to reduce its placements of paper through open market operations.

In terms of the reaction of central banks to public sector indebtedness, Baliño tends to portray the figure of a concessional central bank attitude toward increasing the government's fiscal deficits. This is not so. The new independent central banks in Latin America have established limitations and prohibitions for extending credit to the government. This is true in Argentina, Chile, Mexico, and Venezuela. In Colombia, unanimity of the board of directors is required. This reduces the direct monetary impact of government debt.

In the same vein, it should be pointed out that in regard to the alternative ways to finance governments cheaply that Baliño described, they are no longer common in Latin America given that the new independent central banks have also attempted to limit indirect ways to finance the government and because ongoing financial reforms have tended to eliminate all sorts of forced investments and interest rate subsidies.

A different type of comment regards Baliño's estimations of financial repression. If the exercises to measure financial repression were to be applied today, contrary to his results, their results would indicate either low or negative repression indexes. In fact, owing to capital inflows, exchange rates in Latin America have been appreciating. Domestic interest rates, if anything, are higher than international interest rates adjusted with exchange rate changes.

In regard to the second part of Baliño's paper, which analyzes the effects of monetary policy and other bank actions on debt management, the author illustrates a number of central bank monetary policy actions that have an impact on public debt management and that lower the cost of government placings: central bank participation in the market with government bonds makes such papers more liquid; the design of a rediscount facility; the design of reserve requirements; the regulation of the payments system; and the regulation of deposit insurance.

There are, in contrast, clear cases not mentioned by Baliño where central bank actions have the opposite effect: they make public debt management more difficult, for example, when the bank places its own securities in the market in an effort to exercise monetary restraint and interest rates rise, and whenever the central bank fixes strict minimum financial (solvency) conditions for public enterprise bond placements.

The author also ignores the impact of foreign exchange regulations and exchange rate policies of the central bank on public debt management. Nowadays, independent central banks in Latin America may restrict public indebtedness by exposing the government to exchange rate risks. Some banks also have the authority to establish capital controls. A case in point is the foreign exchange deposit established in Chile and Colombia, whereby foreign and domestic interest rates are equalized.

To finish my comments, I would like to refer to the last section of the paper, which discusses the case for central bank independence. Baliño develops the arguments found in the economic literature in favor of central bank independence and describes the experiences, including the more recent ones, of some Latin American countries. To begin with, it is worth nothing that Argentina, Chile, Colombia, and Venezuela have introduced central bank independence in the past few years; that Mexico has approved the constitutional changes for introducing an independent central bank; and that it has also been discussed in Bolivia, Ecuador, and Peru.

Also, I would like to emphasize that the institutional changes undertaken have been significant and that the new independent central banks in Latin America are among the most independent banks in the world. Colombia, in terms of the Cuckierman Index, can be classified in fourth place, and Chile would be ranked even higher.

There is also evidence that independence is not simply formal but operational. The relatively new experience also indicates that central bank independence has been key to the adoption of macroeconomic policies that have contributed to the lowering of inflation at least in Chile and Colombia.

The issue then is not so much to discuss the merits of central bank independence in Latin America but to foresee the challenges that the new central banks face in order to guarantee their survival. They may be summarized in four points:

(1) The loss of monetary independence with the elimination of capital controls. Monetary policy is the principal instrument assigned to central banks to lower inflation.

(2) The pressures to backslide in stabilization efforts when anchoring the exchange rate result in severe real exchange rate appreciation.

(3) The limited capacity that central banks have in terms of persuading government to reduce public expenditures and fiscal deficits.

(4) The coordination issues with the government, especially with the incoming administrations that may not share the priority that should be given to price stability and that are not committed to the idea of having an independent central bank.

Recent Tax Policy Trends and Issues in Latin America

Parthasarathi Shome

The past decade has witnessed wide-ranging economic reform in several Latin American countries. There is little resemblance between the economies of the early 1990s and their more controlled, poorer performing counterparts of the early 1980s. The new atmosphere reflects, in part, support for sound economic policymaking at the highest political levels and a change in attitudes that now permits the consideration of deregulation, privatization, and the opening up of the economy. Deregulation has spurred economic activity. The opening of the economy, with its impact of increased imports, has led to higher revenue from this source.[1] Where privatization occurred, it has also led to increases in revenue. Significant efforts to reduce the fiscal deficit—even though in most instances the improvement was mainly the result of revenue-enhancing rather than expenditure-tightening efforts—and sensible credit policies have led to success in the control of often runaway inflation. In some countries, the role of the state itself has undergone careful scrutiny. Consequently, government has become less involved in running public enterprises, which began to respond more to market signals; there have been some efforts to contain the government payroll; and, in a few instances, social security has passed from public to private management.

Tax reform comprised not only an integral part of the overall reform effort but often represented its strongest element. A majority of the Latin American countries undertook major tax reforms, even though a small but important minority do not seem to have been able to generate the critical mass of political support for significant change. The fact that tax reform represented such an important policy instrument in overall macro-management and economic growth suggests, to no small extent, that country authorities recognized fiscal policy—and especially tax policy—as "their" policy, that is, more amenable to influence, with results that are

---

[1]This has been the case, in particular, for revenue from the value-added tax (VAT) on imports.

more directly measurable than are the ramifications of other economic policies, at least in the short to medium run.[2]

This paper reviews Latin American countries' recent experiences with tax policy, mainly since the mid-1980s. Based on those experiences, the paper points in the direction of further necessary reforms. In what follows, the main trends in tax policy among Latin American countries in recent years are examined. The next section compares and contrasts important elements of tax reform—or the lack of it—focusing on Argentina, Bolivia, Brazil, Chile, Colombia, and Mexico.[3] The final section outlines future directions for tax reform, especially as the economies, their fiscal institutions, and, perhaps more important, the thinking on these matters mature. These relate to various issues, such as the realization that a tax system—both policy and its administration—cannot be viewed in isolation, especially as a country becomes more integrated with the rest of the world, the need to widen the universe of taxpayers as economic growth begins to result in an expanding middle class; the constraint put on fiscal management by the dearth of tax and expenditure responsibility at lower levels of government; the emergence of new and dynamic concerns, such as those of the environment, with implications for the design of a tax system; and so on. The main findings are summarized and some concluding remarks offered.

Recent Trends in Tax Reform[4]

At the beginning of the 1980s, most Latin American tax structures were complex and cumbersome. Often, they consisted of hundreds of taxes but yielded little revenue. Consumption and production taxes were hampered by multiple rates and led to difficulties with tax administration. The taxes were inefficient because of "cascading"; that is, they were levied not only on the value of production but also on the taxes that were paid at earlier stages of production. They tended to impair international competitiveness because they were often levied at the manufacturing rather than at the retail stage, so that, effectively, exporters also paid the tax. Income taxes were riddled with multiple exemptions and incentives, high rates, a lack of integration between personal and corporate incomes, and a lack of indexation, in general leading to low revenue productivity, inequities caused by narrow tax bases, and inefficiencies in resource allocation, including biases in the debt-equity composition of business financing. On the whole, the tax systems depended on a few highly distortive

---

[2]This experience has been common also among Asian countries. On the role of tax policy in the development strategies of these countries, see Tanzi and Shome (1992).

[3]For selected country studies, see also Bird (1992).

[4]For a description of recent trends in tax reform and IMF recommendations in tax policy, see Shome (1995a).

domestic taxes or on international trade taxes, including export duties, to generate revenues.

The tax reforms that followed comprised either a series of steps over a number of years, as in Colombia (an incremental approach), or what amounted to a sea change, as in Argentina (a revolutionary approach). In general, though, the common experience was one of continuous formulation of reform policies and their steady, sequenced application. Reform-minded countries attempted to simplify their tax structures, focusing, in the early stages, on income taxation but increasingly moving toward taxing production and consumption. As the economies matured and became more integrated with the rest of the world, such as the Mexican economy, their focus reverted to fine-tuning particular aspects of the income tax, which had international ramifications.

Changes in Overall Tax Structure

Among the important changes that the Latin American tax structures underwent, the following pertain to the main tax categories.

Personal Income Tax

With respect to the personal income tax, first, the band was narrowed through a reduction in the number of rates, and the rates themselves were scaled down. Between 1985–86 and 1991, the rates declined, on average, to 5–36 percent from 7–47 percent (Table 6.1). Indeed, few countries had a top marginal rate over 50 percent, while many had brought it down to the 30 percent range.

Second, there was a tendency to reduce the burden of taxation on low-income groups as indicated by an increase in the threshold level at which the personal income tax applied. Thus, on average, the threshold more than doubled from 0.8 times per capita GDP to 1.8 for Central American countries, while for South American countries it more than doubled from 0.4 times per capita GDP to 1 (Table 6.2).

Third, as the top marginal rate came down, it began simultaneously to be applied at lower levels of income for Central American countries. An important difference between Central American and South American countries is that, in the former, the income at which the highest marginal rate applied fell by half, from over 200 times per capita GDP to over 100 times. By contrast, in South American countries, it remained almost the same, decreasing slightly from just over 13 times per capita GDP to just under 13 times.[5]

---

[5]The difference in the upper income bracket in terms of per capita GDP in the two country groups should represent, to an important extent, the different income levels of the two groups of countries. But it also probably reflects measurement problems in hyperinflationary environments. However, there is considerable variation even within the two groups.

Table 6.1. Cross-Country Comparisons: Personal Income Tax Rates
(In percent)

Country	1991	1985 or 1986
Argentina	6–30	16.5–45
Bolivia	13	…–30
Brazil	10–25	0–60
Chile	5–50	0–57
Colombia	5–30	…–49
Costa Rica	10–25	5–50
Dominican Republic	3–70	2–73
Ecuador	10–25	19–40
El Salvador	10–50	3–60
Guatemala	4–34	11–48
Honduras	3–40	3–40
Mexico	3–55	3–55
Nicaragua	6–50	15–50
Panama	2.5–56	13–56
Paraguay	0	5–30
Peru	5–56	2–56
Uruguay	0	0
Venezuela	4.5–45	12–45
Regional average	5–36	7–47[1]

Sources: IMF, Tax Policy Division; secondary, published sources such as publications of tax summaries by Price Waterhouse, Coopers and Lybrand, International Bureau of Fiscal Documentation, the IMF, and other similar sources.

[1] The average shown is a joint average of the two years.

Among other objectives, such as simplicity and greater neutrality, the personal exemption level was raised so as to improve vertical equity and ease administration, while better tax compliance was the main reason for reducing top rates. These steps were usually undertaken simultaneously with reducing other types of exemptions and deductions from the personal income tax, with the goal of improving horizontal equity.

Corporate Taxes

Improving simplicity, neutrality, and equity (through attempts to reduce evasion) were equally important objectives with respect to corporate taxation. First, rate dispersion of the corporate income tax was reduced, and its top marginal rate fell. Thus, between 1986 and 1992, for Latin American countries as a whole, the rate structure was scaled back on average from 3–43 percent to 9–37 percent (Table 6.3).

Second, greater simplicity was achieved by other means. For example, in the 1970s and the early 1980s, the majority of countries in Central and South America changed positions with respect to the treatment of capital gains. Countries that treated capital gains as ordinary income suddenly

Table 6.2. Cross-Country Comparisons: Personal Income Tax Exemption and Upper Bracket

(Multiples of per capita GDP)

Country	Personal Exemption Level		Upper Income Bracket	
	1991	1985 or 1986	1991	1985 or 1986
South America				
Argentina	0.53	0.83	13.66	21.42
Bolivia	0.51	0.96	0.51	10.09
Brazil	1.16	0.32	2.78	10.14
Chile	2.26	0.19	22.60	2.83
Colombia	0.41	0.02	25.30	20.46
Ecuador	2.87	0.43	35.80	29.16
Paraguay	—	0.47	—	10.39
Regional average[1]	0.97	0.40	12.58	13.06
Central and North America				
Costa Rica	2.85	1.20	5.30	1.38
Dominican Republic	0.17	1.10	74.30	413.54
El Salvador	2.34	...	32.50	171.66
Guatemala	2.34	0.85	31.70	355.99
Honduras	6.87	0.00	686.80	600.36
Mexico	0.18	0.65[2]	11.70	21.30
Nicaragua	—	1.71	9.90	56.87
Panama	0.49	0.27	97.80	88.96
Regional average[1]	1.84	0.83	118.75	213.76

Sources: Secondary, published sources such as publications of tax summaries by Price Water-house, Coopers and Lybrand, International Bureau of Fiscal Documentation, the IMF, and other, similar sources.

[1] Averages are taken over the set of countries for which data for both 1991 and 1985 or 1986 are available.

[2] Allowance equals 12 months' minimum wage in zone of residence (13 months with Christmas bonus). The data provided correspond to Mexico City.

exempted them or taxed them at a reduced rate, only to shift back within a few years to treating them as ordinary income for tax purposes.[6] This instability disappeared, however, as most countries settled on the policy of treating capital gains as ordinary income and applying the same tax rates to both.[7]

Third, Latin American countries reduced tax evasion by improving tax administration, such as through rapid computerization of collection procedures and processing of taxpayer information. The payment of taxes

---

[6] The instability in the treatment of capital gains was apparent in a similar table that compared information between 1980 and 1990 in Shome (1992). There, other taxes were also similarly compared. While the trends between 1980 and 1990 seem, in general, to continue for the period beginning the mid-1980s to the early 1990s (which is the focus of this paper), some important differences emerge, for example, stability in the treatment of capital gains.

[7] Bolivia abolished its corporate income tax in 1986 and did not tax capital gains either.

Table 6.3. Cross-Country Comparisons: Corporate Income Tax Rates

(In percent)

Country	1992	1986
Argentina	20	0–33
Bolivia	0	0–30
Brazil	25–40	29–50
Chile	15–35	10–37
Colombia	30	40
Costa Rica	30	0–50
Dominican Republic	0–49.3	0–49.3
Ecuador	0–44.4	0–59
El Salvador	0–25	0–30
Guatemala	12–34	0–42
Honduras	0–40.2	0–55
Mexico	0–35	5–42
Nicaragua	0–35.5	0–45
Panama	2.5–45	0–50
Paraguay	0–30	0–30
Peru	0–30	0–40
Uruguay	0–30	0–30
Venezuela	20–67.7	18–67.7
Regional average	8.6–36.5	3.4–43.3

Sources: IMF, Tax Policy Division; secondary, published sources such as publications of tax summaries by Price Waterhouse, Coopers and Lybrand, International Bureau of Fiscal Documentation, the IMF, and other, similar sources.

was facilitated, for example, through banks, selective auditing, and the establishment of large taxpayer units[8] but also through tax policy measures entailing estimating the extent of tax evasion and enacting presumptive taxes and minimum taxes. Measuring and taxing income at the company level is a difficult task that not only involves complex technical issues but also elicits severe and continuous threats from highly sophisticated tax "planners" looking for ways to erode the tax base. Several countries have been looking for schemes to ensure that at least a minimum contribution is obtained from company income. Some countries—Argentina, Ecuador, Mexico, and Peru—introduced a minimum contribution to the income tax based on gross assets, and many others began considering such a tax. Colombia, Costa Rica, and Uruguay legislated a similar tax based either on fixed assets or on net worth, probably owing to the greater political feasibility of this alternative even though these variants are less revenue productive (Table 6.4). Bolivia replaced its corporate income tax with only a net worth tax.

---

[8]For a full view of tax administration in developing countries, see Bird and Casanegra (1993).

Table 6.4. Cross-Country Comparisons: Assets-Based Taxes
(In percent)

Country	1986	1992	1993
Argentina	1.5 on net worth[1]	2 on gross assets	2 on gross assets
Bolivia	—	3 on net worth	3 on net worth
Brazil	—	—	—
Chile	—	—	—
Colombia	8 on net worth	7 on net worth	5 on net worth[1]
Costa Rica	0.36–1.17 on fixed assets	0.36–1.17 on fixed assets	0.36–1.17 on fixed assets
Dominican Republic	—	—	—
Ecuador	0.15 on assets	0.15 on net worth	0.15 on net worth
El Salvador	0.1–1.4 on net worth	0.90–2 on assets	0.90–2 on assets
Guatemala	0.3–0.8 on real estate[2]	0.3–0.9 on real estate[2]	0.3–0.9 on real estate[2]
Honduras	—	—	—
Mexico	—	2 on gross assets[1]	2 on gross assets[1]
Nicaragua	1 on real estate[2]	1.5–2.5 on net worth	1 on real estate[2]
Panama	1 on net worth[3]	1 on net worth[3]	1 on net worth[3]
Paraguay	1 on real estate[2]	1 on real estate[2]	1 on real estate[2]
Peru	1–2.5 on net worth	2 on net worth	2 on gross assets
Uruguay	2.8 on net worth	2 on net worth	2 on net worth[4]
Venezuela	—	—	—

Sources: Secondary, published sources such as publications of tax summaries by Price Water-house, Coopers and Lybrand, and International Bureau of Fiscal Documentation.

[1]Minimum corporate income tax; can be credited against normal corporate tax. In Mexico, the income tax can be credited against the gross assets tax to avoid the foreign investors' problem of crediting against tax liability in the home country.

[2]The base is real estate. The tax, however, is conceived not as a property tax but as an additional corporate tax.

[3]This tax has the form of a license to do business. The maximum tax amount is US$20,000 a year.

[4]Although it is called a net worth tax it is, in effect, a gross assets tax because liabilities can no longer be deducted.

Fourth, the rates of withholding taxes on foreign remittances fell, thereby bringing closer the domestic and foreign components of corporate taxation (Table 6.5). Finally, in Latin America as a group the overall structure of the corporate income tax was improved, for example, through the introduction of indexation in the face of an inflationary environment.

Consumption Taxes

A significant focus of Latin American taxation was consumption, in particular the VAT. By the early 1980s, some ten Latin American countries had introduced a VAT. By 1994, almost all of them had implemented one (Table 6.6).

In many instances, a rudimentary VAT had been introduced and was levied up to the manufacturing-importing stage or as a production-type VAT that disallowed credit for capital goods purchases. Many of them continued in this form through the mid-1980s. In the latter half of the 1980s and into the 1990s, Latin American countries began to reform their VATs, reducing the number of rates (Bolivia, Chile Colombia, and Mexico), expanding the base by reducing the number of previously exempted goods and covering a greater number of services (Argentina, Bolivia, Chile, Colombia, and Mexico), converting to consumption-type VATs (Argentina, Chile, Colombia, and Mexico), and improving administration.

The VAT played the most important role in improving the revenue performance of the tax system. To enhance revenue, those countries with a VAT measured evasion[9] to assess the need for improvement, consequently strengthening VAT administration. Countries that experienced high increases in their tax-GDP ratios, such as Argentina and Chile, often achieved the increases with the VAT instrument.[10] Most countries increased the rate of the VAT, owing, once again, to the leading role it played in generating revenue.

Commensurate with VAT reform, countries reduced the long list of excises, attempting to tax only such items as beverages, tobacco, petroleum products, electrical and electronic consumer durables, and automobiles. In the last few years, the excises on electrical goods have been rapidly disappearing, further shortening the list.

Taxes on International Trade

Finally, the late 1980s and early 1990s have been witness to fundamental reform of the taxation of international trade. All major countries have basically done away with export duties, which had been a mainstay of tax revenue a decade earlier. Customs tariff reform became common. The dispersion of tariff rates was reduced and their levels fell drastically. Tariff reform was carefully sequenced, with rates usually ending up within a band of 10-20 percent. Some countries hastened to reduce tax rates faster than originally planned (for example, Colombia), some introduced one tariff rate (such as Chile, with 11 percent), and some considered the elimination of import tariffs.

Revenue Consequences of Tax Reform

Table 6.7 presents data on the ratio of tax revenue to GDP of selected Latin American countries. It compares data from the early 1980s with data from the mid- or late 1980s and the 1990s. It divides the sample countries into three groups: high-tax (ratios of more than 20 percent of GDP); medium-tax (ratios of 15-20 percent); and low-tax (ratios of less

---

[9]A beginning was made with the case of the Mexican VAT (Aguirre and Shome, 1988). Many other countries followed with similar estimation procedures.

[10]A few countries, such as Mexico, successfully used the income tax instrument to increase revenues.

Table 6.5. Withholding Taxes on Foreign Remittances
(Percent of remittances)

Country	1986				1992				1993			
	Dividends	Interest	Royalties	Average[1]	Dividends	Interest	Royalties	Average[1]	Dividends	Interest	Royalties	Average[1]
Argentina	18[2]	16	36[3]	23	20	14	25	20	—	12	21	17
Bolivia	25	25	25	25	10	10	—	10	13	—	—	13
Brazil	25	25	25	25	25	25	25	25	15[4]	25	25	22
Chile	40	40	40	40	35	40	40	38	35	40	40	38
Colombia	40	40	—	40	—	—	—	—	12	12	12	12
Costa Rica	15	10	20	15	15	15	25	18	15	15	25	18
Dominican Republic	20	20	20	20	35	35	35	35	30[5,6]	30[6]	30[6]	30
Ecuador	—[7]	—[8]	40	40	36	—	36	36	36	—	36	36
El Salvador	22	22	22	22	—	25[9]	—	25	—	13[9]	—	13
Guatemala	13	10	25	16	13	5	34	17	13	5	25	14
Honduras	15	5	10	10	15	—	35	25	15	—	35	25
Mexico	55	25[10,11]	32[10]	37	none	20[12]	24	22	none	20[13]	24[14,15,16]	22
Nicaragua	20	—	30	25	—	35	35	35	—	30	30	30
Panama	10	—	50	30	10	6	50	22	10	6	50	22
Paraguay	10	30	30	23	10	30	30	23	5	35	35	25
Peru	30	40[17]	55[18]	42	37[17]	10	28[19]	25	10	37[17]	10[18]	19
Uruguay	—	—	30	30	—	—	—	—	—	—	—	—
Venezuela	20	20	—	20	—	—	15	15	—	—	15	15
Simple average	24	23	31	27	22	21	31	24	17	21	28	22

Sources: Secondary, published sources such as publications of tax summaries by Price Waterhouse.

[1]Simple average of figures presented.

[2]Pertains to dividends in cash or kind, other than stock dividends. The beneficiary must be identified; otherwise, the rate is 22.5 percent. Dividends and remittances of branch profits in excess of 12 percent of registered investment are subject to a special remittance tax ranging from 15 percent to 25 percent.

[3]Services derived from agreements ruled by the Foreign Technology Law: (a) technical assistance, technology, and engineering—27 percent (45 percent on assumed profit of 60 percent); (b) cession of right or licenses for inventions, patents, exploitation, and others—36 percent (45 percent on assumed profit of 80 percent); and (c) nonregistered agreements—45 percent (profit of 100 percent is assumed).

[4]This rate was reduced from 25 percent to 15 percent starting January 1, 1993. Treaty rates in excess of 15 percent are automatically reduced.

[5]Payments of interest (loans) to foreign financial institutions are subject to a withholding tax of 15 percent.

[6]Withholding tax will be reduced as indicated above for dividends.

[7]Taxes on dividends are withheld at the basic tax rate with surcharges. If the dividends are paid from undistributed profits of prior years, credit is allowed for the tax already paid on such profits by the company.

[8]No withholding required on interest remitted or credited abroad on loans. A special tax of 0.5 percent to 2 percent on the portion of the loans payable up to two years is levied (only once) at the time loans are registered at the Central Bank of Ecuador. If the loan is due after two years, the special tax is not payable.

[9]Interest on cash foreign-source loans brought into the country is not subject to withholding taxes.

[10]The withholding taxes are an average of different interest and royalties rates.

[11]Interest payments to nonresidents are exempt of Mexican income tax in the case of (a) loans to the federal government; (b) fixed-rate loans for five or more years, by duly registered financial institutions; and (c) certain securities and bank acceptances issued in foreign currency.

[12]Interest payments to nonresidents are exempt from Mexican income tax for (a) loans to the federal government; and (b) loans for three or more years by duly registered financial entities that promote exports by special financing; (c) these gains are taxable as interest. (d) When royalties are paid for the use of patents in connection with the technical assistance required for their use under the same contract, both the licensing fee and amounts paid for the technical assistance will be subject to the lower 15 percent rate. (e) The nonresident taxpayer may elect to pay at the regular corporate tax rate on net profit if he has a resident representative and advises the customer accordingly. The latter, then, makes no withholding.

[13]Treaty signed but not in force at time of publication.

[14]The rate will be reduced to 10 percent five years after the treaty enters into force.

[15]This rate applies where share ownership is at least 10 percent.

[16]The 10 percent rate, applicable to interest on loans from banks and insurance companies, will be reduced to 4.9 percent five years after the treaty enters into force.

[17]Under certain circumstances, exemptions are granted.

[18]Taxable income is determined as gross rentals less depreciation computed as provided by law.

[19]Payments for transfer of technology or for information regarding commercial, industrial, or scientific knowledge are deemed to be royalties.

Table 6.6. Value-Added Tax: Percentage Rates[1]

Country	Date VAT Introduced or Proposed	At Introduction	March 1994
Argentina	Jan. 1975	16	18,26,27[2]
Bolivia	Oct. 1973	5,10,15	14.92[3]
Brazil[4]	Jan. 1967	15	9,11
Brazil[5]	Jan. 1967	15	17
Chile	Mar. 1975	8,20	18
Colombia	Jan. 1975	4,6,10	8,14,20,35,45
Costa Rica	Jan. 1975	10	8
Dominican Republic	Jan. 1983	6	6
Ecuador	Jul. 1970	4,10	10
El Salvador	Sep. 1992	10	10
Guatemala	Aug. 1983	7	7
Haiti	Nov. 1982	7	10
Honduras	Jan. 1976	3	7,10
Jamaica	Oct. 1991	10	12.5
Mexico	Jan. 1980	10	10
Nicaragua	Jan. 1975	6	5,6,10
Panama	Mar. 1977	5	5,10
Paraguay	Jul. 1993	12	10
Peru	Jul. 1976	3,20,40	18
Venezuela[6]	Oct. 1993	10	—

Source: IMF.

[1]Rates shown in bold type are so-called effective standard rates (tax exclusive) applied to goods and services not covered by other especially high or low rates. Most countries use a zero rate for a few goods, and Ireland and the United Kingdom use it extensively to ensure that substantial amounts of goods and services are free of the VAT.

[2]Supplementary VAT rates of 8 percent and 9 percent on noncapital goods imports; through "catch-up," these can revert to 18 percent retail.

[3]Effective rate (legislated tax-inclusive rate is 13 percent).

[4]On interstate transactions depending on region.

[5]On intrastate transactions.

[6]Venezuela was the last country to introduce a VAT in late 1993, but had removed it by March 1994.

than 15 percent). It estimates the tax revenue for the general government—rather than only for the central government—wherever possible. Total tax revenue has been broken down into different types of tax to the extent that such information was available.[11] The, high-tax group includes Brazil, Chile, Costa Rica, Nicaragua, and Uruguay. The medium-tax group includes Argentina, Colombia, Ecuador, Mexico, Panama, and Venezuela.[12]

---

[11]Nevertheless, the information should be used only for purposes of broad comparisons, given the multiple sources used and the recency of some of the data.

[12]It is clear from the cross-country data that those countries that depend heavily on revenue from petroleum have not had to push significantly in the direction of raising the taxation of the nonpetroleum sector. Examples are Ecuador and Venezuela, which are in the medium-tax group because they rely on petroleum as the main source of tax revenue.

The low-tax group includes Bolivia, Guatemala, Paraguay, and Peru.[13]

Table 6.7 shows that most countries that carried out tax reform with the objective of improving the efficiency, equity, neutrality, and administrative feasibility (simplicity) of their tax systems also experienced a perceptible increase in their ratio of tax revenue to GDP, of between 2 percent and 4 percent of GDP, at least at the central government level, the usual target of tax reform. This outcome resulted whether, at the start of the reform, their ratio of tax revenue to GDP was low or high. It is understandable because a typical preoccupation of authorities undertaking reform was a downward slide in tax revenue, which they attributed to the tax structure that they wished to correct. Thus, even though tax reform need not necessarily be linked to a revenue increase, in effect, it invariably was.

Countries whose ratio of tax revenue to GDP is low initially might continue to have rather low ratios—compared with other countries—after implementing reforms, although their own ratio would increase.[14] Thus, throughout the 1980s, and especially from the mid-1980s, most Latin American countries experienced increases in their tax revenue-GDP ratios at the same time as the tax reform was being implemented, a trend that seems to have continued into the early 1990s.[15] As a result, high expectations regarding continuing increases in these ratios are unrealistic. Thus, to achieve fiscal balance, a much greater effort to curtail public expenditures may be necessary. This point will be taken up in the context of future directions for reform.

Anatomy of Tax Reform: Case Studies

The forces behind the tax reform and its main components in selected cases merit a more detailed analysis. Not all country cases can be considered here even though each would provide a unique view of the tax reform process. The countries being considered—Argentina, Bolivia, Brazil, Chile, Colombia, and Mexico—were selected with a view to discussing a variety of experiences, highlighting similarities and contrasts. Nevertheless, given the restriction of space, descriptions will focus on those aspects of the tax reforms that stand out as the most striking. In

---

[13]These classifications are affected to the extent that the ratios may fall within one group in one period and another group in another period.

[14]An exception is Bolivia, which moved recently from the low-tax group to the medium-tax group, or Costa Rica, which moved from the medium-tax group to the high-tax group.

[15]An exception would be Guatemala, which, in the absence of reform, has experienced a lowering in its tax revenue-GDP ratio. Peru has recently introduced reform measures, with an observable recovery in the ratio since its collapse during the heterodox period.

Table 6.7. Cross-Country Comparisons: Tax-to-GDP Ratios

High-Tax Countries

Tax Revenue	Brazil 1980	Brazil 1986	Brazil 1992	Chile 1981	Chile 1988	Chile 1992	Costa Rica 1980	Costa Rica 1986	Costa Rica 1992	Nicaragua 1980	Nicaragua 1988	Nicaragua 1992	Uruguay 1980	Uruguay 1986	Uruguay 1992
General government	22.0	22.1	24.7	25.9	25.1	23.4	17.7	21.2	24.5	...	28.4	25.6	...	...	...
Central government, of which	17.4	...	...	25.2	24.4	22.7	17.0	16.2	18.5	20.1	27.6	23.2	21.0	20.1	24.8
Income taxes	3.0	4.5	4.4	5.2	8.5	6.7	2.4	2.4	2.2	1.8	5.9	3.0	2.3	1.5	2.0
Social security tax	6.1	5.5	5.1	4.1	1.9	1.8	5.1	2.3	2.2	2.0	1.5	3.2	5.2	4.9	7.3
Property and wealth taxes	—	0.3	—	0.0	0.1	0.1	0.4	0.3	0.5	1.4	0.6	0.7	0.8	1.0	0.9
VAT, sales tax	10.6	9.1	12.0	11.1	8.8	9.6	1.7	3.3	6.5	8.6	3.5	2.4	9.6	6.3	8.3
Excises	...	1.3	0.4	1.4	2.3	2.1	3.8	2.7	3.1	...	13.0	8.4	...	3.7	5.0
Trade taxes	1.5	0.6	0.6	1.7	2.8	2.4	3.4	5.2	4.0	5.8	1.8	4.0	2.1	2.7	1.3

Medium-Tax Countries

Tax Revenue	Argentina 1985	Argentina 1988	Argentina 1992	Colombia 1980	Colombia 1987	Colombia 1992	Ecuador 1980	Ecuador 1988	Ecuador 1992	Mexico 1980	Mexico 1988	Mexico 1992	Panama 1980	Panama 1988	Panama 1992	Venezuela 1982	Venezuela 1988	Venezuela 1992
General government, of which	—	—	—	12.3	12.7	14.5	...	...	...	17.2	18.3	18.8[1]	20.3	—	—	25.6	18.5	17.9
Petroleum	—	—	—	—	—	—	...	6.9	8.5	...	3.5	3.4	—	—	—	16.9	10.4	11.7
Central government, of which	14.1	11.2	16.0	10.2	11.5	13.5	12.3	9.5	10.2	16.8	14.5	14.8	19.9	16.1	20.0	8.7	8.1	6.2
Income taxes	0.7	0.8	1.1	3.5	3.5	5.3	5.7	1.2	1.3	5.5	5.0	5.5	5.8	4.3	5.4	3.2	2.9	1.6
Social security tax	3.4	3.0	4.3	1.4	1.9	2.2	0.0	2.4	2.9	2.1	2.4	2.9	5.7	5.8	6.3	1.2	0.9	1.0
Property and wealth taxes	0.7	0.4	0.3	0.3	—	—	0.1	—	0.2	0.3	...	...	0.5	0.8	0.6	—	—	—
VAT, sales tax	2.1	1.9	5.9	2.5	2.8	3.9	1.5	2.6	3.0	4.5	3.6	2.9	4.5	1.1	2.0	1.3	—	—
Excises	3.5	1.2	2.1	1.4	0.7	0.8	0.7	1.1	1.0	...	2.8	1.7	...	2.2	2.0	...	1.4	1.2
Trade taxes	2.3	0.8	0.8	2.5	2.4	1.1	3.9	2.0	1.8	4.2	0.4	1.1	2.8	1.2	2.7	2.4	2.4	2.0

Low-Tax Countries

Tax Revenue	Bolivia			Guatemala			Paraguay			Peru		
	1984	1988	1992	1980	1988	1992	1980	1988	1992	1980	1988	1992
General government, of which	4.5	...	18.6	10.6	9.0	8.5	10.4	9.0	13.4	22.1	11.3	10.8
Petroleum	—	6.5	5.6	—	—	—	—	—	—	—	—	—
Central government, of which	2.9	8.7	12.3	10.1	8.8	8.3	10.1	8.9	11.1	18.9	10.8	9.9
Income taxes	0.0	0.5	0.5	1.3	2.1	1.9	1.8	1.6	2.0	6.0	1.1	0.7
Social security tax	1.0	0.6	0.7	1.3	—²	—²	1.4	1.5	1.6	2.2	2.2	1.5
Property and wealth taxes	0.0	0.8	1.1	0.1	0.2	0.1	0.7	0.3	0.4	0.7	0.4	0.5
VAT, sales tax	0.0	3.3	5.8	1.5	2.4	2.6	2.0	1.0	1.8	5.7	1.0	2.0
Excises	1.9	1.0	2.6	1.2	0.9	1.1	...	1.4	1.3	1.8	4.0	4.5
Trade taxes	1.0	2.1	1.4	3.4	2.4	2.1	2.7	0.9	1.6	5.6	2.0	0.7

Source: IMF staff estimates.
¹Only Mexico City; does not include provincial tax revenues.
²Contributions are classified as nontax revenue.

contrast, Brazil's tax system is complex and provides a unique opportunity for examining in detail a case that demands attention.

Argentina

Among all Latin American countries, Argentina's tax reform probably took place in the most revolutionary manner. As late as 1989, the tax system was riddled with complexities. The VAT had multiple rates, its base had eroded, and it yielded less than 2 percent of GDP in tax revenue. An array of tax incentives ate into the base of the corporate income tax, and revenue from it had become negligible. Tax administration needed all-around improvements. These were just a few of the system's shortcomings.

The 1990s have witnessed the most radical changes in Argentina's tax structure and administration. In many countries, tax structure improvements are not necessarily accompanied by reform of the tax administration, the latter following slowly, if at all. The benefits from such an approach to reform are very often minimal. In Argentina, by contrast, the concurrent efforts made in tax policy as well as in tax administration were probably mainly responsible for the success of the reform. There was a phenomenal rise in the ratio of tax revenue to GDP. Between 1988 and 1992, it jumped from 11 percent of GDP to 16 percent of GDP.

VAT revenue jumped from less than 2 percent of GDP to nearly 6 percent of GDP. Evasion seems to have been minimized, buttressed by tax administration measures. Innovative and imaginative ideas, focused especially on VAT administration, have been tried. Businesses that fail to make timely or correct declarations are closed immediately—*clausura preventiva*—for three days (Durán and Gómez-Sabaini, 1994). In 1990, 700 taxpayers were penalized in this way. In 1992, the number rose to 12,000. This response had a strong impact on VAT compliance. New invoicing requirements and controls, as well as an increased VAT rate for when registered enterprises sell to nonregistered vendors, were also introduced. Improved information on VAT taxpayers, such as the number of sales to which the VAT applies, and relations between credits and debits also helped improve collection from other taxes.

A tax on gross assets was introduced as the basis for a minimum contribution by enterprises. This measure was intended to counter the erosion of the income tax base that had been caused by the widespread prevalence of tax incentives, indexation only on the side of accumulated liabilities and losses, and other factors. The income tax had basically degenerated to a withholding tax on interest. The introduction of the minimum tax, effectively eliminating the possibility of using accumulated losses to reduce tax liability, had a positive impact on income tax revenue, which rose from 1 percent of GDP in 1989 to almost 2.5 percent in 1992. Once revenue from the corporate income tax stabilized, the minimum tax was abolished in 1994. In terms of tax administration, criminal proceedings against enterprises that abused tax incentives—which had been found to be quite widespread—were begun. A large taxpayer unit was introduced to monitor and control more closely 1,000 or so taxpayers initially; it quickly expanded to include 150,000 (progressively smaller) taxpayers.[16]

International trade tax reform also helped improve efficiency. Quantitative restrictions on imports were eliminated in 1991, import duties were sharply reduced, and a minimum import duty was introduced. Export duties that had been used in earlier years to generate revenue were also abolished. Dynamic, younger personnel were hired for the customs administration. Deterrent measures were initiated, including a rolling publication naming importers whose declarations had been modified by the customs administration.

The total number of taxes was drastically reduced. Small taxes, such as stamp taxes, and particularly distortionary taxes, such as one on bank drafts, were abolished. The disappearance of small taxes made the tax system more transparent and easier to administer. Only a few taxes were necessary to generate much of the revenue.

In addition to the administrative measures implemented with respect to particular taxes, personnel reform in the tax administration was undertaken. Corruption and absenteeism, which had vitiated earlier attempts at genuine reform, were reduced by making it easier to fire and hire employees. To conclude, the change that occurred in Argentina was possible only because reform had the support of the highest authorities, who, with a concomitant basic change in philosophy, communicated to the general populace that tax evasion would no longer be tolerated.

Bolivia

Bolivia was one of those Latin American countries that had become dependent on petroleum as the main source of government revenue. Faced with falling international petroleum prices and a heavy external debt burden, it was further burdened by a complicated tax structure that led to the collapse of tax revenue in a hyperinflationary environment. The resultant rise in the fiscal deficit inevitably fed hyperinflation and made it impossible to achieve macroeconomic stabilization. Thus, in the context of an imperative need to correct overall economic policies, Bolivia embarked on fundamental tax reform in 1986 (see Harberger, 1988).

The tax reform could be said to have emphasized a drastic simplification of the tax structure, commensurate with the reality of tax administration

---

[16]For coverage of various factors that lead to tax evasion, methods to measure it, and means to control it, refer to Tanzi and Shome (1993).

standards. The focus of the tax structure became the VAT, with available resources concentrated on its administration. The VAT law was simple yet covered most goods and services, with few exemptions. Other taxes were given a minor role. The corporate income tax was abolished, and a 3 percent tax on the net worth of enterprises was put in place.[17] The primary objective of the personal income tax—taxing all sources of individual income in an equitable fashion—became less important. Instead, it was given the role of acting as a "complementary regime" for the control of the VAT. Thus, the tax would be retained—at the same rate as the VAT—from different sources of income, such as wages, interest, and dividends, and the VAT paid on purchases could be used as a credit against such withholdings. Selected excises continued to be levied. The total number of taxes was drastically reduced so that tax administration could be better targeted. The result of the reform was that tax revenue from sources other than petroleum jumped from less than 4 percent of GDP in 1985 to over 8 percent in 1988. That ratio increased steadily to over 12 percent by 1993.

Nevertheless, revenue pressures at the time of the tax reform made it necessary to consolidate some of the earlier distortionary production taxes into a 1 percent tax on all transactions. Despite its cascading nature, its revenue generation capacity—yielding almost 1 percent of GDP for every percentage point in tax rate—subsequently led to its being increased to 2 percent.

Other difficulties with the tax system also seem to have crept in. First, little revenue is collected from the personal income tax, and most of that revenue is derived from foreign remittances. A secondary market for VAT receipts has developed, so that VAT receipts bought in this market are used for claiming credit for almost all of the personal income tax withheld from other sources of income. Second, some small nuisance taxes, such as a double tax on airline tickets purchased by Bolivians, have been introduced. Third, special regimes for preferred sectors, such as transportation—irrespective of the size of the business—ensure them a lower tax liability. With an effective 15 percent tax rate, the VAT currently yields less than 6 percent of GDP (and less than 5 percent if the petroleum sector is excluded). Finally, there remains the question of whether a country with an overall ratio of nonpetroleum tax revenue to GDP that is not high in a cross-country comparison can continue to avoid a regular income tax, especially if, as is typical, it is unable to withstand expenditure pressures from both the central as well as the lower levels of government.[18]

---

[17]The income tax was abolished also in Uruguay as part of a tax reform that focused on the VAT as the leading tax.

[18]Tanzi (1993) has recently argued that the time may have come in Latin America to renew efforts to legislate and administer a properly structured income tax.

To conclude, the overall success of the Bolivian tax reform cannot be doubted. Simplicity was achieved. By crossing different taxes, the authorities introduced imaginative forms of control into a much reduced tax structure. The revenue objective was achieved. However, this success does not suggest that the time is not ripe for a revamping of the tax system with the objectives of removing remaining impurities and further developing the overall tax structure.

Brazil

The Brazilian tax system continues to be very complex for a number of reasons. Brazil has made numerous attempts to modify its structure in recent years to achieve multiple objectives. Many special incentives are granted through the tax system by various government ministries at all tiers of government. These result in a wide range of effective rates of taxation that could be very different from the nominal rates. Despite the complexity of the tax structure, or perhaps because of it, its resultant burden is not low by standards of middle-income economies (23–24 percent in terms of GDP in recent years) and also reflects the generally high nominal rates of taxation.

Brazil depends on the taxation of production and consumption for almost half its tax revenue. Some of these taxes operate on the credit principle, while some are cascading taxes with negative effects on the efficiency of production. Indeed, the various Brazilian variants would translate into the equivalent of a 25 percent pure consumption VAT. The second largest generator of revenues is payroll taxes, which yield about one-fourth of total tax revenue. Income taxes yield somewhat less than one-fifth of total tax revenue. The personal income tax base has declined through legislative changes, while incentives have tended to erode the corporate income tax base. Because the economy has been relatively closed, import duties have not yielded much revenue. The share of international trade taxes in total tax revenues is less than 2 percent. Rural property is, in general, difficult to tax; urban property and services are lightly taxed by municipalities except in certain larger cities such as São Paulo, where reform has taken place. Thus, the amount of revenue derived from property taxes is negligible.

The VAT in Brazil is limited to certain sectors of activity. It uses a great variety of tax rates and exemptions. It does not allow credit for the purchase of capital goods in general but accords preferential treatment to selected investment goods and other inputs. Thus, it is neither a consumption-type nor a production-type VAT. Both the IPI (a multiple-rate federal tax on manufactured products) and the ICMS (a state-level VAT) systems have become complex, and their economic and distributional effects are difficult to gauge. Professional services are taxed on their turnover through the ISS (a tax at the municipal level), with a negligible collection of revenue.

In general, the personal income tax remains an area of neglect in many Latin American tax systems. That of Brazil is no exception. Tax laws allow generous deductions from the tax base, suggesting that the personal income tax has a dormant revenue-raising potential. The exemption level in U.S. dollar terms is also one of the highest among medium- and high-income countries. Law No. 8383 of 1991 increased the low marginal tax rate from 10 percent to 15 percent. However, the exemption level was raised to 2.4 times per capita GDP—one of the highest in Latin America;[19] also, some deductions from the tax base were increased. This combination must have resulted in some revenue loss.

Five different taxes have been levied on corporate profits in recent years: an ordinary corporate income tax as well as a surcharge yielding an average effective tax rate of 30 percent, plus a social contribution tax, a withholding tax, and a state tax, which result in a high cumulative tax rate.[20] The overall rate, which is high by Latin American standards, must be computed by taking all the taxes into account in the appropriate order. The rate for the first $150,000 a year in profits is about 40 percent and about 50 percent for amounts that exceed this figure.

The administrative cost of dealing with five taxes on corporate profits plus several other taxes and surcharges could be assumed to be quite high for taxpayers. All taxes have their complexities, are calculated on different bases, and are paid at different times. Many medium-size firms have a special department just to administer tax assessments and payments.

Argentina, Mexico, and Peru have implemented a minimum business tax based on gross assets. Those schemes usually impose a benchmark, a minimum contribution to the corporate tax, that is levied on either gross income or gross assets. Other Latin American countries are considering a similar approach. Brazil has not yet attempted to legislate a minimum corporate tax based on gross assets.

In Brazil, many sectors are restricted from foreign investment. There are limits on the acquisition of rural property (no more than 50 defined units of rural land), participation in banks (30 percent of voting shares), the petrochemical industry (one-third of shares), and transportation (limited participation in water transportation). Foreign ownership of newspapers, radio, and television is prohibited. The computer market is basically reserved for Brazilian companies. Road transportation of freight is restricted to Brazilian individuals or to corporations whose voting capital is

---

[19]In general for Latin America, targeting about 20 percent of the population for the personal income tax net may be administratively feasible. This would reduce the exemption level to 1.6 times per capita GDP in the case of Brazil.

[20]The state tax has recently been repealed.

at least four-fifths Brazilian. Without government permission, no enterprise can be established in the 150 kilometer-wide border zone unless it can prove that at least 51 percent of its capital belongs to Brazilians and that two-thirds of the workers and the management are Brazilian.

The current rate of taxation of financial intermediaries' income is over 60 percent. This high rate may be viewed in the context of excess inflationary profits generated under high inflation. However, with a decline in inflation, the tax on most financial transactions would play a negative role. Even under high inflation, the use of monetary policy, such as raising the reserve ratio on demand deposits, is preferable. Brazil considered introducing a tax on bank debits. Such a tax may in general be expected to burden financial intermediation and could damage the financial system.

Brazil's various social security contributions represent about one-tenth of GDP and about one-fourth of total revenue of the general government. The flow of resources among the different agencies and programs is directed through a multitude of funds, which add to the complication of a system characterized by fractioning and partial overlapping of responsibilities. In summary, the system has become increasingly complex, raising the standard compounded corporation tax rate significantly. Both the top marginal rates of the payroll tax structure and the average tax rate on workers' incomes are high by international standards. Also, the very base of the tax—payrolls—tends to be strongly procyclical, thus contributing to the creation of financial problems for the social security system during economic slowdowns and downturns.

Imports as a share of GDP, at less than 5 percent, are quite small. The government recently undertook tariff reform, announcing a stepwise reduction of the average unweighted tariff at an accelerated pace, to slightly over 14 percent, while reducing the maximum tariff to 40 percent. However, unlike the norm in a growing number of countries, including Argentina and Mexico, Brazil has no minimum import duty. A minimum duty can be justified on several grounds: it is efficient in that it provides uniform effective protection, it minimizes import misclassifications, and it serves as a tax handle as imports rise. The authorities recently also curtailed explicit export taxes although a few are still levied at a low rate, for example, on hides and skins and unprocessed minerals. There is also implicit export taxation in that credit for two federal turnover taxes earmarked for social expenditures is not allowed to exporters. Except for those on windfall profits, direct and indirect taxes on exports result in a fall in the international competitiveness of Brazil's exports. There is therefore no role for export taxes in a modern taxation environment.

The scope of fiscal federalism in Brazil is unique among countries with similar levels of income. As may perhaps be expected in a large country, rules of tax assignment do not always conform to commonly accepted economic criteria. Revenue sharing among tiers of government involves complicated formulas for various combinations of tiers (for example, union-state, union-municipality, and state-municipality). Different consumption taxes are assigned to different tiers of government; their revenues are used for general budgetary expenditures, for earmarked expenditures—mainly for social security benefits—and for revenue sharing among the different tiers. Income taxes are put to general as well as specific use and are also shared among government tiers. Payroll taxes are used entirely for social security.[21]

Recent trends toward greater fiscal decentralization have eroded the union's control over the use of total tax revenue. The stabilization capacity of federal finances is thus weakened. The high proportion of shared tax revenue has also tended to limit the union's efforts to improve the yield of shared income and encouraged instead the use of alternative, unshared, but often distortionary sources of federal revenue. At the same time, the wide scope of unconditional vertical tax transfers and limited decentralization of expenditure responsibilities could have led local governments to underutilize their own revenue bases, such as user charges and property taxes. Current fiscal federalism arrangements have also generated tax competition. The states' operation of the ICMS will gradually erode the tax base through special treatments and incentives.

In general, local jurisdictions can enhance their tax revenue efforts by reducing the scope of unconditional vertical tax transfers, decentralizing expenditure responsibilities, setting, at a national level, minimum property tax rates and valuation methods, and providing technical assistance on tax administration matters to the smaller municipalities. To increase the efficiency and yield of property taxes, tax schedules should be as simple and flat as possible, and the tax base should be automatically linked to an inflation index. Provided that standards of property taxation are defined nationally, the administration and proceeds of the rural property tax could be viewed as a local government jurisdiction.

To conclude, it seems clear that Brazil is at an ideal juncture to undertake fundamental tax reform. Given the country's continental dimensions, however, the scope of the effort has to be grand, not only touching upon the structure of the tax system itself, but also carefully determining tax assignment rules within its overall fiscal federal structure.

Chile

Over the years, Chile has used the tax system for specific objectives. Major tax policy changes in 1984 reflected an ongoing economic strategy

---

[21]For a detailed description of the system, see Shah (1991).

from the previous decade toward greater emphasis on private sector activity. The objectives of the changes seemed to be focused on encouraging savings of individuals and enterprises. Average tax rates were effectively reduced through integration of the corporate and personal income taxes as well as through simplifying the income tax, while income tax incentives were provided for stock market investments. Although many of the changes concentrated on income taxes, the VAT base was expanded and some small taxes abolished.

The common view of income tax incentives is that they are not very effective for generating savings and investment. Recent, selected studies on Chile arrive at a similar conclusion that the incentives seemed to have generated some short-run gains in savings and economic activity, although an actual reduction in the tax rates may have been more beneficial in the longer run (Toro, 1994). Also, the incentives gave rise to some important loopholes that particularly benefited the banking sector, which was able to skim off interest differentials through its lending operations to incentive-seeking industry. In sum, the household sector, which historically saved little, did not change its savings behavior, while the enterprise sector increased reinvestment through retained profits, more as a result of increased economic stability than as a result of tax changes. It is noteworthy that between 1986 and 1989, the economy grew by more than 7 percent a year.

In 1990, another set of tax policy changes followed, with the objective of improving equity, reflecting the Chilean authorities' desire to consolidate the benefits of economic growth by increasing social expenditures on health, education, and housing. Their specific goal, which was to increase revenue by US$600 million, resulted in all-around increases in the rates of major taxes, including an increase in the VAT rate to 18 percent from 16 percent. Recognizing that these changes might lead to increased evasion, the authorities also stepped up administrative measures, focusing mainly on intensified auditing. The result in terms of revenue was impressive. From less than 15 percent of GDP in 1989, domestic tax revenue increased to over 18 percent in 1993. In terms of the VAT, a rate of 18 percent produces 9 percent of GDP in tax revenue. Thus, each 1 percentage point of tax rate now generates about 0.5 percent of GDP—one of the highest yield rates in the world. It is also worth mentioning that international trade taxes were reformed, with export taxes being abolished and a single import tariff being imposed at 11 percent.

To conclude, the real rate of growth of the Chilean economy between 1990 and 1992 continued to be remarkably high—nearly 6.5 percent annually. First, the increased tax rates, the higher social expenditures, and the fortification of tax administrative measures did not seem to curb economic growth. Rather, the overall economic environment seems to have been responsible for supporting economic growth.[22] Second, Chilean tax policy cannot be said to have conformed at all times to the general philosophy of simplification, base expansion, and rate reduction. Sometimes, it reflected other economic strategies and resulted in an income tax system with high tax rates and differentiated taxation and with preferred sectors and individuals identified within the system. To what extent those strategies were helped by manipulating the tax system remains open to question. The system's success in revenue generation depended in large measure on a broadly based VAT and an efficient tax administration supported by a small, efficient staff.

Colombia

Tax reform in Colombia has been a continuous effort over a number of decades. Many special commissions have been set up to examine broad or specific aspects of the tax system. Colombia's highly qualified tax professionals and the authorities' open welcome of cross-fertilization of ideas attracted the attention of international tax experts, and many commission reports were submitted to the Colombian government.[23] Important reform-oriented measures were taken in 1983, 1986, 1990, and 1992–93, which gradually improved the country's tax structure.

The objectives of the 1983 reform (like those of the 1984 reform), were to encourage economic activity through the reduction of double taxation and tax incentives. Among the measures actually taken were wide-ranging improvements in various taxes that simply attempted to correct some of the structural deficiencies of the prevailing tax system. The personal income tax structure underwent changes, such as a reduction in tax rates to reduce "fiscal drag." At the same time, an increase in the personal exemption level reduced the number of taxpayers and facilitated tax administration. Other changes included monetary correction for financial incomes of individuals and presumptive taxation for commerce and financial intermediation. The tax rate for limited companies was reduced (multiple corporate income tax rates prevailed), and double taxation was eliminated, although various incentives were granted. The sales tax was converted to an income-type VAT, and the tax base was extended to include several previously exempted services.

The 1986 Colombian reform (like the 1990 Chilean reform) attempted to achieve greater neutrality and equity, especially through restructuring the income tax, as well as to improve tax administration. Individual income tax rates were further reduced, 90 percent of salary earners began to pay tax through retentions only, corporate income tax rates were uni-

---

[22]This argument, which may be seen in the same vein as that of Toro (1994) for the 1984 reform, is made by Larrañaga (1994) for the reform of 1990.

[23]See Musgrave and Gillis (1971), McLure (1988), and Shome (1995b) for descriptions.

fied, and attempts were made to correct any continuing biases in the debt-equity ratios of companies caused by the tax system. On the administration side, the reform simplified tax declaration forms, introduced tax payments through banks, thereby releasing many tax officials for other functions, and created large taxpayer units.

The 1990 tax policy changes were carried out in the context of economic restructuring and modernization. They focused on promoting savings, improving the capital market through, among other measures, the encouragement of repatriation of capital, and opening up the economy through customs tariff reform. Actual measures included a reduction in the corporate income tax rate, but the authorities also saw fit to introduce special provisions with the objectives mentioned above. Thus, they introduced a much lower tax rate for income from repatriated capital, exempted income tax from stock market incomes, and halved the withholding tax rate on repatriated income from foreign capital. The VAT rate was unified at 12 percent and its base was further expanded. The import surcharge applicable to all imports was reduced to 13 percent from 16 percent (eventually to be reduced to 8 percent in 1994), while the average tariff was reduced to 7 percent from 16 percent. On the administration side, a national directorate for taxes was created, with a view to consolidating tax evasion strategies. This action was complemented by a further, drastic reduction in the number of taxpayers who needed to file declarations.

Tax policy changes continued in 1992–93 with the objective of lowering the fiscal deficit in the face of inflation, which hovered stubbornly near 30 percent. Tax rates tended to be increased. An income tax surcharge of 5 percent was introduced to fund national security expenditures. Public commercial and industrial enterprises, mixed enterprises, public funds, and financial cooperatives became taxable. However, the withholding tax on foreign remittances was reduced, with the intention of reducing it gradually to 7 percent by 1996. The rate of the VAT, which was converted to a consumption-type VAT to reduce cascading, was increased to 14 percent for five years and its base was broadened. Import restrictions were virtually eliminated. On the administration side, domestic taxes and customs were consolidated into one directorate to improve cross control and facilitate anti-evasion measures.

In summary, the Colombian tax policy changes can be characterized as incremental, combining particular short-run goals, such as the encouragement of savings, investment, and capital inflow, and medium-term goals consisting of corrective features to remove distortions, improve equity, and simplify the tax system.[24] Colombia experienced no revolutionary

---

[24]For further elaboration on the ramifications of tax reform, see Torres and Gutiérrez Sourdis (1994).

change—such as those that occurred in Argentina or even Bolivia—its style resembling more the Chilean-style reform, which was based on a wide scope of tax policy mixes. Nevertheless, Colombia's success with the VAT has been somewhat less complete than that of Argentina or Chile, and, in its dependence on income taxes, it can be compared with Mexico. As in all the other countries being examined, the tax policy changes progressively increased the ratio of tax revenue to GDP over the years under consideration.

Mexico

Mexico is another country in which tax reform is neither a recent nor a onetime phenomenon but can be characterized as an ongoing process. The VAT and fiscal federal arrangements were developed in the early 1980s, while further modernization of the tax system—responding to changing economic conditions—and even sophistication—based on theoretical or conceptual merit—have been achieved in the 1990s. Just as in Bolivia in the mid-1980s, Mexico in 1986–87 faced rapid inflation, high real interest rates, and a heavy debt-service ratio together with a fiscal deficit-GDP ratio of nearly 16 percent. Among other policy improvements, a fiscal strategy was engineered to achieve macroeconomic stabilization through improved revenue productivity as well as to induce economic growth through eliminating inefficiencies in the tax system. The result is that the Mexican tax structure and its administration are markedly different today from the way they were a decade ago.

The tax system had become a mixture of ad hoc arrangements, as manifested, for example, in piecemeal statutes for monetary correction. Consequently, distortionary investment decisions abounded, raising the debt-capital ratio. Additional deductions for losses in real asset values were permitted, which, in combination with a nominal interest deduction for enterprises, led to a depletion of real revenues. In the tax reform that followed, Mexico's experience seems to have occurred in stages: tax policy reform and the innovative administration reform that followed later. This experience presents an interesting contrast to that of Argentina, where, as described above, those two facets of reform proceeded together.[25] Further, in Mexico, subsequent reductions in consumption tax rates accompanied the implementation of a social contract among government, workers, and entrepreneurs.

During the first period (1986–88), Mexico's focus was on recovering the real value of tax revenues and reducing the distortionary elements of the tax system through appropriate policy measures. Advance monthly payments for the income tax, the VAT, and excises were required for the

---

[25]See Organization for Economic Cooperation and Development (1993).

first time. Indexation was introduced: only real interest could be taxed or deducted, depreciation was adjusted for inflation, inventories were immediately expensed, capital contributions by stockholders were adjusted, and enterprises were allowed to index previous years' losses.

The changes were made with some caution, however. Because enterprises were heavily indebted, an immediate monetary correction would have led to a sudden rise in their tax base. Such a move could have caused liquidity problems. As a result, a transition period of five years was introduced for the full correction to be achieved. First, the corporate tax rate was effectively reduced to 35 percent from 42 percent over the period. Second, a gradual increase was made toward the full use of the new expanded tax base.

Interestingly, some cash-flow properties were also built into the corporate income tax without inciting reaction from foreign governments. Thus, with the objective of recuperating private investment, enterprises were allowed to deduct fully—without authorization—the present value of the depreciation in new investments in fixed assets (at a discount rate of 7.5 percent), while a whole class of distortionary tax incentives was abolished.

The top personal income tax rate was reduced to 50 percent from 55 percent, and the standard deduction of one minimum wage was converted to a tax credit of 10 percent of that wage. The authorities, however, continued to experiment with the VAT, retaining more than one rate, which reflected distributional and developmental objectives.

The emphasis during the second period of tax reform (1989–92), following a change in government, was on containing evasion mainly through control measures. The authorities held the view that tax rates should not be increased so that economic growth would not be hampered, while the stabilization goal would remain intact. Furthermore, as a result of the previously implemented monetary and other corrections, the new corporate tax base turned out to be considerably smaller than originally expected, and the private sector preferred to adopt the new tax base in full immediately. This was granted in 1989, increasing the need for compensatory revenue measures that would be focused on base expansion through improved control and administrative mechanisms.

The first such measure was a 2 percent gross assets tax that would act as a minimum contribution to the corporate income tax, immediately yielding almost ½ of 1 percent of GDP in revenue in 1989 (similar to that of Argentina).[26] The second was a rapid expansion in the number of taxpayers, which increased from 13 million to 18 million between 1988 and 1992. The number of taxpaying enterprises increased more than

---

[26]For an elaboration on the operation and method of calculating the liability of this tax, see McLees (1991).

100 percent. The third measure was a reorientation of special regimes. These had originally been created to facilitate the administration of small taxpayers but had become enclaves for privileged sectors—agriculture, livestock, fisheries, transportation, and publishing—which, irrespective of the size of operations, had become immune from any revenue contribution. These regimes were simply replaced by an innovative cash-flow tax that simplified tax calculations but had a higher revenue potential. Also, there were few international repercussions of the cash-flow tax given the sectors that were affected.

Administrative improvements included redefining several types of tax-related behavior—such as delays of more than six months in filing taxes or committing acts with the purpose of obtaining unjustified fiscal benefits—as tax fraud and, thus, criminal acts. As a result, the number of tax-related criminal cases jumped from 3 during 1980–88 to 300 during 1989-93. The tax administration was also thoroughly revamped, with increased integration of various functional areas, such as collection and audit, rapid automation, and random selection for audits and customs checks.

Nevertheless, some important tax policy changes took place in this period. First, the top individual income tax rate was reduced to match the corporate income tax rate of 35 percent, while fringe benefits were taxed at higher rates than was cash income. Second, the integration provisions for the corporate and individual income taxes were simplified to reduce the burden at the individual level. Third, the corporate tax was brought closer to the cash-flow tax by allowing immediate deductions for new investments outside Mexico City, Guadalajara, and Monterrey and immediate expensing of inventories. Whether some of these complicating features, the last one in particular, necessarily constitute reform is debatable.[27] Nonetheless, sincere attempts were being made to simplify tax calculations for many taxpayers and accounting for tax purposes in general.

Interestingly, in Mexico—in contrast with Argentina—much of the focus of tax reform was on the income tax rather than on the consumption tax. When the two countries are compared, this focus is also observed in the differences in the relative shares of income and consumption taxes in total tax revenue. Thus, beginning in 1989, the VAT on selected goods and services, such as nonalcoholic beverages, telephone services, and insurance premiums, was eliminated, and the general VAT rate was reduced to 10 percent from 15 percent, while the preferential rate of 5 percent on food and medicine was reduced to zero.[28] Excises on automobiles, alco-

---

[27]For the pros and cons of a cash-flow tax, see Shome and Schutte (1993).

[28]However, exempted purchases made in worker unions' stores and the lower tax rate applicable in the border regions—*zona frontera*—were eliminated, and interest on credit card and financial consumer loans was included in the tax base.

holic beverages, and tobacco products were slashed, and the mineral extraction tax was eliminated. It is not surprising, therefore, that the revenue productivity of the Mexican VAT has not been high; it hovered at less than 4 percent of GDP until 1991 when the VAT rate was still 15 percent (it was reduced to 10 percent in November 1991) and fell to less than 3 percent of GDP in 1992 with the decrease in the tax rate. In contrast, the revenue from income taxes increased steadily from just over 4 percent of GDP in 1987 to nearly 5.5 percent of GDP in 1992.

In conclusion, the selected country experiences demonstrate a certain common philosophy of relying on tax reform to achieve such objectives as simplicity, neutrality, and overall efficiency in the tax structure. Nevertheless, there were perceptible differences among countries in the use of particular tax instruments to achieve, for example, greater savings and investment. Differences also appeared as economies matured at different rates. Those that developed faster became more concerned with equity and international compatibility and with modernizing the administration of their tax systems.

Future Issues and Directions for Reform

Although Latin American countries have significantly reformed their tax structures, important tasks remain to be addressed. These tasks take various forms and emerge from different directions. First, their tax structures retain certain elements that are reminiscent of archaic, distortionary systems and should be corrected. Second, as the Latin American economies grow and become more open and integrated into the world economy, their tax systems will be expected to incorporate more modern features. Third, much of the fiscal reform that has already taken place reflects a much greater effort on the tax than on the expenditure side, a problem that becomes exacerbated as new tax assignment rules tend to allocate greater resources to lower levels of government. Therefore, there seems to be a strong need for the reform of fiscal federalism rules.

Remaining Distortionary Elements

In every tax system, even after major reform has taken place, some distortionary elements are likely to remain or to creep in because of successful lobbying or populist promises made by politicians or to meet the authorities' urgent revenue needs. Latin America is no exception. The technician's role under those circumstances is to work steadfastly toward eliminating the distortions. The purpose of this section is not to list all such elements in Latin American tax systems but rather to provide some examples of how otherwise neutral tax systems may become subject to inefficiencies.

To generate revenue in the short run, Argentina introduced a tax on financial transactions—essentially on checks. The tax had an initial positive revenue impact but soon encouraged financial transactions to go underground, for example, through the multiple use (endorsement) of a check. The tax was eventually repealed. The news of the initial success of the tax in yielding revenue, however, had a significant demonstration effect in neighboring countries. A strong movement for a unique tax on checks—to replace the tax system—received credibility, albeit temporarily, in Brazil. Quite a few other countries continue to consider the tax quite seriously. Needless to say, such a tax has the potential to inflict lasting damage on the domestic banking system. For example, if many agents switched to foreign accounts, it would become convenient to open an account abroad and to transact with foreign checks. The tax could also reduce the overall attractiveness of financial markets and hamper tax auditing by driving transactions underground.

Despite the almost universal implementation of the VAT by Latin American countries, some country authorities burden the system with additional distortionary taxes on production or transactions. Bolivia's 2 percent cascading tax on all transactions, for example, is highly revenue productive—as might be expected because there is no credit mechanism—but distortionary. Other countries may levy excises, including on small household appliances, that are difficult to administer. A few countries levy other nuisance taxes for fear of losing even the smallest amount of revenue.

These types of tax seem to thrive, owing, sometimes, to campaign promises not to increase the VAT rate or even to repeal the VAT. Indeed, many statements have recently been made against the VAT. Interestingly, opposition seems not to lie with the VAT itself because, in the countries where the statements are generally made, the VAT bases have typically been eroded to accommodate various interest groups, while the tax rate of the VAT might have had to be sequentially increased to compensate for the base erosion. It is obvious that the VAT should not be eliminated but rather that its base should be extended. Those countries in which the VAT base is broad and the rate is judged to be at a ceiling may do better to explore the feasibility of expanding the role of income taxes instead of introducing additional distortionary taxes on production.

Modernization

At least those countries of Latin America that can be said to be modernizing very rapidly will need, in the not too distant future, to give due consideration to the tax systems of industrial countries. Three areas that need attention are the taxation and administration of incomes, property, and agriculture.

Many Latin American countries, at the early reform stage, quite rightly simplified both their tax structure and tax administration, focusing mainly on the VAT. As their tax systems and economies mature, however, many of them continue to generate insignificant revenue from income taxes. The time may have come for many of them to consider reforming, rather than eradicating, income taxes. It is not necessary to link an income tax with a global approach, based on compulsory declarations, right from the start. A beginning could be made with a simple, even schedular, structure, using withholding and retention mechanisms. Such an approach should facilitate administration of the tax and make it more productive.

In almost all Latin American countries, property taxation has been virtually ignored except, perhaps, in certain large cities, particularly those in fiscally federal states. Typically, the rate structure is unrealistic, with high tax rates, while the base remains uncorrected for inflation sometimes for decades. There seems to be little reason not to introduce in Latin America the model used by various local governments in the United States, which relies on published sale values to determine the assessed values of different properties rather than on a completed cadastral survey. The model that has been used to assess properties and the administration of the property tax in São Paulo also merits examination for broader applicability.

Essentially, the same argument may be made for agricultural taxation. Any modern tax system must include at least a simplified mechanism for taxing agriculture appropriately. Some Latin American countries are at the economic threshold at which they should seriously consider such a mechanism.

A number of European countries—Finland, Netherlands, Norway, and Sweden—have already implemented a carbon tax for environmental considerations, and other countries are seriously considering one. The tax variants are on sulfur emissions, sulfur dioxide, chlorofluorocarbons, heavy metals, chemical fertilizers, pesticides and herbicides, phosphates, and methane, as well as the "classical" taxes on mineral oil, natural gas, and coal. There are proposals for taxes on specific forms of industrial and agricultural waste and waste produced by the construction industry, as well as taxes on tropical wood, plastic bags, aluminum cans and foil, batteries, light bulbs, and water consumption. Most member countries of the Organization for Economic Cooperation and Development have expressed their willingness to reduce carbon dioxide emissions, as manifested by their participation in the 1988 World Climate Change Conference in Toronto and the 1992 United Nations Environment Conference in Rio de Janeiro.

The rationale for a carbon tax is as follows. First, scientists have linked carbon emissions to a global warming phenomenon. Second, studies have correlated carbon emissions and energy prices inversely. An appropriately designed carbon tax should therefore help curb global warming. It is time that Latin American countries legislate the means to reduce emissions. In this context, it is surprising that, as their economies have been opened and import tariffs reduced, including those on automobiles, many authorities have continued to reduce domestic excises on automobiles. The introduction of a carbon tax would correct this anomaly and help modernize the tax structure.

Tax Assignment and Fiscal Federalism

The Latin American experience with fiscal federalism, for example, in Argentina and Brazil,[29] reveals that, over time, the lack of reform, unfinished reform, or reform that is countered by policies precipitated by short-term exigencies may increase the burden on higher-level governments. This outcome may, in turn, lead to mounting difficulties for the federal government in its macromanagement functions. Sometimes even the onset of reform may increase the burden on the federal government, as explained below.

Important taxes in terms of revenue productivity—such as income and consumption taxes—are usually subject to revenue sharing. Typically, the federal government has sole control over the revenue from international trade taxes. With tariff reform, as average tariff rates have fallen and the tax bases have diminished, the federal government has had to look elsewhere for a steady source of revenue.

As revenue shares from shared taxes have tended to increase for lower-level governments, federal governments have devised unshared taxes that are often inefficient, such as the one mentioned on financial transactions. These taxes can be temporary at best and are unable to alleviate the revenue problem at the federal level in the long run.

As the revenue performance of shared federal taxes has improved, lower-level governments have had windfall revenue gains and therefore have little incentive to improve their own revenue performance. Thus, it may be necessary to require a minimum revenue effort by lower-level governments before federal funds are dispensed to them. The challenge for the federal government would be to adhere to such requirements, once introduced.

A certain volatility caused by a lack of specific rules has characterized the distribution of tax revenue. However, distributional changes have usually had the twofold effect on lower-level government shares of increasing the strain for macromanagement and causing their revenue efforts to stagnate. The lack of rules has also plagued certain categories of expenditure.

---

[29]See Fundación de Investigaciones Económicas Latinoamericanas (1993) for Argentina, Prud'homme (1989) and Shah (1991) for Brazil, and, for a comparative analysis, Shome (1994).

Tax assignment and revenue-sharing reform take place faster than expenditure assignment reform. This has essentially implied that taxes get assigned to lower levels (and revenue shares of lower levels increase) faster than the rate at which larger expenditures are assigned to lower-level governments. Indeed, intergovernmental negotiations for expenditure assignment tend to leave large responsibilities to the federal government, generally in excess of what its revenue share would imply.

The common experience has been for lower-level governments to be able to finance their expenditure through provincial banks virtually without constraint. Thus, reform may be carried out at the level of revenue sharing and tax assignment. Nevertheless, unless financing reform stipulates a ceiling on lower-tier financing, fiscal federal reform cannot be complete.

To conclude, with greater decentralization of tax revenue, greater decentralization must follow for expenditure responsibilities. Furthermore, given a tax and expenditure assignment mix, guidelines are needed for deficit financing rules if serious macromanagement is not to be jeopardized. While local governments have to be provided some budgetary discretion so that the efficiency gains of decentralization can be obtained, an argument may be made for local governments to earn that discretion by relying on their own tax efforts. To the extent that they are dependent on federal financing, general equilibrium and dynamic stability of the macroeconomy must eventually entail a limit on free financing of local government deficits. Thus, first, lower-level governments should be required to report their finances regularly to the next higher level, and, second, their borrowing capacity must be curbed.

Summary and Conclusions

Much of the prereform tax policy in Latin America over the past decade reflected the need for basic economic reforms that were initiated in the face of hyperinflation, stagnating or negative economic growth, expanding balance of payments deficits, and difficulty with pursuing sufficiently tight monetary policy. The concomitant growth in fiscal deficits resulted in correction, especially on the tax side, because governments were unable to reduce expenditures quickly owing to high interest costs or wage bills that were politically difficult to curtail. In that event, authorities often found that tax policy was a relatively easy instrument to wield and used it to the maximum extent possible.

Many countries initiated, and followed through with, important tax policy reform. While steadfastly keeping the revenue goal in mind, as manifested in a steadily increasing tax revenue-GDP ratio to the extent of 2–4 percent of GDP over a few years, countries that undertook reform typically revealed a number of strong trends: personal income tax rates and their dispersion went down, the tax began to be applied at higher incomes in terms of GDP, fiscal drag was corrected, corporate income tax rates were unified and decreased, withholding rates on foreign remittances were lowered, capital gains began to be treated as ordinary income, it became more common to consider or even require a minimum contribution to the corporate income tax as an anti-evasion measure, the VAT structure was improved and its base universally expanded, excises became more selective, export taxes were generally abolished, and the customs tariff structure and dispersion were scaled back.

On the tax administration side, imaginative measures were taken in many countries although, in others, improvements lagged behind. Closing businesses and treating more evasion-related behavior as criminal acts became important deterrent measures. Personnel reform and structural consolidation of tax and customs administration made it possible to induct officials who took bold steps, supported at the highest political levels, toward curbing evasion. As a result, the general population began to believe that taxes—recently rationalized and often lowered—had to be paid to avoid high penalties.

Despite the common trends, there was considerable variation in individual country experiences in conducting particular aspects of tax policy. While in some countries, neutrality of the tax system was a stated objective, in others, income taxes were used at particular times with the express purpose of encouraging savings and investment.[30] Colombia and Mexico, for example, relied considerably more on income taxes than did Argentina or Bolivia, which focused on the VAT, while Chile emphasized both areas. The revenue productivity of the VAT in Chile is among the highest in the world today. Bolivia simplified its tax structure more than any other country and, in a relative sense, perhaps experienced the most dramatic revenue increase.

As Latin American economies became more integrated with the rest of the world, their tax systems responded to varying degrees, for example, with respect to the withholding tax on foreign remittances. In addition, with foreign investors in mind, Argentina and Mexico attempted to increase the sophistication of their income tax structures by incorporating international issues, such as transfer pricing, a foreign tax credit, and so on.

A key reason for country differences has been the fact that a critical mass in favor of tax reform has been slow in forming in Brazil and Venezuela. Thus, these countries have been slow to respond to pressure to carry out fundamental tax reform based solely on the evidence from neighboring countries. Clearly, the dynamics of political consensus buttressed by support from the highest political levels are essential for the implementation of tax reform.

---

[30]Such a policy did not always turn out to be successful, however.

The reforming countries did not always succeed in eliminating completely inefficient or inadequate features of their tax systems. Some that remain are the inadequate taxation of property and agriculture. Moreover, some inefficient elements have been introduced into the tax structure with the sole purpose of generating revenue. For example, Argentina introduced a tax on financial transactions, and Bolivia and Brazil considered one; Bolivia continues to implement a distortionary and cascading turnover tax at a 2 percent rate that covers all manufactured goods; and small taxes, including on business net worth, continue despite their failure to yield much revenue. Complex fiscal federal relations in large countries like Brazil tend to hamper the implementation of efficient tax assignment principles, for example, in the case of the VAT.

In conclusion, the directions in which Latin American countries should look to conduct their tax policies are clear. One important area is that of fiscal federal relations and the determination of rules for tax assignment to the various levels of government. Decentralization must also proceed for both taxes and expenditures if the objective of a low fiscal deficit is to be pursued.

Second, as economies mature, they must consider to what extent the administered tax system resembles the legislated tax structure. For example, to simplify tax administration, potential taxpayers often have to be ignored or eliminated from the functioning ambit of certain taxes, such as the VAT or income taxes. It is important, therefore, to consider to what extent the universe of taxpayers can be increased over time to include more and more so-called minor taxpayers. Third, and relatedly, while the role of "large" taxpayer units in improving auditing and revenue performance should not be minimized, the rate at which the coverage of these units can be expanded—if not merged with the general taxpayer population—should certainly be considered an important criterion for the measurement of the maturity of a tax system. Fourth, and in the same vein, the rate at which the use of tax amnesties declines may be taken as an indicator of the maturity of the tax administration.

Fifth, the two areas that have been largely overlooked—property and agriculture—cannot go untaxed for too long if the tax structures of the more advanced of the Latin American countries are to become fully comparable with those of industrial countries. Sixth, it would seem feasible for Latin American countries to give serious consideration to selected new concepts in modern taxation, such as eco-taxes (those levied for ecological purposes, such as the carbon tax). These would comprise some of the important elements of future tax reform that may be envisaged as the Latin American countries approach the twenty-first century.

References

Aguirre, Carlos, and Parthasarathi Shome, "The Mexican Value-Added Tax (VAT): Methodology for Calculating the Base," *National Tax Journal*, Vol. 41 (December 1988), pp. 543-54.

Bird, Richard M., "Tax Reform in Latin America: A Review of Some Recent Experiences," *Latin American Research Review*, Vol. 27 (1992), pp. 7-36.

———, and Milka Casanegra de Jantscher, *Improving Tax Administration in Developing Countries* (Washington: International Monetary Fund, 1992).

Durán, Viviana, and Juan C. Gómez-Sabaini, "Lecciones sobre Reformas Fiscales en Argentina: 1990-1993," paper presented at the sixth Comisión Económica para América Latina y el Caribe (CEPAL) seminar, Santiago, Chile, January 1994.

Fundación de Investigaciones Económicas Latinoamericanas, *Hacia una Nueva Organizacion del Federalismo Fiscal en la Argentina* (Buenos Aires, Argentina: FIEL, 1993).

Harberger, Arnold C., "Introduction," in *Bolivia 1952-1986*, by Jeffrey Sachs and Juan A. Morales (San Francisco: International Center for Economic Growth, 1988).

Larrañaga, Osvaldo, "Casos de Exito de la Política Fiscal en Chile: 1980-1993," paper presented at the sixth CEPAL seminar, Santiago, Chile, January 1994.

McLees, John A., "Fine Tuning the Mexico Assets Tax," *Tax Notes International*, Vol. 3 (February 1991), pp. 117-20.

McLure, Charles E. Jr., "Analysis and Reform of the Colombian Tax System," Working Paper in Economics No. E-88-15 (Stanford, California: Stanford University, Hoover Institution, 1988).

Musgrave, Richard A., and Malcolm Gillis, *Fiscal Reform for Colombia; Final Report and Staff Papers of the Colombian Commission on Tax Reform* (Cambridge: Law School of Harvard University, 1971).

Organization for Economic Cooperation and Development, "Mexico's Recent Tax Policy," a note by Mexico, Committee on Fiscal Affairs, Meeting of June 30-July 1, 1993 (Paris: OECD, 1993).

Prud'homme, Remy, *State and Local Finance and Public Policy in Brazil*, OEIL Report for World Bank, University of Paris XII (Paris, June 1989).

Shah, Anwar, "The New Fiscal Federalism in Brazil," Discussion Paper No. 124 (Washington: World Bank, 1991).

Shome, Parthasarathi, "Fiscal Federalism—Revenue, Expenditure, and Macro Management," inaugural address at the sixth CEPAL seminar, Santiago, Chile, January 1994.

———, "Trends and Future Directions in Tax Policy Reform: A Latin American Perspective," *Bulletin for International Fiscal Documentation*, Vol. 46 (September 1992), pp. 452-66.

———, ed. (1995a), *Tax Policy Handbook* (Washington: International Monetary Fund).

———, ed. (1995b), *Comprehensive Tax Reforms: The Colombian Experience*, Occasional Paper No. 123 (Washington: International Monetary Fund).

————, and Christian Schutte, "Cash-Flow Tax," *Staff Papers*, International Monetary Fund, Vol. 40 (September 1993), pp. 638-62.

Tanzi, Vito, *Tax Notes Today* (July 27, 1993).

————, and Parthasarathi Shome, "The Role of Taxation in the Development of East Asian Economies," in *Taxation and Development in East Asian Countries*, ed. by Anne O. Krueger and Takatoshi Ito (Chicago: Chicago University Press, 1992), pp. 31-61.

————, "A Primer on Tax Evasion," *Staff Papers*, International Monetary Fund, Vol. 40 (December 1993), pp. 807-28.

Toro, Juan, "Aspectos Exitosos y Lecciones de Reformas Tributarias en Chile," paper presented at the sixth CEPAL seminar, Santiago, Chile, January 1994.

Torres, Fabio Sánchez, and Catalina Gutiérrez Sourdis, "Casos de Exito en Reformas Fiscales: Colombia, 1980-1992" (January 1994).

Comment

Miguel Rodríguez

Mr. Shome's paper offers an excellent analytical summary of the progress made over the past decade in tax reforms in the context of structural adjustment programs in Latin America. It also describes with great lucidity the future challenges facing governments with respect to taxation.

As we know, efforts aimed at restructuring the public sector and finding a solution to structural fiscal instability have become the cornerstone of the structural reforms being successfully implemented by several Latin American countries. The sharp reduction in inflation in Argentina, Bolivia, Chile, and Mexico is the result of the extraordinary progress these countries have made in restructuring their public sectors and in eliminating or substantially reducing their fiscal deficits. Mr. Shome points out how important tax reform has been in improving these countries' fiscal situation and alerts us to the fact that the delay in implementing appropriate tax reforms in countries such as Brazil and Venezuela explains, in large measure, the persistent fiscal and macroeconomic instability in their economies.

Venezuela's case perhaps best illustrates the importance of the role of fiscal adjustment and tax reform in economic reform. After the successful launch of its economic reform program in 1989, when trade liberalization, early efforts to restructure the public sector, rationalization of exchange and monetary policies, and debt renegotiation fueled sharply accentuated growth and reduced inflation until 1992, the Venezuelan economy plunged into a severe recession. The recession was accompanied by a resurgence of inflation and the onset of a crisis in the financial sector, which quickly led to capital flight. At the root of this grave macroeconomic instability lies a sizable structural fiscal deficit (more than 10 percent of GDP) owing to the failure to implement an appropriate tax reform to diversify the government's non-oil revenue base. In a country with a high potential for noninflationary growth, the absence of a solid tax base has led to a marked fiscal imbalance, which is hurting the economy and threatening to cancel out all of the gains achieved as a result of the liberalization effort.

Mr. Shome's paper stresses the major progress achieved in tax matters in the region and the positive effects on the adjustment process. First, he reviews the progress achieved in this past decade with the establishment of more rational and efficient tax systems, which are decreasingly distortionary and in which collections have increased significantly. In some countries, collections increased dramatically owing to a more efficient tax environment, laying the groundwork for further progress. The basis of the reforms (which, of course, took on different forms in different countries) was the simplification of the personal and corporate income tax structure, the introduction of a minimum tax on corporate income (such as the tax on assets), the introduction or restructuring of consumption taxes (basically the value-added tax), and customs tariff reforms. However, the countries that have made the most progress in developing taxes and that have achieved relatively high ratios of tax revenue to GDP are those that were able to undertake major changes in their tax codes. These countries clearly defined tax violations and penalties and have relied on dynamic finance ministers, who have strictly enforced the new tax laws as is done in industrial countries.

But the most significant observations in Mr. Shome's paper pertain to the agenda for the future. First, it is necessary to build upon the efficiency gains in tax administration and legislation by eliminating the sources of distortion that still exist in most countries. In extreme cases, such as Venezuela's, the authorities intend to abolish the VAT—which was approved only last year—and to introduce a highly distortionary tax on bank debit balances that will foster financial disintermediation, in connection with a thoroughly political economic policy that is likely to delay even further the tax reform and the resulting stabilization of the economy. Fortunately, most countries are past this phase, and the general trend seems to be toward greater progress in eliminating these distortions and promoting substantially efficient tax systems.

Second, progress in the major decentralization process occurring in several countries must be accompanied by an appropriate delegation of spending authority and sharing of tax responsibilities among the various regions and government authorities. All of these efforts would lead to greater efficiency in fiscal administration and keep the fiscal deficit under control.

Last, besides suggestions for modernizing taxation in areas such as the environment, I believe that the proposals to develop the property tax scheme and to increase income tax collections are the most important ones on the tax agenda that Mr. Shome suggests for our countries. Through an institutional effort that stresses improved administration and the use of legal mechanisms to ensure that these taxes are collected, it is possible to achieve elsewhere in Latin America results similar to those that Argentina and Chile obtained with the VAT or that Mexico achieved with the income tax.

Nevertheless, a major effort with respect to the property tax and the personal income tax would help our countries adopt a progressive tax structure, with positive results on redistribution. If, at the same time, Latin American countries also adopted a progressive social spending program, long-term productivity would increase. One of the reasons income is so unevenly distributed in Latin America is the governments' extremely regressive fiscal policy, which has played a role in maintaining, or, rather, in aggravating the appalling distribution of wealth inherited from our feudal colonial past. Traditionally, government action in the fiscal area has been based on distortionary, regressive tax policies—with the wealthiest segments of the population paying insignificant amounts—and on a public spending policy that, associated with a populist discourse, has led to large subsidies and the transfer of income and wealth to the most privileged sectors in our countries. One of the fundamental challenges Latin America faces in restructuring its public sector—building upon the rationalization achieved in recent years—is to promote a progressive tax policy on both revenue and expenditure, thereby helping to set a pattern of economic growth through a more equitable distribution of income and wealth.

To that end, our countries will have to pattern themselves increasingly after the industrial countries, with respect to government action in the fiscal realm. On the revenue side, in addition to sustaining substantial collections from the consumption tax, revenue must also be obtained effectively from income and property taxes, with the wealthy bearing a significantly higher burden. On the expenditure side, we should invest intensively and efficiently in education and health and establish the infrastructure essential to development. In a population that is generally healthy and well trained for productive purposes, such investment would reduce the sharp disparities in relative wages that are found in Latin America and that account for 70 percent of the regressive income distribution in our countries. This is precisely what the industrial countries have done: they have invested heavily in human capital using the resources obtained from progressive taxation, endowing their populations with the ability to engage in productive work. These steps, in turn, have had a decisive impact on the level of real wages and relative remuneration, and thus on income distribution. Similar trends can be observed in the successful, newly industrializing economies in Asia, which have used progressive tax policies, encouragement of savings, and major educational efforts to establish, in their growth and development process, much more equitable distribution patterns than those found in Latin America.

These remarks on the government's recommended fiscal actions lead me to comment on a proposition reiterated by Mr. Shome in his paper, namely, the need to persist in efforts to reduce public spending as a part of long-term fiscal adjustment. I disagree slightly, perhaps because of my familiarity with Venezuela's experience, but also because of my conversations with many Latin American ministers and officials and my observation from time to time of the Latin American expenditure figures and how they compare internationally. Although I fully agree that public expenditure should be rationalized and every effort made to eliminate unproductive expenditure,

I believe that it is going to be very difficult for many countries to reduce public expenditure further. On the contrary, when we achieve greater efficiency in the allocation and execution of expenditure, that is, when we are spending the appropriate amounts on education, health, infrastructure investment, social programs, and environmental protection, I suspect that we will have to increase public spending in comparison with current Latin American practice, including in relatively more developed countries. For this reason, despite the great progress that several countries have already achieved, we must step up our tax efforts in the future so as to be able to provide noninflationary financing for forward-looking public spending programs that are consistent with our foremost development objectives.

Last, I believe that such a comprehensive, high-quality work as Mr. Shome's should have devoted a portion of the analysis to social security, an important component of the reform that Latin America must undertake, and to its possible repercussions in fiscal matters, promotion of savings, and macroeconomics in the region's countries.

Comment

Luis Viana

The paper by Mr. Shome is an interesting survey of recent changes in tax policy in Latin America. It is a rich paper that stimulates discussion about tax issues. The main results seem to show that the reforms that have taken place in most of the countries were steps in the correct direction. From the paper, it can be concluded that tax reforms improved tax neutrality at the same time that tax revenues increased and the inequality of the tax system was dampened.

Based on cross-country evidence on tax rates and country case studies, the paper concluded that tax neutrality was achieved through

- a lower dispersion of tax rates,
- a reduction in corporate and income tax rates,
- an increase in the tax base, mainly as a consequence of tight controls and enforcement of penalties on tax evasion and the elimination of tax exemptions, and
- the replacement of cascading turnover taxes by a value-added tax.

After reading the paper carefully, I am left with the impression that perhaps the paper was too ambitious in tackling so many issues at the same time. Even though it is mainly a survey, many times I had difficulty evaluating the main conclusions about tax neutrality, equality, and other aspects of tax administration. These three objectives are not necessarily achieved without any cost. What is missing from Mr. Shome's paper is an explicit consideration of the trade-offs among the objectives, which should be put forward to balance the discussion.

For example, we can conclude that per capita taxes may be the most neutral tax or, at the same time, the most regressive. We can also infer that increasing the tax base on corporate taxes will increase tax neutrality, but that, simultaneously, neutrality can be achieved only at a high administrative cost. Furthermore, it might be argued that the trade-offs among neutrality, equality, and revenue-enhancing objectives must be taken into account if we are to evaluate the evidence correctly.

The second gap in Mr. Shome's paper is the lack of a discussion of how the objectives can be achieved independently. The criteria for evaluating tax neutrality are based mainly on uniform tax structures and a broad tax base. In this paper, little attention has been paid to the effects of the overall tax structure. First, social security taxes have not been considered, and, second, the inflation tax and implicit taxes raised through public enterprises have not been taken into account. Some conclusions for inflation taxes and implicit taxes on public enterprises can be inferred insofar as stabilization and privatization policies were pursued during the period under review. However, analyzing tax neutrality without discussing social security and inflation taxes in Latin America may be misleading.

In addition, the impact of the tax structure on the structure of industry is underestimated. The tax system may influence this structure in at least two ways: first, by discriminating among sectors, and, second, by discriminating among the sizes of firms within a sector.

Both of these effects appear to be extremely important for private sector development in Uruguay.[1] These were the main results of a survey of two hundred export firms that attempted to identify barriers to private development. Information was stratified by firm size and exporting sector. The results of the survey showed that the tax burden was one of the most important obstacles for the private sector, in particular for large firms. Small firms not only enjoy tax advantages through the tax system, but are also less likely to have their taxes audited. Social security tax evasion was estimated at 3 percent of GDP, while evasion of the value-added tax was estimated at 1.8 percent of GDP.

The above findings also underscore the importance of presenting information other than marginal tax rates to evaluate tax systems. For example, information on average tax rates to compare with marginal tax rates might have been useful. Such a comparison would have revealed a truer picture of the tax base. Average tax rates can be estimated from tax collections and potential tax bases. Comparisons by sector and by the size of the firms within a sector would have been useful for evaluating tax policy.

Finally, the paper raises two issues concerning tax inequality on which I would like to elaborate. Both of them are related to tax incidence considerations. First, no explicit comment is made in the paper about the implications of capital taxation, both property and corporate taxes. The common view is that capital taxation improves equality; in my view, it does the opposite. For a small open economy with a given rate of return on capital, taxes, in the long run, are paid by low-skill workers when investment falls. Capital taxes not only depress growth, but at the same time fall on low-income groups.

Second, the paper by Mr. Shome implicitly favors income taxes over consumption taxes as a tool for improving income equality. This view presumes that savings are never going to be spent or ignores the existence of a life income profile. I believe income distribution policies should be addressed with focalized expenditure policies rather than with tax policy.

---

[1]Gustavo Michelin and L. Viana Martorell, "Desarrollo de la Actividad Privada en el Marco del Proceso de Regulación" (Bogota: Centro de Estudios de la Realidad Económica y Social, 1992).

7

Trade and Industrial Policy Reform in Latin America

Sebastián Edwards

Most Latin American countries began to open up to the rest of the world in the late 1980s. This process is perhaps the most impressive achievement of the structural adjustment programs that followed the debt crisis and has effectively put an end to more than four decades of active industrial policies based on import substitution.

However, the process leading to these trade reforms has not been easy. As recently as the mid-1980s, the protectionist view was still influential in many parts of Latin America. In fact, the debt crisis of 1982 provided a new impetus to the protectionist paradigm. In a way that resembled the arguments of the 1930s and 1940s, a number of authors interpreted the crisis as a failure of "the world economic order" and argued that the only way for Latin America to avoid a recurrence of this type of shock was to further isolate itself from the rest of the world through selective protectionism and government intervention (Griffith-Jones and Sunkel, 1986). This perspective was vividly defended by Lance Taylor (1991, p. 119), who argued that the "trade liberalization strategy is intellectually moribund" and that "development strategies oriented internally may be a wise choice towards the century's end" (p. 141).

In the mid-1980s, Latin America's external sector was the most distorted in the world. For example, as can be seen in Table 7.1, Central America had the highest degree of import protection in terms of both tariff and nontariff barriers (NTBs)—among developing countries, with South America following closely behind. However, by 1987–88 it became apparent that a permanent solution to the region's economic problems would imply a fundamental change in its development strategy. In particular, policymakers began to realize that the long-standing protectionist trade policy was at the heart of the region's problems. During the late 1980s and early 1990s, and with the assistance of the multilateral institu-

Note: I am indebted to my discussants and conference participants for useful comments. I am thankful to Fernando Losada for excellent research assistance.

Table 7.1. Import Protection in the Developing World, 1985
(In percent)

Region	Total Tariff Protection[1]	Nontariff Barrier Coverage[2]
South America	51	60
Central America	66	100
Caribbean	17	23
North Africa	39	85
Other Africa	36	86
West Asia	5	11
Other Asia	25	21

Source: Erzan and others (1989).
[1]Includes tariffs and para-tariffs.
[2]Measures as a percentage of import lines covered by nontariff barriers. Data on both tariffs and NTBs reported here are weighted averages.

tions, a larger and larger number of countries began to reduce their levels of protection and to reform their development views. Reforms on the trade front have accelerated: tariffs have been drastically slashed, in many countries import licenses and prohibitions have been completely eliminated, and a number of nations are actively trying to sign free trade agreements with other Latin American countries as well as with the United States.

This paper documents and evaluates the process of trade reform in Latin America.[1] The next section provides an analytical and historical discussion of the consequence of the traditional industrial policies in Latin America. A distinction is made between policies based on strict import substitution and policies that combined high and uneven import tariffs with export promotion. The paper deals also with the analytics of trade liberalization reforms, including a discussion of the role of supporting policies in assuring the success of trade liberalization reforms. Important questions related to the sequencing of economic reform are discussed in some detail. In particular, emphasis is given to the issue of the appropriate sequencing of stabilization and trade reform policies. The extent of trade reform in Latin America is discussed, and some of the results of the reforms are analyzed. The analysis concentrates on productivity and exports and deals with the experiences of several countries. The role of real exchange rates in a trade liberalization process is carefully taken into account, and the recent trend toward real appreciation in most countries in the region is assessed. Finally, the paper studies the recent attempts at reviving regional integration agreements, the future prospects for free trade agreements with the United States, and the significance of the recent

---

[1]The material presented in this paper is based on some of the author's work over the past few years. In particular, it draws on Chapter 5 of World Bank (1993b). See the references to this paper for a list of works related to this topic.

agreement of the General Agreement on Tariffs and Trade (GATT) for the Latin American countries.

Protectionism, Industrial Policy, and Export Promotion

The recent trade liberalization programs in Latin America have sought to reverse protectionist policies that for decades have been at the heart of the region's development strategy. To place these reforms in perspective, it is useful to first analyze the way in which the protectionist policies affected the economic structure of Latin America and to discuss what the expected effects of the liberalization policies were.

Economic Consequences of Protectionist Industrial Policies

The Great Depression had a fundamental impact on the Latin American economies. Terms of trade plummeted—in Brazil, Chile, and Colombia by almost 50 percent—capital inflows stopped, and real income was severely reduced. The effects of the decline in the worldwide demand for raw materials in 1929–30 were compounded by the adoption of protectionist policies in the United States and Europe through, for example, the Smoot-Hawley Tariff Act in 1930 and the British Abnormal Importations Act of 1931.

Most Latin American countries reacted to these events by abandoning convertibility, devaluing their currencies, and imposing tariff barriers. Díaz-Alejandro (1981) has described these policies as follows:[2] "Exchange rate devaluations were not the only measures undertaken. . . . [T]here were also increased tariffs, import and exchange controls, bilateral clearing agreements and . . . multiple exchange rates" (p. 340).

It has generally been thought that sustained protectionism became dominant throughout Latin America in the early 1930s, if not earlier.[3] However, Thorp (1992) has recently argued that in the mid- to late 1930s a number of countries in the region—especially Argentina, Brazil, and Chile—implemented substantial trade liberalization policies aimed at encouraging openness and outward orientation. She has argued that export expansion played a key role in the Latin American recovery toward the end of the 1930s. The eruption of World War II put an end to this episode of export-led growth, and once again the Latin American countries responded to the adverse world shocks by resorting to protectionism and inward-looking policies. However, the end of the foreign disturbances was not followed by a new period of openness and the region's reinsertion into the world economic system. By the late 1940s and early 1950s,

---

[2]See also Furtado (1969) and Bianchi and Nohara (1988).

[3]See Leff (1969) on Brazil. Bianchi and Nohara (1988) discuss this issue for Latin America as a whole.

protectionist policies based on import substitution were well entrenched and constituted, by far, the dominant perspective (Díaz-Alejandro, 1981).

The creation of the UN Economic Commission for Latin America and the Caribbean (ECLAC) provided an intellectual underpinning for the protectionist position. In particular, the writings of Raúl Prebisch (1950)[4] and Hans Singer (1950) imparted an aura of respectability to import-substitution policies. These authors' thinking was based on two fundamental premises: (1) a secular deterioration in the international price of raw materials and commodities would result, in the absence of industrialization in the developing countries, in a widening of the gap between rich and poor countries, and (2) to industrialize, the smaller countries required temporary assistance in the form of protection for the newly emerging manufacturing sector. This reasoning was closely related to the *infant industry* argument for industrialization.[5] Between the 1950s and 1970s, a large number of development economists embraced the inward-oriented view and devoted enormous energy to designing planning models that relied heavily on the import-substitution ideas. This view became dominant and was taught with great zeal in most Latin American universities.[6]

Prebisch's position developed as a criticism of outward orientation, which he considered to be incapable of permitting the full development of the Latin American countries. He argued that development required industrialization through import substitution and that this approach could be "stimulated by moderate and selective protection policy" (Prebisch, 1984, p. 179). Eventually, however, the degree of protection to the incipient industries became anything but moderate, as more and more sectors required additional tariffs and other types of government support to continue facing foreign competition (Balassa, 1982, and Little, Scitovsky, and Scott, 1970).

During the early years of import substitution, important heavy industries were created in the larger countries, and the basis for the development of

---

[4]Raúl Prebisch was a remarkable intellectual force who greatly shaped early Latin American economic thinking. He was the governor of the Argentine central bank in the 1930s and early 1940s, a period when he applied orthodox policies. In 1947, Prebisch published the first Spanish language guide to Keynes's *General Theory*. On the evolution of his thinking, see Prebisch (1984). See also, Chapter 1 of Iglesias (1992) and Solís (1988).

[5]An interesting summary of this view can be found in Prebisch (1984). Hirschman (1968) provided an early "soul-searching" assessment of the disappointing results experienced under the import-substitution strategies. A review of import-substitution theories appears in Bruton (1989). For a discussion of trade policies in the context of Latin America's historical development, see Fishlow (1991).

[6]See, for example, the popular Paz and Sunkel (1970) textbook for a discussion of economic policy in the context of the structuralist and protectionist views. See also the text on international economics by Ffrench-Davis and Griffin (1967). Castro and Lessa (1969) provided a popular, and widely used, principles text that discussed basic economic issues from a structuralist perspective.

a domestic manufacturing sector was set. During the 1950s, the industrial sector grew at rapid real rates, topping in some countries—Brazil and Mexico, for example—8 percent a year (Elías, 1992). With industrialization, however, an array of restrictions, controls, and often contradictory regulations evolved. In most countries, lobbying developed swiftly as a way to secure the rents created by the maze of controls. It was, in fact, because of import restrictions that many of the domestic industries were able to survive. As a consequence, many of the industries created under the import-substitution strategy were quite inefficient. Krueger (1981) and Balassa (1982) found that this inward-looking strategy generated rent-seeking activities and resulted in the use of highly capital-intensive techniques, which hampered the creation of employment throughout the region.

In most countries, starting in the late 1940s, import substitution was accompanied by an overvalued domestic currency that precluded the development of a vigorous nontraditional export sector.[7] In an early study using data from the 1960s, Balassa (1971) found that the Latin American countries in his sample—Brazil, Chile, and Mexico—had some of the most distorted foreign trade sectors in the world. These findings coincide with those obtained by Little, Scitovsky, and Scott (1970) in their pioneer study on trade policy and industrialization in the developing world. These authors persuasively argued that the high degree of protection granted to manufacturing in Latin America resulted in serious discrimination against exports, resource misallocation, inefficient investment, and deteriorating income distribution. They further argued that the reversal of the protectionist policies should be at the center of any reformulation of Latin America's development strategy. The agricultural sector was particularly harmed by real exchange rate overvaluation. The lagging of agriculture became one of the most noticeable symptoms of many countries' economic problems of the 1950s and 1960s. The overvaluation of the real exchange rate played an important political role during this period because it kept down the prices of imported goods consumed by urban dwellers.[8]

In many countries—especially in Argentina, Brazil, Chile, Colombia, Peru, Uruguay, and Venezuela—fiscal imbalances became a staple of government policies. However, the dominant view did not consider this to

---

[7]This point was strongly made by Díaz-Alejandro (1970) in his monumental study on the external sector in Argentina. See also Díaz-Alejandro's (1976) work on Colombia. See Edwards (1988, 1989) for discussions on real exchange rate misalignment. It may be argued that, given the level of protectionism that prevailed during this period, observed (and appreciated) real exchange rates were at an "equilibrium" level. However, under this interpretation, the highly appreciated real exchange rates still discouraged nontraditional exports.

[8]The discrimination against agriculture during this period contrasts sharply with the case of East Asia, where serious efforts were made to avoid harming that sector. See World Bank (1993a).

be an overly serious matter; it was, in fact, believed that fiscal disequilibrium was only indirectly related to inflation.[9] The inflationary problem became particularly serious in Chile, where the rate of increase of consumer prices averaged 36 percent a year during the 1950s, reaching a peak of 84 percent in 1955.

The discouragement of export activities took place through two main channels: first, import tariffs, quotas, and prohibitions increased the cost of imported intermediate materials and capital goods used in the production of exportables, reducing their effective rate of protection. In fact, for years a vast number of exportable goods, especially those in the agricultural sector, had *negative* protection of their value added. Second, the maze of protectionist policies resulted in real exchange rate overvaluation that reduced the degree of competitiveness of exports. This antiexport bias explains the poor performance of the export sector, including the inability to aggressively develop nontraditional exports, during the twenty years preceding the debt crisis. Paradoxically, policies that were supposed to reduce Latin America's dependency on the worldwide business cycle ended up creating a highly vulnerable economic structure where the sources of foreign exchange were concentrated in a few products intensive in natural resources, and where imports were concentrated in a relatively small group of essential goods (United Nations, 1992).

A second general and important consequence of traditional protective trade policies was the creation of a manufacturing sector that, in most countries, was largely inefficient. Instead of granting short-term protection to help launch new activities, high tariffs, quotas, and prohibitions became a fixture of the region's economic landscape. An important consequence of the pressures exercised by lobbyists and interest groups was that the protective structure in Latin America became extremely uneven, with some sectors enjoying effective tariff rates of more than 1,000 percent, and others suffering from negative value-added protection (Edwards, 1992). Moreover, as is argued below, in the 1970s interest group pressures resulted in the superimposition of an array of special export subsidies for a handful of firms that were deemed to be strategically important (Nogués, 1990).

The protectionist policies also had serious effects on labor markets. In particular, the protection of capital-intensive industries affected the region's ability to create employment. A number of studies have shown that in developing countries more open trade regimes have resulted in higher employment and in a more even income distribution than protectionist regimes. For example, after analyzing in detail the experiences of ten

---

[9]See Sunkel (1960) for the classic piece on the structuralist view of inflation. Dornbusch and Edwards (1990) examine these issues from the more extreme, populist perspective.

countries, Krueger (1983) concluded that exportable industries tended to be significantly more labor intensive than import-competing sectors. In the conclusions to this massive study, Krueger argues that employment has tended to grow faster in outward-oriented economies and that the removal of external sector distortions will tend to help the employment creation process in most developing countries. These results were broadly supported by other cross-country studies, including those by Balassa (1982) and Michaely, Papageorgiou, and Choksi (1991).

In terms of income distribution, the protection system largely benefited local industrialists—in particular, those able to obtain import licenses and concessions—and urban workers, but at the cost of depressing the incomes of rural workers. As discussed in Edwards (1993b), for example, during the 1970s income distribution was significantly more unequal in Latin America than in Asia.

In summary, although several decades of protectionist policies succeeded in creating an industrial sector in Latin America, this goal was achieved at high cost. Exports were discouraged, the exchange rate became overvalued, employment creation lagged behind, and massive amounts of resources—including skilled human resources—were withdrawn from the productive sphere and devoted to lobbying for an ever-favorable treatment of different sectors of the economy.[10] An increasing number of comparative studies in the 1980s made the shortcomings of the Latin American development strategies particularly apparent. In the aftermath of the debt crisis, the long stagnation, and even retrogression, of the region's export sector—with an average rate of *decline* of 1 percent a year between 1965 and 1980—became particularly painful to the local public, analysts, and policymakers.

Industrial Policy and Export Promotion

As discussed above, after an auspicious beginning, the import-substitution strategy began to run into difficulties during the late 1950s and early 1960s. At that time most of the obvious substitutions of imported goods had already taken place, and the process was rapidly becoming less dynamic (Hirschman, 1968). For example, during the 1960s total real industrial production grew in most countries at one-half the annual rate of the previous decade (Elías, 1992). Also, an increasing number of politicians and economists began to agree that Latin America was facing long-run economic problems. It was generally recognized that the easy phase

---

[10]As discussed in some detail in Chapter 3 of World Bank (1993b), most authors agree that the import-substitution process rapidly ran into difficulties once low-technology consumer goods had been "substituted." As countries tried to move toward producing more sophisticated goods—including capital goods and machinery—they faced an increasingly uphill battle. See Hirschman (1968) and Fishlow (1985).

of the import-substitution process had ended and that inflation and the recurrent crises of the external and agricultural sectors had become serious obstacles to growth. Furthermore, the increasingly unequal distribution of income and the unemployment problem represented serious challenges to any new economic program. Although most experts pointed out that low rates of domestic savings and investment represented an important obstacle to growth, they differed markedly on some other aspects of their diagnosis and on the proposed policy packages to take the country out of its relative stagnation.[11] At this time, the simple import-substitution policies came under attack from two flanks: on the one hand, a small number of economists, sometimes associated with the monetarist position, argued for orthodox stabilization programs based on fiscal restraint and a greater reliance on market forces.[12] On the other hand, a growing number of intellectuals in the Marxist tradition—including the group known as *dependencistas*—argued that there was too little government presence in economic decisions and postulated a massive move toward full-fledged planning, in the Eastern European style.[13]

Facing this two-pronged attack, the structuralist thinkers eventually concluded that their policies had to be reformed. Fishlow (1985) notes that the dominant economic view in Latin America experienced two important developments during the 1960s. First, import substitution was expanded from the country sphere to the regional level, and a number of attempts to create regional trading agreements were undertaken. Perhaps the most comprehensive of these was the Andean Pact created in 1969 and grouping Bolivia, Chile, Colombia, Ecuador, Peru, and, later, Venezuela. However, the proposed regional arrangements did not tackle the high levels of protection and distortions imposed in the previous twenty years. In fact, in the Andean Pact, the proposed common external tariff was extremely high and uneven, representing the expansion of the traditional structuralist thinking to a supranational level (see Edwards and Savastano, 1988). The evolution of integrationist attempts in the region is addressed in greater detail below.

The second development discussed by Fishlow (1985) was the recognition of the importance of capital inflows as a way to supplement domestic savings and finance higher rates of capital accumulation. However, this option was centered around official capital flows through multilateral

---

[11]The UN Economic Commission for Latin America and the Caribbean played an important role in developing this diagnosis.

[12]No serious recommendations were made, however, to introduce deep structural changes, such as privatizing government-owned firms.

[13]See Fishlow (1985) for a discussion of these competing criticisms of import substitution. Edwards and Edwards (1991) discuss this problem from Chile's perspective. See, also, Sheahan (1987) and Cardoso and Helwege (1992). Vuskovic (1970) provides one of the most eloquent defenses of the *dependencista* position.

institutions and did not give private flows a significant role. Also, no specific recommendations were made to alter the basic incentive structure of the economy or to provide a greater role to market forces in long-run development strategies.

In the late 1960s and the 1970s, the structuralist view continued to evolve, as it became increasingly evident that the dynamism of most Latin American economies was in rapid decline. In particular, in a number of countries the expansion of exports became an important component of otherwise traditional economic programs. Brazil provides, perhaps, the clearest example of a strategy for expanding manufacturing exports with the aid of an aggressive industrial policy based on export subsidies, tax allowances, and subsidized credit to selected industries. At the macroeconomic level, this industrial policy was supplemented by an active crawling peg exchange rate system aimed at avoiding real exchange rate overvaluation.[14]

Although this policy resulted in a very rapid rate of growth of GDP and manufacturing exports, Brazil's economic base remained somewhat rigid and fragile.[15] As Fishlow (1991) has argued, after decades of an industrialization strategy based on protective policies, Latin America, and especially Brazil, had relatively high wages and its exports could not become the "engine of growth" as in East Asia. In spite of expanding at a rapid pace, exports still failed to relax the required foreign exchange constraint that for years had affected most countries. As a consequence, during the 1970s virtually every country in the region resorted to heavy foreign borrowing to obtain foreign exchange. The rapid accumulation of debt made these economies particularly vulnerable, as the region painfully learned in 1982.

Why wasn't export promotion more successful in Latin America? After all, industrial policies explicitly aimed at encouraging exports were implemented aggressively and very successfully in many East Asian countries. For example, in the 1960s an aggressive export-promotion scheme became an important complement of the Korean trade liberalization strategy. Throughout the years, exports have been subsidized through a number of channels, including (1) direct cash subsidies (until 1964); (2) direct tax reductions (until 1973); (3) interest rate preferences; (4) indirect tax reductions on intermediate inputs; and (5) tariff exemptions to imported intermediate materials.[16] Kim (1991) has recently calculated that these subsidies were reduced from 23 percent to zero between 1963 and 1983.

---

[14]See Rabello de Castro and Ronci (1991) for a critical view of sixty years of development policy in Brazil.

[15]Coes (1991) provides a thorough evaluation of Brazil's attempts at encouraging exports during the 1970s.

[16]See Kim (1991) for details on the different export-promotion schemes used.

He has argued, as others have, that in Korea, export subsidies played an important role during the earlier years of the country's export boom.[17] A recent massive study undertaken by the World Bank (1993a) has explored with great detail the reasons for the East Asian export success. It is argued that in most cases the government organized "contests" among private firms, with export performance as the main criterion to determine "winners." Those firms with a strong export record were rewarded with access to preferential credit and other types of special treatment. This study suggests that by picking exports as the general activity to be rewarded, rather than production in a particular sector (for example, steel), the East Asian countries avoided major distortions and, in particular, were able to minimize the extent of rent-seeking activities. It may be argued that while the Latin American export-promotion policies—especially those developed in Brazil—subsidized selected industries that were deemed to have export potential, East Asian government policies were based on whether the final destination of production was, in effect, the world market.

Lin (1988) has compared trade policies in Korea, Taiwan Province of China, and Argentina. His computations indicate that in the 1970s the overall rate of effective protection was 10 percent in Korea, 5 percent in Taiwan Province of China, and 47 percent in Argentina. The contrast was even greater in the manufacturing sector, where the effective rates of protection were -1 percent in Korea, 19 percent in Taiwan Province of China, and almost 100 percent in Argentina. These differences in protective rates affected relative incentives, generating a substantial antiexport bias in Argentina. Modern theories of economic growth have linked openness with productivity growth: more open economies tend to engage in technological innovation faster, exhibiting more rapid productivity improvements. According to Lin (1988), labor productivity increased at an annual rate of 8.7 percent in Korea during 1973–85 and at only 0.5 percent a year in Argentina. The vigorous growth experienced by other East Asian countries—including the second generation "miracle" countries of Indonesia, Malaysia, and Thailand—since the late 1980s has added impetus to the idea that a development path based on openness and market orientation can be extremely rewarding. Increasingly, Latin American leaders are turning toward East Asia for inspiration and economic partnership.

A number of authors have argued that the conduct of macroeconomic policy constitutes a second crucial difference between East Asia and Latin America (see Sachs, 1987). As has been extensively documented by a number of authors, inflation has been significantly higher in the Latin American countries than in the East Asian countries. Moreover, Latin America has also been affected by higher inflation variability and real

---

[17]In Latin America, there has been a controversy on the actual effectiveness of export subsidies. See, for example, Nogués and Gulati (1992).

exchange rate volatility. The greatest advantage of a stable macroeconomic environment is that it reduces uncertainty, thereby encouraging investment. Moreover, to the extent that the real exchange rate is stable, investment in the tradables sector will increase, as will exports. Sachs (1988) and Fischer (1988), among others, have pointed out that in the adjustment-cum-reform process, the achievement of macroeconomic stability should *precede* trade liberalization in the developing countries. Based on the experiences of Korea, Taiwan Province of China, and Japan, Sachs (1988) has argued that massive and deep tariff reduction should take place only after macroeconomic stabilization is firmly in place.[18] This issue is addressed with greater detail in the next section.

Trade Liberalization: Expected Results and Transitional Problems

The main objective of trade liberalization programs is to reverse the negative consequences of protectionism and, especially, its antiexport bias. According to basic theory, trade liberalization will result in a reallocation of resources, according to comparative advantage, in a reduction of waste, and in a decline in the prices of imported goods.[19] Moreover, to the extent that the new trade regime is more transparent—for example, through a relatively uniform import tariff—it is expected that lobbying activities will be greatly reduced, releasing highly skilled workers from unproductive jobs. According to traditional international trade theory, it is expected that once negative effective rates of protection and overvalued exchange rates are eliminated, exports will not only grow rapidly, but will also become more diversified.

From a growth perspective, the fundamental objective of trade reform is to transform international trade into the engine of growth. In fact, newly developed models of endogenous growth have stressed the role of openness.[20] For example, Romer (1989) has developed a model in which, by taking advantage of larger markets—the *world* market—an open economy can specialize in the production of a larger number of intermediate goods and, thus, grow faster. Other authors have recently concentrated on the relationship between openness, technological progress, and productivity growth. Grossman and Helpman (1991) and Edwards (1992), for

---

[18]See Edwards (1992) for a general discussion on the sequencing of economic reform.

[19]Of course, this amounts to the important textbook notion that freer trade increases the level of domestic welfare. However, modern approaches go beyond this goal and also consider the acceleration of growth as a goal of trade policy (see Edwards, 1992).

[20]Traditional neoclassical growth models concentrated on the effect of national economic policies on the *level* of income per capita. The new generation of endogenous growth models has shifted attention to the relationship between different policies and the rate of growth of the economy (see Lucas, 1988).

example, have argued that openness affects the speed and efficiency with which small countries can absorb technological innovations developed in the industrial world. This idea, based on an insight first proposed by John Stuart Mill, implies that countries with a lower level of trade distortions will experience faster growth in total factor productivity and, with other things being equal, will grow faster than countries that inhibit international competition.[21]

In recent papers, a number of authors have tested the general implications of these theories using cross-country data sets.[22] Although different empirical models have yielded different results, the general thrust of this line of research is that countries with less distorted external sectors appear to grow faster. As Dornbusch (1990) pointed out, openness possibly affects growth through not just one channel, but through a combination of channels, including the introduction of new goods, the adoption of new methods of production, the reorganization of industries, the expansion of the number of intermediate goods available, and the conquest of new markets that permit the expansion of exports.

The importance placed by liberalization strategists on the reduction of the antiexport bias has resulted in significant emphasis on the role of exchange rate policy during a trade reform effort. A number of authors have argued that a large devaluation should constitute the first step of trade reform. Bhagwati (1978) and Krueger (1978) have pointed out that in the presence of quotas and import licenses, a real exchange rate depreciation will reduce the rents received by importers, shifting relative prices in favor of export-oriented activities and, thus, reducing the extent of the antiexport bias (see Krueger, 1978, 1981, and Michaely, Papageorgiou, and Choksi, 1991).

Speed and Sequencing of Trade Liberalization Reform

Two fundamental problems must be addressed in the transition toward freer trade: first, it is important to determine the adequate speed of reform. For a long time, analysts argued for gradual liberalization programs (Little, Scitovsky, and Scott, 1970; Michaely, 1985), because they maintained that gradual reforms would give firms time to restructure their productive processes and, thus, would result in low dislocation

---

[21]In Chapter 17 of his *Principles of Political Economy* (1848), Mill said that "a country that produces for a larger market than its own can introduce a more extended division of labor, can make greater use of machinery, and is more likely to make inventions and improvements in the process of production." Arthur Lewis makes a similar proposition in his classic 1955 book on economic growth.

[22]See Tybout (1992) for a general survey of empirical models of the relationship between trade orientation and growth of total factor productivity. See also Edwards (1992) and De Gregorio (1992).

costs in the form of unemployment and bankruptcies. These reduced adjustment costs would, in turn, provide the needed political support for the liberalization program. Recently, however, the gradualist position has been under attack. There is increasing agreement that slower reforms tend to lack credibility, inhibiting firms from engaging in serious restructuring. Moreover, the experience of Argentina in the 1970s has shown that a gradual (and preannounced) reform allows those firms negatively affected by it to lobby successfully against reductions in tariffs. According to this line of reasoning, faster reforms are more credible and thus tend to be sustained over time (Stockman, 1982).

The thinking on the speed of reform has also been influenced by recent empirical work on the short-run unemployment consequences of trade liberalization. Contrary to conventional wisdom, a World Bank study directed by Michaely, Papageorgiou, and Choksi (1991) on liberalization episodes in 19 countries strongly suggests that, even in the short run, the costs of reform can be small. Although contracting industries will release workers, those sectors that expand as a result of the reform process will tend to create a large number of employment positions. The study shows that, in sustainable and successful reforms, the *net* effect—that is, the effect that nets out contracting and expanding sectors—on short-run employment has been negligible.

The second problem that must be addressed when designing a liberalization strategy is the sequencing of reform (Edwards, 1984). This issue was first addressed in the 1980s in discussions dealing with the Southern Cone (Argentina, Chile, and Uruguay) experience and emphasized the macroeconomic consequences of alternative sequences. It is now generally agreed that resolving the fiscal imbalance and attaining some degree of macroeconomic reform should be a priority of structural reform. Most analysts also agree that trade liberalization should precede liberalization of the capital account and that financial reform should be implemented only after a modern and efficient supervisory framework is put in place.[23]

The behavior of the real exchange rate is at the heart of this policy prescription. The central issue is that liberalizing the capital account, under some conditions, results in large capital inflows and an appreciation of the real exchange rate (McKinnon, 1982; Edwards, 1984; Harberger, 1985).[24] The problem with this scenario is that an appreciation of the real exchange rate will send the "wrong" signal to the real sector, frustrating the reallocation of resources called for by the trade reform. The effects of

---

[23]Lal (1985) presents a dissenting view. Hanson (1992) has argued that under some circumstances the capital account should be liberalized early on. See Chapter 7 of World Bank (1993b) for a discussion on sequencing issues with financial reform.

[24]This would be the case if the opening of the capital account were done in the context of an overall liberalization program, where the country becomes attractive to foreign investors and speculators.

this real exchange rate appreciation will be particularly serious if, as argued by McKinnon (1982) and Edwards (1984), the transitional period is characterized by "abnormally" high capital inflows that result in temporary real appreciations. If, however, the opening of the capital account is postponed, the real sector will be able to adjust and the new allocation of resources will be consolidated. According to this view, only at this time should the capital account be liberalized.

More recent discussions on the sequencing of reform have expanded the analysis to include other markets. An increasing number of authors have argued that the reform of the labor market—in particular the removal of distortions that discourage labor mobility—should precede the trade reform as well as the relaxation of capital controls. As argued by Edwards (1992), it is even possible that the liberalization of trade in the presence of highly distorted labor markets will be counterproductive, generating overall welfare losses in the country in question. Discussions on the sequencing of reform have addressed in detail only the order in which the liberalization of various "real" sectors in society should proceed. For instance, only a few studies, such as those by Krueger (1981) and Edwards (1984), have dealt with the order of reform of agriculture, industry, government (i.e., privatization), financial services, and education. The key question is the extent to which independent reforms will bear all their potential fruits or whether the existence of synergism implies that in a broad liberalization process the reforms in different sectors reinforce each other.[25]

As the preceding discussion has suggested, real exchange rate behavior is a key element during the transition to trade liberalization. According to traditional manuals on how to liberalize, a large devaluation should constitute the first step of trade reform. Maintaining a depreciated and competitive real exchange rate during trade liberalization is also important in order to avoid an explosion in import growth and a balance of payments crisis. Under most circumstances, a reduction in protection will tend to generate a rapid and immediate surge in imports. On the other hand, the expansion of exports usually takes some time. Consequently, there is a danger that trade liberalization will generate a large trade balance disequilibrium in the short run. This, however, will not happen if there is a depreciated real exchange rate that encourages exports and curbs imports.

Many countries have historically failed to sustain a depreciated real exchange rate during the transition, mainly because of expansionary macroeconomic policies that generate speculation and international reserve losses and, in many cases, lead to a reversal of the reform effort. In the conclusions to the massive World Bank project on trade reform Michaely, Papageorgiou, and Choksi (1991) succinctly summarize the key role of the real exchange rate in determining the success of liberalization programs: "The

---

[25]Of course, this discussion is related to a second-best analysis of policy measures.

long term performance of the real exchange rate clearly differentiates 'liber-alizers' from 'non-liberalizers' " (p. 119). Edwards (1989) used data on 39 ex-change rate crises and found that, in almost every case, real exchange rate overvaluation led to drastic increases in the degree of protectionism.

Order of Stabilization and Trade Liberalization Policies

The question of sequencing macroeconomic stabilization and structural reform—especially trade reform—has recently become an important pol-icy issue in a number of places, including Latin America, Eastern Europe, and the countries of the former Soviet Union. Analysts have asked whether fiscal reform should precede structural reform or whether both types of policies should be implemented simultaneously. By the late 1980s, most analysts began to agree that in countries with serious macroeconomic imbalances the most appropriate sequencing required early and decisive action on the macroeconomic front, including the elim-ination of the debt-overhang problem.[26] It was argued that the uncer-tainty associated with high inflation, including high relative price variability, would reduce the effectiveness of market-oriented structural reforms, especially trade liberalization policies. This high degree of uncer-tainty would result in low investment and, in some cases, could even direct investment toward the "wrong" sectors (Fischer, 1986).

A second argument for the "stabilization-first" sequence is based on the contribution of foreign trade taxes to public revenues: if public finances have not been brought under control, the reduction of import tariffs would make things worse by increasing the fiscal deficit. This argument is considered to be particularly valid for low-income countries that rely heavily on taxes on international trade.

As in the case of trade versus capital account liberalization, the real ex-change rate is at the center of the debate. Under a set of plausible condi-tions, macroeconomic stabilization programs will tend to result in an appreciation of the real exchange rate, while, as pointed out above, a suc-cessful trade reform will require a real depreciation.

A limitation of the approach that advocates stabilization before liberal-ization is that it does not distinguish between different degrees of macro-economic disequilibria at the time the reforms are initiated. While the relative price variability and real exchange appreciation arguments are eminently plausible for high-inflation countries, they are unlikely to be as important in countries that start from moderate inflation. For example, Krueger (1981) has argued that the Asian and Middle Eastern experiences suggest that there is little connection between the determinants of infla-tion and the orientation of the trade regime. Along similar lines, Edwards

---

[26]For early discussions of the sequencing debates, see Edwards (1984) and Fischer (1986).

(1992) has argued that, in countries with moderate rates of inflation, trade liberalization and macroeconomic stabilization will tend to reinforce each other. In particular, the reduction of import tariffs and the exposure of the domestic industry to foreign competition will tend to introduce "price discipline." Moreover, the increase in productivity growth usually associated with trade reforms will tend to offset mild real exchange rate appreciations that take place during the stabilization effort. A second limitation of this approach is that it tends to ignore the political economy of reform. Two points are in order regarding this issue. First, once embarked on a major transformation process, reform-minded policymakers tend to take advantage of whatever opportunity they have. Second, in many cases it is easier to attack the protectionist lobby—which is fairly well defined and concentrated in specific industries—than to deal with the interest groups that lead to fiscal imbalances and inflation.

In spite of these limitations, the stabilization-first approach has become the dominant view among policy analysts, including the staffs of multilateral financial institutions such as the International Monetary Fund and the World Bank. However, as documented in World Bank (1993b), almost every country in Latin America ignored this piece of advice and either embarked on trade reform first or implemented trade liberalization and stabilization policies simultaneously.

Determinants of Successful Trade Liberalization Policies

Two economic aspects of trade liberalization are particularly important for analyzing the political economy of transition and the likelihood that reforms can be sustained over time. First, it takes time for the structural reforms to bear fruit. This means that even though in the long run the reforms will have a positive effect on the aggregate economy, there will be some short-run costs. These transitional costs, however, will not be even and will affect some groups more heavily than others. Second, even in the long run some groups will lose and will see their real incomes diminish. These groups will be those that have benefited from the preform maze of regulations, and, in most cases, they will tend to oppose the reforms from the beginning. Politically, then, trade reforms will survive only if they show some benefits early on and if these benefits expand gradually, affecting larger and larger segments of society.

The extensive comparative studies by Little, Scitovsky, and Scott (1970), Balassa (1971, 1982), Krueger (1978, 1980), Bhagwati (1978), and Michaely, Papageorgiou, and Choksi (1991) have provided abundant evidence on the key determinants of a successful trade reform that will change the trade structure of a country. These elements can serve as a guide for policymakers who want to implement trade liberalization policies that will be sustained over time. Existing historical evidence suggests that successful (i.e., sustained) reforms have been characterized, in the short and medium run, by at least some of the following elements:[27]

- Exports, particularly nontraditional exports, expand at a pace that exceeds the historical rate.
- Productivity growth increases rapidly, helping generate rapid growth for the economy as a whole.
- The trade balance does not exhibit "unreasonable" deficits. If such deficits exist, the public will be skeptical about the viability of the reform and will speculate against the domestic currency.
- The overall level of unemployment stays at a relatively low level.
- Real wages increase, at least in the medium run. For this increase in wages to affect a broad sector of society, trade liberalization should be supplemented by other structural reforms aimed at deregulating and liberalizing other sectors of the economy.

Recent Trade Liberalization Reforms in Latin America and the Caribbean

The pioneer in the Latin American trade liberalization process was Chile, which, between 1975 and 1979, unilaterally eliminated quantitative restrictions and reduced import tariffs to a uniform level of 10 percent. After a brief interlude with higher tariffs (at the uniform level of 35 percent), by 1992 Chile had reduced its degree of protection to a uniform tariff of 11 percent, totally abolishing licenses and other forms of quantitative controls. Uruguay implemented its reform in 1978 and, after a brief reversal, pushed forward once again in 1986. Bolivia and Mexico embarked on their reforms in 1985–86, followed by a number of countries in the late 1980s. By early 1992, a number of Latin American countries, including Brazil, were proceeding steadily with scheduled rounds of tariff reduction and the dismantling of quantitative restrictions. However, at the time of this writing, it is still unclear whether all these reforms will become a permanent feature of the Latin America economies or whether some of them will be reversed. Recent developments in Argentina and Colombia indeed suggest that in some countries higher tariffs may be implemented, once again, in the near future.

The Latin American trade reforms have been characterized by four basic components: (1) the reduction of the coverage of nontariff barriers, including quotas and prohibitions; (2) the reduction of the average level of import tariffs; (3) the reduction of the degree of dispersion of the tariff structure; and (4) the reduction of export taxes. These measures have

---

[27]These elements have been present in most sustained reforms studied in recent times. See, for example, Little, Scitovsky, and Scott (1970), Krueger (1978), and Michaely, Papageorgiou, and Choksi (1991) for extensive case studies.

generally been supported by exchange rate policies aimed at maintaining a competitive real exchange rate.

Nontariff Barriers

A key component of the trade reform programs has been the elimination, or at least the severe reduction, of the coverage of NTBs. During the early and mid-1980s in some countries, such as Colombia and Peru, more than 50 percent of import positions were subject to licenses or outright prohibitions. In Mexico, as in most of Central America, NTBs covered almost all import categories in 1985 (Table 7.1).

Table 7.2 contains data on protectionism in 1985–87 and 1991–92 and shows that in almost every country the coverage of NTBs has been substantially reduced.[28] In fact, in a number of countries they have been fully eliminated. The process through which NTBs have been eased has varied from country to country. In some cases, such as Honduras, they were initially replaced by quasi-equivalent import tariffs and then slowly phased out. In other countries, like Chile, they were eliminated rapidly without a compensating hike in tariffs.

As Table 7.2 shows, in spite of the progress experienced in the past few years, significant NTB coverage remains in a number of countries. In most cases, these NTBs correspond to agricultural products. For example, in approximately 60 percent of Mexico's agriculture sector, tariff positions were still subject to import licenses in mid-1992. Those for U.S. imports were scheduled to be eliminated as a result of the North American Free Trade Agreement. An important feature of the region's liberalization programs is that they have proceeded much slower in agriculture than in industry. This has largely been the result of the authorities' desire to isolate agriculture from fluctuations in world prices and unfair trade practices by foreign countries.[29] Although, according to a recent study by Valdés (1992), this approach based on quantitative restrictions entails serious efficiency costs,

---

[28]These are *unweighted* averages, and are thus not comparable to those presented in Table 7.1. There has been a long discussion in applied international trade theory on whether tariffs and NTBs should be measured as weighted or unweighted averages. Both views have some merits and some limitations. An obvious problem of the weighted-average approach (where the weights are the import shares) is that more restrictive distortions will tend to have a very small weight. In the extreme case, prohibitive tariffs that effectively ban the importation of a particular item will have a zero weight. Corden (1966) provides an early and still highly relevant discussion on these issues.

[29]Protecting local producers from "dumping" is an important issue in the design of the new, liberalized trade regimes. The crucial problem is to enact legislation that is able to distinguish true cases of unfair trade practices from simple cases of increased foreign competition stemming from more efficient productive processes. Approving a dynamic and flexible antidumping legislation should be high on the region's current agenda for legal and institutional reform.

Table 7.2. Selected Latin American Countries: Decline in Level of Protection
(In percent)

Reforming Countries	Tariff Protection, Including Para-tariffs[1]		Nontariff Barrier Coverage[1]	
	1985	1991–92	1985–87	1991–92
First group				
Bolivia	20.0	8.0	25.0	—
Chile	36.0	11.0	10.0	—
Mexico	34.0	4.0	12.7	20.0
Second group				
Costa Rica	92.0	16.0	0.8	—
Uruguay	32.0	12.0	14.1	—
Third group				
Argentina	28.0	15.0	31.9	8.0
Brazil	80.0	21.1	35.3	10.0
Colombia	83.0	6.7	73.2	1.0
Guatemala	50.0	19.0	7.4	6.0
Nicaragua	54.0	...	27.8	...
Paraguay	71.7	16.0	9.9	—
Peru	64.0	15.0	53.4	—
Venezuela	30.0	17.0	44.1	5.0
Fourth group				
Ecuador	50.0	18.0	59.3	...

Sources: World Bank; UNCTAD, *Handbook of Trade Control Measures of Developing Countries*; and Erzan and others (1989).
[1]These figures are unweighted averages.

more and more countries are addressing these concerns by replacing quantitative restrictions with variable levies and by introducing a system for smoothing price fluctuations based on price bands.

Tariff Dispersion

The development strategy based on import substitution that Latin America pursued for decades created highly dispersed protective structures. According to the World Bank (1987), Brazil, Chile, and Colombia had some of the highest degrees of dispersion in effective protection in the world during the 1960s. Also, Heitger (1987) shows that during the 1960s Chile had the highest rate of tariff dispersion in the world—with a standard deviation of 634 percent—closely followed by Colombia and Uruguay. Cardoso and Helwege (1992) have pointed out that highly dispersed protective structures generate high welfare costs by increasing uncertainty and negatively affecting the investment process. These highly dispersed tariffs and NTBs were the result of decades of lobbying by different sectors to obtain preferential treatment. As the relative power of the different lobbies changed, so did their tariff concessions and the protective landscape.

Table 7.3. Range of Import Tariffs

(In percent)

Country/Most Recent Observation	1980s		1990s	
	Minimum	Maximum	Minimum	Maximum
First group				
Bolivia (1985)	0	20	5	10
Chile (1987)	0	20	11	11
Second group				
Costa Rica (1986)	1	100	5	20
Uruguay (1986)	10	45	10	30
Third group				
Argentina (1987)	0	55	0	22
Brazil (1987)	0	105	0	65
Colombia (1986)	0	200	0	15
Guatemala (1986)	1	100	0	10
Nicaragua (1986)	1	100	0	10
Paraguay (1984)	0	44	5	86
Peru (1987)	0	120	5	15
Venezuela (1987)	0	135	0	50
Fourth group				
Ecuador (1986)	0	290	2	40

Sources: World Bank; UNCTAD, *Handbook of Trade Control Measures of Developing Countries*; Erzan and others (1989).

An important goal of the Latin American trade reforms has been the reduction of the degree of dispersion of import tariffs. Table 7.3 contains data on the tariff range for a group of countries for 1985–87 and 1991–92 and clearly documents that the reforms have indeed reduced the range between minimum and maximum tariffs. In many cases this has meant *increasing* tariffs on goods that were originally exempted from import duties. In fact, this table shows that in many countries the minimum tariff was zero in the mid-1980s. Generally, zero tariffs have been applied to intermediate inputs used in the manufacturing process.[30] From a political-economy perspective, the process of raising some tariffs while maintaining a pro-liberalization rhetoric has not always been easy. Those sectors that had traditionally benefited from the exemptions tried to oppose them strongly as they suddenly saw their privileged situation coming to an end.

---

[30]This system with low (or zero) tariffs on intermediate inputs and high tariffs on final goods generated high rates of effective protection or protection to domestic value added. In recent years, a number of authors have argued that the use of effective protection is misleading. The reason for this is that effective rates of protection are unable to provide much information on the general equilibrium consequences of tariff changes (Dixit, 1985). In spite of this, such measures are still useful because they provide an indication of the degree of "inefficiency" a country is willing to accept for a particular sector.

An important question addressed by policymakers throughout the region is: By how much should tariff dispersion be reduced? Should a *uniform* tariff be implemented or is some dispersion desirable? Although from a strict welfare perspective, uniform tariffs are advisable only under special circumstances, they have a strong administrative and political-economy appeal. In particular, a uniform tariff system is transparent, making it difficult for the authorities to grant special treatment to particular firms or sectors (Harberger, 1990).

Average Tariffs

Reducing the average degree of protection is, perhaps, the fundamental policy goal of trade liberalization reforms. Traditional policy manuals on the subject suggest that once the exchange rate has been devalued and quantitative restrictions have been reduced or eliminated, tariffs should be slashed in such a way that both their range and average are reduced.[31] Table 7.2 contains data on average total tariffs (tariffs plus para-tariffs) in 1985 and 1991-92. As can be seen, the extent of tariff reduction has been significant in almost every country. Even countries that have acted somewhat cautiously on the reform front have experienced important cuts in import tariffs, making the environment more competitive and reducing the degree of antiexport bias of the trade regime.

Countries that have embarked on trade liberalization in recent years have moved much faster than those that decided to open up earlier. There has, in fact, been a clear change in what is perceived to be *abrupt* and *rapid* removal of impediments to imports. What only 15 years ago were seen as brutally fast reforms are now viewed as mild and gradual liberalizations. When Chile initiated its trade reform in 1975, most analysts thought that the announced tariff reduction from an average of 52 percent to 10 percent in four and a half years was an extremely aggressive move that would cause major dislocations, including large increases in unemployment. The view on the speed of reform has changed in the early 1990s, as an increasing number of countries have opened up their external sectors very rapidly. For instance, Colombia slashed total import tariffs by 65 percent *in one year*, reducing them from 34 percent in 1990 to 12 percent in 1991. This fast approach to liberalization has also been followed by Argentina, Nicaragua, and Peru. Nicaragua eliminated quantitative restrictions in one bold move and slashed import tariffs from an average of 110 percent in 1990 to 15 percent in March 1992.

---

[31]However, the term "tariffs" is sometimes misleading because many countries have traditionally relied on both import duties (that is, tariffs proper) and import duty surcharges or para-tariffs. See Harberger (1990) for a discussion on the actual mechanics for reducing uneven tariffs.

Table 7.4. Real Exchange Rates in Selected Latin American Countries
(1985 = 100)

Country	1980	1983	1987	1992	1993[1]
Argentina	35.8	96.4	80.8	36.9	34.0
Bolivia	88.1	84.6	107.9	109.6	113.3
Brazil	70.7	88.7	78.0	51.7	45.7
Chile	55.3	75.3	94.8	75.1	75.2
Colombia	79.2	78.3	115.9	119.9	102.6
Costa Rica	65.8	103.0	94.9	88.2	82.9
Ecuador	105.6	104.5	153.3	165.7	153.9
El Salvador	172.6	133.9	121.0	103.7	...
Guatemala	124.9	120.5	162.0	149.5	...
Honduras	121.6	106.2	93.2	141.5	152.3
Jamaica	60.1	54.8	80.1	94.5	70.7
Mexico	83.3	119.8	123.9	68.7	63.8
Panama	102.0	100.7	98.8	107.8	106.5
Paraguay	74.4	60.7	111.4	113.0	...
Peru	77.3	80.6	46.2	21.7	23.6
Trinidad and Tobago	152.9	117.3	122.8	112.1	129.0
Uruguay	49.7	89.4	77.2	55.5	40.5
Venezuela	84.2	70.3	134.8	122.3	119.1

Source: Calculated using data from IMF, International Financial Statistics database.
[1]Preliminary.
Note: Increases indicate currency depreciation against the dollar.

Exchange Rate Policy

In the vast majority of countries, the first step in the recent trade reform process was the implementation of large nominal devaluations. In many cases, this measure represented a unification of the exchange rate market. Most countries implemented large exchange rate adjustments as early as 1982 in order to address the urgent needs of the adjustment process. The purpose of these policies was to generate *real* exchange rate devaluations as a way to reduce the degree of antiexport bias of incentive systems.

Many countries adopted crawling peg regimes, characterized by a periodic, small devaluation of the nominal exchange rate to protect the real exchange rate from the effects of inflation.[32] Table 7.4 contains data on real exchange rates for a group of Latin American countries for 1980, 1987, and 1992. Once again, an increase in the index represents a real exchange rate *depreciation* and thus an improvement in the degree of competitiveness. Between 1980 and 1987, almost every country in the

---

[32]Some countries, notably Brazil, Chile, and Colombia, experimented with crawling pegs as early as the 1960s. However, only Colombia maintained a regime that avoided real exchange rate overvaluation.

sample experienced large real depreciations (see World Bank, 1993b), although in many countries they have been partially reversed in the past few years. The reversals have been the consequence of a combination of events, including the inflow of large volumes of foreign capital into these countries since 1990 and the use of the exchange rate as the cornerstone of the disinflation policies. This subject is addressed below. Overall, however, in most countries the real exchange rate was depreciated significantly more by late 1991 than it was in 1981. This greatly encouraged exports, helping revert decades of discriminatory policies.

Effects of Trade Liberalization

The trade liberalization reforms implemented in Latin America had three fundamental objectives: (1) to reduce the antiexport bias of the old regime and, thus, to encourage exports; (2) to help create an increase in total factor productivity growth through greater competition and enhanced efficiency; and (3) to increase consumer welfare by reducing the real prices of importable goods. In this section, the evolution of productivity and exports in the postreform period are analyzed in some detail.

Trade Liberalization and Productivity Growth

The relaxation of trade impediments has had a fundamental impact on the region's economies. Suddenly, Latin America's industry, which to a large extent had developed and grown behind protective walls, was forced to compete. Many firms have not been able to survive this shock and have become bankrupt. Others, however, have met the challenge of lower protection by embarking on major restructuring and have increased their level of productivity.

The ability, and willingness, of firms to implement significant adjustment depends on the degree of credibility of the reform and the level of distortions in the labor market. If entrepreneurs believe that the reform will not endure over time, they will have no incentives to incur the costs of adjusting the product mix and increasing the degree of productive efficiency. In fact, if the reform is perceived as temporary, the optimal behavior is not to adjust but to speculate through the accumulation of imported durable goods. This approach, as Rodríguez (1982) has documented, was adopted in Argentina during the failed Martinez de Hoz reforms.[33]

In their studies on the interaction between labor markets and structural reforms, Krueger (1980) and Michaely, Papageorgiou, and Choksi (1991) found that most successful trade reforms have indeed resulted in major increases in labor productivity. In most countries in which this has

---

[33]See Corbo, Condon, and De Melo (1985) for a detailed microeconomic account of the process of adjustment in a large group of Chilean manufacturing firms.

happened, labor markets have been characterized by some degree of flexibility. Countries with rigid and highly distorted labor markets—including countries with high costs of dismissal, limitations on temporary contracts, and rigid minimum wage legislation—have generally exhibited modest improvements in labor productivity since the reform.

Some of the early Latin American reformers have experienced important labor productivity improvements. For example, according to Edwards and Edwards (1991), labor productivity in the Chilean manufacturing sector increased at an average annual rate of 13.4 percent between 1978 and 1981. The available evidence also suggests that the increases in labor productivity in the Mexican manufacturing sector in the postreform period have been significant. According to Sánchez (1992), labor productivity in Mexico's manufacturing sector increased at an annual rate of almost 4 percent between 1986 and 1991. This figure is more than double the historical annual rate of growth of labor productivity of 1.6 percent in the manufacturing sector between 1960 and 1982 (Elías, 1992).

As discussed above, recent models of growth have suggested that countries that are more open to the rest of the world will exhibit a faster rate of technological improvement and productivity growth than countries that isolate themselves from the rest of the world. From an empirical point of view, countries that open up their external sectors and engage in trade liberalization reforms will experience an *increase* in total factor productivity (TFP) growth relative to the prereform period. The empirical regression analysis presented in the appendix to this chapter supports the idea that, when other variables (such as human capital formation, government size, political volatility, and the development gap) are held constant, the degree of openness of the economy is positively associated with the rate of growth of productivity. What is particularly important is that this result appears to be robust to the proxy used to measure trade policy orientation.

Table 7.4 contains data on the change in aggregate TFP growth in the period following the implementation of trade liberalization reform in six Latin American countries.[34] Although these data cannot be interpreted as capturing causality, they are still suggestive. As can be seen, Chile and Costa Rica, two of the earliest reformers, experienced very large increases in the growth of TFP in the postreform period. The results for

---

[34] The original TFP growth data comes from Martin's (1992) study on sources of growth in Latin America. The countries in Table 7.4 are those that initiated the reform before 1988. To compute series on TFP growth, Martin analyzed the contributions of capital and labor and explicitly incorporated the role of changes in the degree of capital utilization. The countries considered in this study are Argentina, Bolivia, Chile, Colombia, Costa Rica, the Dominican Republic, El Salvador, Guatemala, Honduras, Mexico, Nicaragua, Panama, Peru, Uruguay, and Venezuela. Harberger (1990) presents data on productivity growth before and after a series of historical trade reform episodes. He finds that in the majority of the countries, productivity growth increased after liberalization.

Table 7.5. Changes in Total Factor Productivity Growth
(In percent)

Country	1978–82 to 1987–91
Argentina	1.91
Bolivia	0.11
Chile[1]	4.96
Costa Rica	3.25
Mexico	−0.32
Uruguay	2.02

Source: Martin (1992).
[1]Prereform period is 1972–78.

Chile coincide with those obtained by Edwards (1985), who found that in the late 1970s after the trade reforms had been completed, TFP growth was approximately three times higher than the historical average.[35] Although the outcome has been less spectacular in Argentina and Uruguay, these countries still exhibit important improvements in productivity growth following the opening up. Bolivia, on the other hand, presents a flat profile of productivity growth. Sturzenegger (1992) argues that the very slow improvement in Bolivian productivity growth has been, to a large extent, the result of negative terms of trade shocks and, in particular, the collapse of the tin market.[36]

Perhaps the most puzzling result in Table 7.5 is the slight *decline* in aggregate productivity growth in Mexico after the reforms. Martin (1992) shows that this finding is robust to alternative methods of measuring TFP growth, including different procedures for correcting for capacity utilization. Also, Harberger (1990) has found a slowing down of productivity growth in Mexico in 1986-90 relative to 1975-82.[37] However, the aggregate nature of the data in Table 7.5 tends to obscure the actual sectoral response to trade reform in Mexico. According to new theories on endogenous growth, faster productivity will be observed in those sectors where protectionism has been *reduced* and not in those that are still subject to trade barriers or other forms of regulation.

---

[35]It may be argued, however, that the major increase in productivity growth in Chile has been the result of the *complete* structural reform package implemented in that country.

[36]In a series of recent studies, Ocampo (1991) has calculated total factor productivity growth in Colombia and found that the increase in protectionism in 1982-85 was accompanied by a decline in productivity growth.

[37]However, according to Harberger's data, TFP growth in 1986-90 exceeds the level of immediate postcrisis years. The actual growth numbers calculated by Harberger are the following: 1950-60 = 3.8; 1960-75 = 3.9; 1975-82 = 2.5; 1982-86 = -2.8; 1986-90 = 0.8. An important difference between the Martin and Harberger computations is that the former does not make corrections for different degrees of capacity utilization.

Table 7.6. Mexico: Total Factor Productivity Growth in Manufacturing, 1940–90
(In percent)

Period	Rate
1940–50	0.46
1950–60	0.53
1960–70	3.00
1970–80	. . .
1985–89	3.40

Sources: Data for 1940–80 are from Elías (1992); for 1985–89, from Ibarra (1992).

A distinctive characteristic of the Mexican reform is that, contrary to the Chilean reform, it proceeded at an uneven pace. In particular, while most of the manufacturing sector—with the exception of automobiles—experienced a significant reduction in protection in the early stages, agriculture continues to be subject to relatively high tariffs and substantial nontariff barriers. Moreover, until very recently, the Mexican land tenure system was subject to a legal system—the *ejido*—that, among other things, severely restricted the market for land and distorted economic incentives in many other directions. Although most agricultural sector regulations were legally eliminated in early 1992, these reforms have not yet had a practical impact because the titling process, where property rights are actually assigned, is still in its infancy. By mid-1993 practically no *ejidos* had yet been converted into private landholdings.[38] Also, during much of the period following the debt crisis, large fragments of the services sector in Mexico—including telecommunications and financial services—were under direct government control and subject to distortions.

Table 7.6 contains data on productivity growth in Mexico's manufacturing sector for 1940–89.[39] These figures indicate that since the trade reform period was implemented, the rate of productivity growth in the Mexican manufacturing sector has *exceeded* every subperiod since 1940 for which there are data. This evidence favors the view that, once the sectors actually subjected to increased competition are considered, Mexican productivity growth has indeed improved since the trade reform. This proposition is supported by results recently obtained by Weiss (1992), who used regression analysis to investigate the impact of the trade reforms on productivity and cost margins.

An important question that arises when the effects of trade reform are evaluated has to do with the speed with which productivity growth will

---

[38]A number of observers have argued that the titling process will, by itself, take between five and ten years.

[39]Because these figures come from two different sources, they may not be fully comparable and should thus be interpreted with care.

react to the new incentives. Will the response be rapid, or will it be necessary to wait for a long time before the reforms yield results? Existing data for Chile provide some support for the idea that total factor productivity growth will react quite fast. For example, Edwards (1985) found that already by 1979—the year the trade reform reached its goal of a uniform 10 percent import tariff—aggregate total factor productivity growth in Chile had reached 5.4 percent, significantly higher than the historical level. More recently, Agacino, Rivas, and Román (1992) found that total factor productivity growth averaged 3.9 percent a year during 1976–81, greatly exceeding the historical average of approximately 1 percent. These author salso found significant variations across industries during 1976–81. In some industries, for example, wood products and glass industries, average productivity growth exceeded 10 percent a year, while in others, for example, nonelectric machinery, it was negative.

Trade Reforms and Exports

An important goal of trade reform has been to reduce the traditional degree of antiexport bias of Latin American trade regimes and to generate a surge in exports. In fact, based on the East Asian model, Latin American leaders have increasingly called for the transformation of the external sector into the region's engine of growth. As pointed out previously, it is expected that the reduction of this traditional antiexport bias will take place through three channels: a more competitive—that is, more devalued—real exchange rate; a reduction in the cost of imported capital goods and intermediate inputs used in the production of exportables; and a direct shift in relative prices in favor of exports.

The volume of international trade in Latin America, and, in particular, that of exports, increased significantly after the reforms were initiated (see, for example, Nogués and Gulati, 1992). Although the *volume* of exports for the region as a whole grew at an annual rate of only 2 percent between 1970 and 1980, it grew at a rate of 5.5 percent between 1980 and 1985 and at an annual average of 6.7 percent between 1986 and 1990. The real *value* of exports, however, has evolved at a somewhat slower pace because the terms of trade in every subgroup of countries underwent a significant deterioration during 1980–93 (see United Nations, 1992). Although, strictly speaking, it is not possible to attribute this export surge fully to the reforms, there is significant country-specific evidence suggesting that a more open economy and, in particular, a more depreciated real exchange rate, has positively affected export growth.[40] Some countries, notably Costa Rica, also implemented a battery of export-promotion schemes, including tax credits—through the *Certificado de*

---

[40] See, for example, Nogués and Gulati (1992).

Table 7.7. Selected Latin American Countries: Value of Exports of Goods and Nonfactor Services

(Annual percentage growth rates in constant prices)

Country	1970–80	1982–87	1987–92	1991–93[1]
Argentina	4.8	–0.1	6.6	1.8
Bolivia	0.6	0.6	8.1	–8.3
Brazil	9.9	9.7	5.5	7.5
Chile	10.2	6.5	10.9	3.9
Colombia	5.7	10.2	6.7	2.9
Costa Rica	5.9	5.7	10.9	12.2
Ecuador	14.0	3.3	9.1	2.6
Mexico	8.3	5.8	3.5	3.1
Paraguay	6.1	5.4	9.5	1.1
Peru	2.7	–4.5	0.8	1.6
Uruguay	7.2	4.2	7.1	–1.7
Venezuela	–7.32[2]	3.6	4.4	–7.0

Source: World Bank, International Economics Department database.
[1]Preliminary.
[2]1974–80.

Abono Tributario—duty-free imports, and income tax exemptions. However, some authors, including Nogués and Gulati (1992), have argued that these systems have been fiscally expensive and have not been an effective way of encouraging exports.[41]

Table 7.7 presents detailed country-level data on the rate of growth of the total value of exports (in constant dollars) for three different periods. Table 7.8 contains information on the evolution of export volume for 1970-93. A number of facts emerge from these tables. First, while exports have grown rapidly for the region as a whole, there are nontrivial variations across countries; some countries have experienced a decline in the real value of exports—for example, Peru. Second, export performance during the subperiods 1982-87 and 1987-92 has not been homogeneous. In the majority of the countries, exports performed significantly better during 1987-92 than in the previous five years, reflecting, among other things, the fact that it takes some time for exports to respond to greater incentives.

An interesting fact that emerges from these tables is that in the country that has lagged behind in terms of trade reform—Ecuador—the performance of export volume has been, in recent years, below the 1970-80 historical average. In contrast, in two of the early reformers—Bolivia and Chile—exports were very strong during 1987-90.

---

[41]This issue, however, remains controversial. Some authors (Sachs, 1987) have pointed to the Korean experience to suggest that government policies in support of exports may be beneficial.

Table 7.8. Selected Latin American Countries: Volume of Exports of Goods
(Annual percentage growth rates)

Country	1970–80	1982–87	1987–91	1991–93[1]
Argentina	2.1	0.8	12.8	–0.1
Bolivia	–1.7	–5.2	13.2	5.3
Brazil	8.2	8.0	1.5	11.2
Chile	7.4	7.6	7.4	10.5
Colombia	3.6	14.8	7.3	12.6
Costa Rica	3.8	6.2	7.5	15.4
Ecuador	14.6	6.8	8.2	6.7
Mexico	10.2	6.1	5.5	8.7
Paraguay	7.3	9.2	17.2	2.2
Peru	2.3	–4.0	1.3	5.2
Uruguay	5.4	–0.5	4.8	–0.6
Venezuela	–5.8	2.1	7.5	6.5

Source: United Nations, Economic Commission for Latin America and the Caribbean, *Statistical Yearbook for Latin America*, various issues.
[1] Preliminary.

The Chilean case is particularly interesting. Since most of its liberalization effort was undertaken prior to 1980, there are enough data points to provide a more detailed evaluation of the export response to the new regime. Between 1975 and 1980—when tariffs were reduced to a uniform 10 percent and nontariff barriers were completely eliminated—the performance of Chilean exports was spectacular, growing (in volume terms) at an average of 12 percent a year—many times higher than the historical average of 1960-70 of only 2.6 percent a year. What is particularly impressive is that most of the export surge took place in the nontraditional sector (United Nations, 1991).

The story of Chile's success in the past few years is closely related to a boom in agriculture, forestry, and fishing exports. During 1960-70, Chile was basically a net importer of agricultural goods, whereas today, agricultural, forestry, and fishing exports play an increasingly important role in the Chilean economy. In 1970, Chile exported US$33 million in agricultural, forestry, and fishing products; by 1991 this figure had jumped to US$1.2 billion. This figure excludes the manufactured goods that are based on the elaboration of the agriculture sector. There is little doubt that economic policy lies behind the stellar performance of the Chilean agriculture and export sectors in the past years. First, the liberalization of international trade substantially lowered the costs of agricultural imported inputs and capital goods, making the sector more competitive. In fact, the liberalization of international trade put an end to a long trend of discrimination against agriculture. In contrast, Mexican agriculture has not yet benefited from the very recent liberalization measures. For example, the reform of the old *ejido* system has not yet occurred. Second, the exchange rate policy pursued aggressively in Chile since 1985 has provided clear incentives for the expansion of exports. However, as is discussed in some detail in the section on real exchange rate behavior and capital flows, the current trend toward real exchange rate appreciation represents a cloud in the future of the sector. A third, fundamental policy-based explanation of the success of the Chilean agriculture has to do with the pursuit of a stable macroeconomic policy. This has allowed entrepreneurs to have confidence in the system and to plan their activities over the longer run. Many of the export-oriented agricultural activities have required sizable investments that are undertaken only in an environment of stability and policy continuity. Fourth, the strict respect for property rights, and the emergence of a stable and legal framework, also had significant, positive effects on the evolution of Chilean agricultural exports.

As Tables 7.7 and 7.8 show, Mexico has exhibited a slower rate of growth of total exports in the postreform period than during 1970-80. This, however, is largely an illusion stemming from the fact that during the 1970s Mexico's oil production increased rapidly—at a rate exceeding 18 percent a year. When nontraditional exports are considered, the postreform performance is remarkable, with an annual average rate of growth for 1985-91 of more than 25 percent (see Table 7.9).[42]

After two successive years of decline, the volume of exports in Brazil increased rapidly during 1992, to 4.9 percent. In 1993, Brazilian exports expanded by almost 12 percent in volume terms. Although it is too early to determine what forces are behind this rapid growth, and whether it will be sustained, there is some indication that the highly depreciated real exchange rate and the reduction in the degree of protection in the country have helped increase the degree of international competitiveness of Brazil's exports.[43] This interpretation is supported by recent empirical results by Bonelli (1992), who found that productivity growth in Brazil's manufacturing sector has been positively affected by export orientation.

A stated objective of trade reforms has been to increase the degree of diversification of exports. Table 7.10 contains data for 12 Latin American countries on the share of manufacturing exports and shows that following the trade reforms their importance has increased steadily in the early reformers—Bolivia, Chile, and Mexico. Also, in the majority of the countries, the share of the ten most important export goods in total exports has declined significantly in the last few years (United Nations, 1991).

---

[42]A large percentage of this growth, however, has been in the *maquiladora*, or in-bond, sector.

[43]Also, the reduction in internal demand could have affected the recent rapid growth in exports.

Table 7.9. Share of Nontraditional Exports
(In percent of total exports)

Country	1980	1982	1985	1987	1991
Argentina	0.27	0.31	0.28	0.31	0.35
Bolivia	0.15	0.09	0.05	0.19	0.30
Brazil[1]	0.57	0.59	0.66	0.69	0.71
Chile	0.38	0.22	0.35	0.39	0.36[2]
Colombia	0.41	0.42	0.41	0.55	0.64[3]
Costa Rica	0.36	0.38	0.37	0.42	0.50
Ecuador[4]	0.24	0.09	0.12	0.14	0.12
Mexico	0.13	0.20	0.18	0.38	0.50
Paraguay	0.58	0.71	0.82	0.68	0.69
Peru	0.21	0.23	0.24	0.27	0.28
Uruguay	0.61	0.58	0.66	0.67	0.71
Venezuela	0.04	0.07	0.09	0.13	0.17

Source: United Nations, Economic Commission for Latin America and the Caribbean, *Economic Survey of Latin America*, various issues.
[1] Industrial products.
[2] 1989 data; subsequent data are classified differently.
[3] 1990 data.
[4] Manufactured products.

A somewhat troublesome recent development is that during 1993 the rate of export growth (measured in constant value) has slowed down significantly in many Latin American countries. The slowdown is the result of a number of factors, including the sluggishness of the world economy, the slowing down of productivity gains, and, especially, the recent trends toward real exchange rate appreciation observed in most countries in the region.

Real Exchange Rate Behavior, Capital Inflows, and the Future of Trade Reforms

In the past few years, competitive real exchange rates have been at the center of the vigorous performance of most of Latin America's external sectors. In fact, trade reforms have been driven by highly competitive real exchange rates, making Latin American products very attractive in world markets. However, as pointed out previously, in most Latin American countries real exchange rates have recently experienced significant real appreciations and losses in competitiveness. Chart 7.1 presents the evolution of real exchange rates for selected countries.

These real appreciations and losses in international competitiveness, which have generated considerable concern among policymakers and political leaders (see Calvo, Leiderman, and Reinhart, 1992), result from two developments: first, a large number of countries are using ex-

Table 7.10. Exports of Manufactured Goods
(In percent of total)

Country	1970	1980	1982	1985	1987	1991
Argentina	0.14	0.23	0.24	0.21	0.31	0.28
Bolivia	0.03	0.02	0.03	0.01	0.03	0.05[1]
Brazil	0.15	0.37	0.38	0.44	0.50	0.55
Chile	0.04	0.09	0.07	0.11	0.09	0.11
Colombia	0.11	0.20	0.24	0.17	0.19	0.33
Costa Rica	0.19	0.28	0.25	0.22	0.24	0.25
Ecuador	0.02	0.03	0.03	0.01	0.02	0.02
Mexico	0.33	0.11	0.10	0.21	0.38	0.44[1]
Paraguay	0.08	0.04	0.09	0.06	0.10	0.11
Peru	0.01	0.17	0.16	0.13	0.17	0.19[1]
Uruguay	0.15	0.38	0.32	0.35	0.55	0.52
Venezuela	0.01	0.02	0.02	0.10	0.06	0.11[1]

Source: United Nations, Economic Commission for Latin America and the Caribbean, *Statistical Yearbook for Latin America*, various issues.
[1] 1990 data.

change rate policy as an anti-inflationary tool, and, second, recent massive capital inflows into Latin America have made foreign exchange "overabundant."

Tables 7.11 and 7.12 contain data on capital inflows into Latin America and show that, after eight years of negative resource transfers, there was a significant turnaround in 1991–92. The increased availability of foreign funds has affected the real exchange rate through increased aggregate expenditure. A proportion of the newly available resources has been spent on nontradables—including the real estate sector—putting pressure on their relative prices and on domestic inflation. An interesting feature of the recent capital movements is that a large proportion corresponds to portfolio investment and relatively little is foreign direct investment. As can be seen, Mexico has been the most important recipient of foreign funds in the region in the past few years. Indeed, this large availability of foreign financing has allowed that country to have a current account deficit of 5–6 percent of GDP. An important question is whether these inflows are sustainable, or whether a decline in the level of funds available is foreseen in the near future.

Real exchange rate appreciations generated by increased capital inflows are not a completely new phenomenon in Latin America. In the late 1970s, most countries in the region, but especially those in the Southern Cone, were flooded with foreign resources that led to large real appreciations. The fact that this previous episode ended in the debt crisis has added drama to the current concern about the possible negative effects of these capital flows.

Chart 7.1. Real Effective Exchange Rates in Selected Latin American Countries
(1985 = 100)

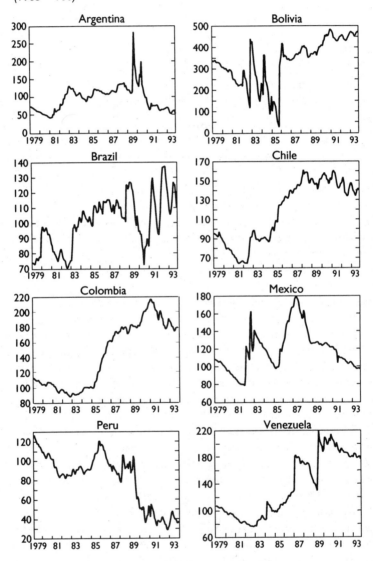

Note: An increase in the index denotes a real depreciation.

Source: IMF, *International Financial Statistics*, various editions.

**Table 7.11. Latin America: Capital Inflows and
Net Resource Transfers**
(In billions of U.S. dollars)

Years	Net Capital Inflows	Interest and Profit Income	Net Resource Transfers
1982–85	55.3	−111.7	−56.4
1986–89	33.5	−138.7	−105.2
1990	17.0	−35.7	−18.7
1991	36.3	−31.1	5.2
1992	42.8	−21.2	21.6

Source: Jaspersen (1992).

Whether these capital movements are temporary—and thus subject to sudden reversals, as in 1982—is particularly important in evaluating their possible consequences. In a recent study, Calvo, Leiderman, and Reinhart (1992) argued that the most important causes of the generalized inflow of resources are external. In particular, their empirical analysis suggests that these capital movements were triggered primarily by the recession in the industrial world and the reduction in U.S. interest rates. These authors suggest that once these world economic conditions change, the volume of capital flowing to Latin America will decline. At that point, the pressure on the real exchange rate will subside, and a real exchange rate depreciation will be required.

The countries in the region have tried to cope with the real appreciation pressures in several ways. Colombia, for instance, tried to sterilize the accumulation of reserves by placing domestic bonds on the local market in 1991.[44] However, to place these bonds, the authorities had to increase the local interest rate to make them more attractive. This move generated a widening interest rate differential in favor of Colombia, which attracted new capital flows that, in order to be sterilized, required new bond placements. This process created a vicious cycle that contributed to a large accumulation of domestic debt without significantly affecting the real exchange rate. This experience shows vividly the difficulties faced by authorities wishing to handle real exchange rate movements. In particular, this case indicates that real shocks—such as an increase in foreign capital inflows—cannot be tackled successfully using monetary policy instruments.

During 1993, Argentina tried to deal with the real appreciation by engineering a pseudo devaluation through a simultaneous increase in import tariffs and export subsidies. Although it is too early to know how this

---

[44]An important peculiarity of the Colombian case is that the original inflow of foreign exchange came through the *trade account*.

Table 7.12. Selected Latin American Countries: Net Capital Inflows

(In percent of GDP)

Country	1982	1983	1984	1985	1986	1987	1988	1989	1990	1991	1992[1]
Argentina	2.5	0.4	2.3	2.8	1.6	2.2	2.8	0.3	0.5	3.0	5.7
Brazil	4.1	2.7	2.4	0.1	0.7	1.5	-0.5	0.3	1.1	0.2	...
Chile	4.2	2.6	10.5	8.6	4.3	5.4	5.0	5.5	11.7	3.0	7.8
Colombia	5.7	3.7	2.5	6.4	3.3	0.0	2.4	1.2	0.0	-1.9	...
Mexico	5.5	-1.6	-0.6	-1.1	0.9	-0.7	-0.8	0.7	3.5	7.1	3.4
Peru	7.8	3.8	5.3	2.4	3.6	3.7	5.4	2.9	3.6	2.2	5.8
Venezuela	-1.9	-4.7	-3.4	-1.7	-1.8	1.1	-1.7	-7.9	-7.4	3.7	

Sources: World Bank, International Economics Department database (GDP); and IMF, *Balance of Payments Statistics* database (capital inflows).

[1] Preliminary.

measure will affect the country's competitiveness, preliminary computations suggest that the magnitude of the adjustment obtained through a tariffs-cum-subsidies package may be rather small. Mexico followed a different route, deciding to postpone the adoption of a completely fixed exchange rate. In October 1992, the pace of the daily nominal exchange rate adjustment was doubled to 40 cents. As the unfolding of the Mexican peso crisis of December 1994 showed, this measure was clearly not enough. At this point, however, it is difficult to know how the implementation of the North American Free Trade Agreement (NAFTA) will affect Mexico's equilibrium real exchange rate and its competitiveness.

Chile has tackled the real appreciation by implementing a broad set of measures, including conducting exchange rate policy relative to a three-currency basket, imposing reserve requirements on capital inflows, allowing the nominal exchange rate to appreciate somewhat, and undertaking significant sterilization operations. In spite of this multifront approach, Chile has not avoided real exchange rate pressures. Between December 1991 and December 1992, the Chilean bilateral real exchange rate appreciated by approximately 10 percent. As a result, exporters and agriculture producers have been mounting increasing pressure on the government for special treatment, arguing that it had broken an implicit contract by allowing the real exchange rate to appreciate. This type of political reaction is becoming more and more generalized throughout the region and has been particularly important in Colombia, adding a difficult social dimension to the real exchange rate issue.

Although there is no easy way to handle the real appreciation pressures, experience shows that the authorities have at least two options. First, in those countries where the dominant force behind real exchange rate movements is price inertia in the presence of nominal exchange rate anchor policies, the adoption of a pragmatic crawling peg system will usually help. This means that, to some extent, the inflationary targets will have to be less ambitious because a periodic exchange rate adjustment will result in some inflation.[45] However, to the extent that this policy is supplemented by tight overall fiscal policy there should be no concern regarding inflationary explosions.

Second, the discrimination between short-term, speculative capital and longer-term capital should go a long way toward alleviating the preoccupations about the effects of capital movements on real exchange rates. To the extent that short-term capital flows are more volatile and capital inflows are genuinely long term—especially if they help finance investment projects in the tradables sector—the change in the real exchange rate will be a "true equilibrium" phenomenon. Policymakers should recognize them as such by implementing the required adjustment resource allocation. In

---

[45]More specifically, with this option the *one-digit* inflationary goal will be postponed.

practice, however, discriminating between "permanent" and "transitory" capital inflows is difficult; ultimately, policymakers are forced to make a judgment call.

Regional Trading Blocks, Multilateralism, and Industrial Country Protectionism

As the twenty-first century approaches, the world economy is moving toward the formation of a small number of trading blocs. Although the European Economic Community and NAFTA are considered the most formidable ones, a number of other trading blocs, with different degrees of cohesion, are rapidly emerging. Among these, the Association of South East Asian Nations (ASEAN), with its dynamic and aggressive members, is especially promising. This is particularly so if the formation of a yen zone in the Pacific—comprising Japan and the ASEAN countries—takes shape in the next few years.[46]

In the last few years, however, some new important trading blocs in the Western Hemisphere have emerged and are now attracting increasing attention from policy analysts. Among these, the Southern Cone Common Market (MERCOSUR) and the Andean Pact, which jointly comprise nine Latin American countries, are two of the most important ones and have a volume of international trade that is expected to approach US$250 billion a year by the year 2000.[47] What makes this new integrationist effort in Latin America particularly interesting is that it is taking place within a context that strongly favors export promotion and the expansion of international trade throughout most of the developing world.

In addition to the somewhat large, multimember trade agreements, there has recently been a proliferation of bilateral integration agreements. Table 7.13 presents a brief summary of trade agreements negotiated since 1990. The majority of the Latin American countries have expressed keen interest in joining NAFTA and see the bilateral—or, for that matter, small multilateral—agreements as an intermediate step. Table 7.14 contains data on the evolution of intraregional trade, and Table 7.15 on bilateral trade for selected countries. Several important facts emerge from these tables. First, after having reached a low in 1985, intraregional trade has expanded greatly in the past few years. Contrary to popular belief, intaregional trade as a proportion of total trade is still significantly below its 1975–80 level. This means that there is significant room for further ex-

---

[46]See Schott (1991) for a general discussion on the recent formation, and prospects, of trading blocs in the global economy.

[47]MERCOSUR comprises Argentina, Brazil, Paraguay, and Uruguay. The members of the Andean Pact are Bolivia, Colombia, Ecuador, Peru, and Venezuela. Chile withdrew from the Andean Pact in 1974.

Table 7.13. Regional Integration Agreements in the Americas After 1990

Name and Membership	Date	Objective	Current Status	Memoranda (1990)
Andean Trade Preference Act Bolivia Colombia Ecuador Peru United States	1991	Duty-free status for US$324 million in imports from Andean countries to the United States.	Operational.	
Chile-Colombia Free Trade Agreement (FTA)	1993	Establishment of a free trade area.	Operational.	
Chile-Mexico FTA	1991	Establishment of a free trade area by January 1996.	Current maximum reciprocal tariff 7.5 percent.	Aggregate GDP: US$241.2 billion Population: 94.9 million Total foreign trade: US$73.8 billion Intraregional trade as % of total foreign trade: 0.1.
Chile-Venezuela FTA	1993	Establishment of a free trade area by 1999.	Maximum tariff on imports from Chile scheduled to be 20 percent in 1994. Chile's tariff rate remains at 11 percent. Tariffs scheduled to reach zero in 1999.	Aggregate GDP: US$76.7 billion Population: 32.5 million Total foreign trade: US$38.9 billion Intraregional trade as % of total foreign trade: 1.4.
Colombia-Venezuela FTA	1992	Establishment of a free trade area by 1992.	Common tariff agreed in 1992. Conversations initiated with Mexico (Group of Three) to establish free trade area.	Aggregate GDP: US$91.3 billion Population: 52 million Total foreign trade: US$34.7 billion Intraregional trade as % of total foreign trade: 1.4.
El Salvador-Guatemala FTA	1991	Establishment of a free trade area.	Entered into operation in October 1991.	

Table 7.13 (continued)

Name and Membership	Date	Objective	Current Status	Memoranda (1990)
North American Free Trade Agreement Canada Mexico United States	1992	Establishment of a free trade area by 2009. Elimination of tariffs in 5, 10, or 15 years depending on the product. Exceptions are Canadian agricultural and Mexican petroleum products. NAFTA contains precedent-setting rights and obligations regarding intellectual property rights, services, trade, and investment. U.S.-Canada dispute-settlement system extended to Mexico.	Agreement signed and ratified. In phase as of January 1, 1994.	Aggregate GDP: US$6,204.6 billion Population: 362.7 million Total foreign trade: US$1,223.8 billion Intraregional trade as % of total foreign trade: 18.8.
Group of Three: Colombia-Mexico-Venezuela FTA	1993	Economic cooperation. In April 1993 the three countries agreed to establish a free trade area by 1994.	Energy sector agreements signed. Negotiations under way. Draft accord of November 1993 provides for an immediate zero tariff for some items and a ten-year transition for others, except in automobiles and agricultural goods. Mexico is to cut tariffs faster than Colombia and Venezuela. Signing date of January 1994 postponed because of Chiapas rebellion. Agreement ratified by new Venezuelan authorities in February 1994.	Aggregate GDP: US$305.8 billion Population: 138.2 million Total foreign trade: US$94.4 billion Intraregional trade as % of total foreign trade: 0.8.
Costa Rica-Mexico FTA	1994	Establishment of a free trade area.	Negotiations in progress. Removal of all tariffs and NTBs between both countries. Mexican exports of goods that Costa Rica does not produce will enter duty free from 1995. Tariffs on the remainder of Mexican exports to be reduced over 5, 10, and 15 years. Most Costa Rican exports will be allowed duty free by Mexico in five years or less. Rigid rule of origin requiring goods to be made with inputs from the region.	

Agreement / Countries	Year	Objective	Status	Statistics
Mexico-Central America FTA Costa Rica El Salvador Guatemala Honduras Mexico Nicaragua	1992	Establishment of a free trade area by December 1996.	Safeguard regime, technical rules, and dispute-resolution agreements under negotiation. Framework agreement for trade cooperation signed August 1992. Costa Rica currently engaged in bilateral negotiations with Mexico.	Aggregate GDP: US$240.3 billion Population: 112.4 million Total foreign trade: US$74.2 billion Intraregional trade as % of total foreign trade: 1.6.
Venezuela-Central America FTA Costa Rica El Salvador Guatemala Honduras Nicaragua Panama Venezuela	1992	Provides for a nonreciprocal transition period in which unilateral tariff cuts will be made by Venezuela, with the eventual goal of a free trade area.	Negotiations gained impetus after G-3 presidential summit in 1993, but have proceeded slowly since.	
Nueva Ocotepeque Agreement El Salvador Guatemala Honduras	1992	Establishment of a free trade area by 1993. Long-run objective is to create a customs union. It includes recent complementation agreements signed by these countries.	Not clear.	Aggregate GDP: US$17.1 billion Population: 19.7 million Total foreign trade: US$7.3 billion Intraregional trade as % of total foreign trade: 11.8.
MERCOSUR Argentina Brazil Paraguay Uruguay	1991	Establishment of a common market by January 1995. Commercial liberalization program, macroeconomic policy coordination, common tariff, sectoral agreements.	Present tariff preferences: 68 percent. Dispute-resolution agreement signed. Products gradually removed from national lists of exclusion. CET negotiations hung up on differences over capital goods and electronics. Liberalization well under way, but doubtful that a customs union will be attained by 1995.	Aggregate GDP: US$492.3 billion Population: 190 million Total foreign trade: US$76.3 billion Intraregional trade as % of total foreign trade: 8.6.

Table 7.13 (concluded)

Name and Membership	Date	Objective	Current Status	Memoranda (1990)
CARICOM-Colombia FTA Antigua and Barbuda Bahamas, The Barbados Belize Colombia Dominica Grenada Jamaica Montserrat St. Kitts and Nevis St. Lucia St. Vincent and the Grenadines Trinidad and Tobago	1991	Provides for a nonreciprocal transition period in which unilateral tariff cuts will be made by Colombia, with the eventual goal of a free trade area.	Negotiations are proceeding slowly due to CARICOM demands for unilateral tariff reductions.	
CARICOM-Venezuela FTA Antigua and Barbuda Bahamas, The Barbados Belize Dominica Grenada Jamaica Montserrat St. Kitts and Nevis St. Lucia St. Vincent and the Grenadines Trinidad and Tobago Venezuela	1991	Provides for duty-free imports from CARICOM nations into Venezuela to be phased in over five years. After five years, negotiations are to begin to eliminate tariffs on Venezuelan exports to signatory countries.	Negotiations are proceeding slowly due to CARICOM demands for unilateral tariff reductions.	

Colombia-Central America FTA	1993	Provides for a nonreciprocal transition period in which unilateral tariff cuts will be made by Colombia, with the eventual goal of a free trade agreement.	Negotiations gained impetus after G-3 presidential summit in 1993, but have proceeded slowly since.
Colombia			
Costa Rica			
El Salvador			
Guatemala			
Honduras			
Nicaragua			
Panama			
Venezuela			

Sources: Lustig (1994); and World Bank.

Table 7.14. Intraregional Trade in Latin America and the Caribbean
(Intraregional exports as percent of total exports)

Country	1970	1975	1980	1981	1982	1983	1984	1985	1986	1987	1988	1989	1990	1991	1992	Jan.–Oct. 1992	Jan.–Oct. 1993
Argentina	21.1	25.9	23.8	19.7	20.4	14.1	18.5	18.7	23.9	21.6	20.5	25.9	26.3	30.3	34.1	35.5	37.3
Bolivia	9.7	35.9	36.7	42.6	51.6	55.0	52.8	60.2	64.5	57.8	47.7	44.0	45.6	51.2	40.7	42.1	44.6
Brazil	11.8	15.7	18.1	19.3	15.6	10.4	11.5	9.7	12.4	12.4	12.1	12.1	11.6	16.7	22.6	22.2	22.9
Chile	12.2	23.7	24.3	21.9	19.4	12.1	15.0	14.5	17.0	17.0	12.8	12.1	12.5	14.4	17.1	16.3	18.5
Colombia	10.5	21.7	17.6	23.7	21.7	14.0	13.5	14.0	11.4	17.3	16.0	16.0	16.9	24.1	23.0	22.5	24.8
Costa Rica	23.9	29.3	35.0	35.7	29.3	30.6	26.6	23.2	17.6	16.6	17.1	17.8	16.5	18.1	19.8	20.2	16.5
Mexico	9.8	14.3	6.9	9.8	8.8	7.5	6.4	5.4	6.7	7.8	7.5	7.1	6.6	4.3	4.8	4.7	4.9
Peru	6.5	16.7	21.2	12.8	15.4	10.4	11.9	14.1	14.5	16.1	14.5	15.3	15.4	16.1	18.1	18.7	21.7
Uruguay	12.8	29.3	37.3	26.6	30.8	23.7	26.2	27.8	39.2	30.3	27.4	36.8	39.0	40.4	41.9	43.2	45.7
Venezuela	33.5	33.2	37.4	36.6	21.4	20.9	19.2	18.3	20.0	23.9	21.6	21.5	22.8	20.1	27.2	27.5	30.3
Latin America and the Caribbean	17.6	21.0	22.2	21.1	17.5	14.0	13.7	12.6	14.1	14.9	14.3	15.4	16.0	16.1	18.6	18.6	19.0

Source: IMF, *Direction of Trade Statistics.*

Table 7.15. Intraregional Exports
(f.o.b. values; percent of total)

From	To	1980	1981	1982	1983	1984	1985	1986	1987	1988	1989	1990	1991	1992	1993[1]
ARG	BRA	9.5	6.5	7.4	4.6	5.9	5.9	10.2	8.5	6.7	11.8	11.5	12.4	13.7	30.4
ARG	CHL	2.7	2.1	2.2	2.4	.8	1.3	2.0	2.3	2.8	3.7	3.7	4.1	4.7	6.7
ARG	COL	0.5	0.6	0.9	0.8	0.7	1.6	0.9	1.0	0.9	0.8	0.6	0.7	0.9	1.0
ARG	PER	1.5	1.0	1.4	1.2	1.6	1.9	2.8	2.2	1.9	1.7	1.5	1.7	1.9	2.2
ARG	VEN	0.8	1.1	1.3	0.7	1.4	0.9	0.7	0.9	1.4	1.0	1.2	1.7	1.7	1.8
BRA	ARG	5.4	3.8	3.2	3.0	3.2	2.1	3.0	3.2	2.9	2.2	2.1	4.7	8.5	9.2
BRA	CHL	2.2	2.7	1.4	1.0	1.0	0.9	1.1	1.4	1.6	2.1	1.5	2.1	2.6	2.8
BRA	COL	0.7	0.9	1.3	0.7	0.6	0.4	0.5	0.5	0.7	0.6	0.5	0.5	1.0	1.0
BRA	PER	0.6	1.2	1.1	0.3	0.5	0.4	0.7	0.8	0.6	0.4	0.5	0.7	0.6	0.6
BRA	VEN	1.1	1.8	2.3	1.2	1.4	1.2	1.6	1.4	1.5	0.8	0.9	1.4	1.2	1.2
CHL	ARG	6.0	4.8	4.1	3.1	3.2	2.2	3.8	3.4	2.3	1.3	1.3	2.9	4.6	5.1
CHL	BRA	9.6	7.3	8.3	4.3	6.2	5.4	6.9	6.8	4.7	6.4	5.7	5.0	4.5	5.2
CHL	COL	1.6	1.8	1.2	1.1	1.2	1.4	1.0	1.0	0.8	1.0	0.9	0.6	0.7	0.9
CHL	PER	1.5	1.8	1.3	1.0	1.2	1.2	1.6	1.7	0.9	0.7	0.9	1.6	1.7	1.5
CHL	VEN	1.7	1.8	1.2	0.8	1.1	0.9	1.0	1.4	1.5	0.4	0.4	0.6	0.7	0.8
COL	ARG	1.7	1.7	1.2	1.4	1.7	1.0	1.3	0.8	1.0	0.6	0.4	0.5	1.0	1.3
COL	BRA	0.2	0.2	0.1	0.2	0.4	0.2	0.2	0.4	0.2	0.4	0.4	0.7	0.9	2.0
COL	CHL	1.6	1.0	0.4	0.4	0.5	0.6	0.6	2.0	2.4	2.3	2.4	2.2	1.3	1.3
COL	PER	0.7	1.5	1.1	0.6	0.7	0.9	1.4	2.4	1.7	1.1	1.3	2.9	4.2	4.6
COL	VEN	7.1	11.5	11.8	3.8	2.8	3.6	2.9	4.4	4.4	3.2	3.0	5.9	6.8	7.3
PER	ARG	1.5	0.6	0.8	1.2	1.1	1.2	2.3	1.5	0.6	0.5	0.9	0.9	0.8	1.0
PER	BRA	3.2	1.5	2.2	2.0	1.5	1.8	2.9	4.2	3.0	4.5	3.9	3.1	4.7	0.0
PER	CHL	1.2	1.8	1.2	1.5	1.6	1.7	2.0	1.2	1.5	1.9	1.7	1.3	1.2	1.2
PER	COL	1.4	2.8	4.2	1.7	2.4	2.5	2.6	2.4	3.1	3.0	2.9	3.2	2.5	3.2
PER	VEN	1.3	1.4	1.7	1.0	1.6	1.4	1.8	2.4	3.1	1.2	1.7	2.4	3.1	3.6

Table 7.15 (concluded)

From	To	1980	1981	1982	1983	1984	1985	1986	1987	1988	1989	1990	1991	1992	1993[1]
VEN	ARG	0.3	0.2	0.1	0.0	0.0	0.0	0.1	0.0	0.2	0.2	0.0	0.1	0.2	0.2
VEN	BRA	3.5	4.7	5.3	3.7	3.2	1.8	0.8	1.4	1.5	2.0	1.9	1.8	2.8	2.9
VEN	CHL	1.3	1.7	1.4	1.4	1.4	1.7	1.4	1.3	1.4	1.2	1.0	0.8	0.8	0.3
VEN	COL	1.4	1.6	1.8	2.2	2.0	1.6	1.2	0.1	1.7	2.1	2.1	1.5	2.2	2.5
VEN	PER	0.1	0.1	0.1	0.1	0.1	0.2	0.4	0.1	0.5	0.2	0.2	0.5	0.8	0.9
World	ARG	0.6	0.5	0.3	0.3	0.3	0.2	0.3	0.3	0.2	0.2	0.1	0.3	0.4	0.4
World	BRA	1.0	1.1	1.1	0.9	0.8	0.8	0.7	0.7	0.6	0.7	0.6	0.6	0.6	0.5
World	CHL	0.3	0.3	0.2	0.2	0.2	0.1	0.2	0.2	0.2	0.2	0.2	0.2	0.3	0.5
World	COL	0.3	0.3	0.3	0.3	0.2	0.2	0.2	0.2	0.2	0.2	0.2	0.1	0.2	0.2
World	PER	0.2	0.2	0.2	0.1	0.1	0.1	0.1	0.1	0.1	0.1	0.1	0.1	0.1	0.1
World	VEN	0.6	0.6	0.7	0.3	0.4	0.4	0.4	0.4	0.4	0.2	0.2	0.3	0.3	0.2

Source: IMF, Direction of Trade Statistics.
[1] Data through October 1993 except for exports from Argentina to Brazil, which correspond to May 1993.

panding intraregional trade. In this context, it is notable that intraregional trade in East Asia accounts for almost 30 percent of total trade. In a recent study, Losada (1993) found that, with reduced trade impediments, distance is the main determinant of bilateral trade.

MERCOSUR

MERCOSUR is a trade agreement signed by Argentina, Brazil, Paraguay, and Uruguay in 1991.[48] Its main goal is to eliminate all tariffs for intraregional trade by December 1994 and to establish a common external tariff that would guide international trade between the member countries and the rest of the world. What is particularly interesting about MERCOSUR is that it groups the two largest countries in South America—Argentina and Brazil—with two of the smallest.[49] Table 7.16 contains data on some basic indicators for these countries, as well as for Andean Pact members (see below). These data highlight some of the differences across the countries, including size, recent performance, and extent of international indebtedness. There is little doubt that the future of MERCOSUR will depend on the policies of Argentina and Brazil; Uruguay and Paraguay, as smaller members, will play a limited role in the political-diplomatic process that will determine the actual characteristics of the agreement.

Table 7.16, however, does not capture some important recent economic developments that are likely to affect the future of this agreement. Although Argentina has recently been able to make substantial progress in attaining macroeconomic stability and in launching an ambitious privatization program, Brazil has faced economic and political problems. The resignation in 1992 of President Fernando Collor de Mello added further uncertainty to the future of Brazil's reform programs. Brazil's inability to control inflation is particularly serious. In fact, there is widespread agreement that many of the troubles encountered by early integrationist attempts in Latin America during the 1960s and 1970s had their roots in the marked differences in countries' macroeconomic performance, including inflation and exchange rate policies.[50]

The differences in strategy regarding the speed and depth of privatization and trade reform suggest that disagreements could easily erupt between Argentina and Brazil on points closely related to MERCOSUR. In

---

[48]The legal document that sets the basis for MERCOSUR is the Asunción Treaty, whose origins lie in an integration act signed between Argentina and Brazil in 1986. New acts were signed between these two countries in 1989 and 1990. For details, see Nogués and Quintanilla (1992).

[49]Chile was invited to join but declined. Chile, however, is moving briskly toward integration with Argentina through the signature of bilateral agreements.

[50]Baldinelli (1991) discusses some of the most important macroeconomic policies in the MERCOSUR countries.

Table 7.16. Economic Indicators for MERCOSUR and Andean Pact Countries

Indicator	MERCOSUR					Andean Pact			
	Argentina	Brazil	Paraguay	Uruguay	Bolivia	Colombia	Ecuador	Peru	Venezuela
GDP, 1992 (million U.S. dollars)	154,400	406,500	6,500	11,400	5,300	46,200	12,400	26,300	61,100
GNP per capita, 1992 (million U.S. dollars)[1]	4,160	2,940[2]	1,410	2,840	680	1,300	1,060	1,080	2,920
GDP growth, 1980–92 (annual average, percent)	0.6	1.2	2.7	0.7	0.7	3.4	2.4	-0.7	2.1
Share of manufacturing in 1992 GDP (percent)	22	22[2]	17	25	16[2]	20[2]	21[2]	...	16
Investment ratio, 1992 (percent)	17	19	24	13	16	18	20	16[2]	23
Merchandise exports, 1992 (million U.S. dollars)	12,000	36,200	920	1,700	600	7,300	3,000	3,500	14,000
Export growth, 1980–92[3] (annual average, percent)	3.5	7.1	7.2	4.2	3.4	5.7	5.0	-0.9[2]	2.0
Total external debt, 1992 (million U.S. dollars)	66,500	118,700	1,800	5,200	4,200	16,700	12,300	21,000	33,700
Inflation, 1980–92[4] (annual average, percent)	341	373	23	63	170	25	38	287	22

Sources: World Bank, *World Development Indicators* (1993); International Economics Department databases; and country department staff estimates.

[1] Calculated according to the *World Bank Atlas* method.

[2] 1991 data.

[3] Exports of goods and nonfactor services, in constant prices.

[4] Growth in GDP deflator, compound rate.

Note: All 1992 data are preliminary estimates.

Table 7.17. Trade Among MERCOSUR Countries, 1992

Country	Exports (percent)	Value (million U.S. dollars)
Argentina	17	2,100
Brazil	11	4,100
Paraguay	37	220
Uruguay	34	540

Source: IMF, *Direction of Trade Statistics.*

particular, an increasingly large number of observers in Argentina are concerned that Brazil will insist on a *higher* common external tariff (CET) than what would be acceptable to Argentina. The current structure of protection in the individual members of MERCOSUR, discussed above, shows that there may indeed be some room for disagreement. Whereas Argentina has recently embraced a significant free trade stance—slashing tariffs, reducing nontariff barriers considerably, and completely eliminating export taxes—Brazil is aiming at a higher and more variable tariff structure.

Table 7.17 contains data on the recent level of intraregional trade for MERCOSUR members. It shows that intraregional trade is more important for Argentina (with 17 percent) than for Brazil (11 percent).[51] This suggests that it is, in fact, Argentina that is bound to lose more if MERCOSUR is aborted. From a political-economy perspective, it is likely that in negotiations regarding policies toward third parties, Brazil may have an important edge. If it does, and if MERCOSUR is implemented around high import tariffs—with a range of 0-40 percent, which corresponds to the Brazilian liberalization target—it is unlikely that its members would experience a net gain over the long run. More specifically, if Argentina joins a trade agreement with a common external tariff set at the Brazilian level, the likely result will be trade diversion, which would more than offset any benefits derived from trade creation.[52]

Table 7.18 presents the expected path of elimination of tariffs for intraregional trade within MERCOSUR. Two main differences with respect to previous attempts at integration immediately stand out.[53] First, there is a

---

[51]The data in the table are for 1992. Historically, Brazil's intraregional trade has been significantly lower—on the order of 4 percent of total exports.

[52]The higher the common external tariff, the more likely it is that a customs union will have net negative welfare effects on its members. The reason is that there will be additional trade diversion. Commodities that, at the original tariff, were imported from the least expensive source will be imported from a less efficient regional member. On trade creation and trade diversion see, for example, Dornbusch (1989). Notice, however, that the General Agreement on Tariffs and Trade does not allow the common tariff to exceed the members' average before the union. It is unclear, however, whether this provision can actually be enforced.

[53]On historical integrationist attempts in Latin America, see Edwards and Savastano (1988).

Table 7.18. Imports Subject to Free Trade in MERCOSUR

Date	Percentage
June 1991	47
December 1991	54
June 1992	61
December 1992	68
June 1993	75
December 1993	82
June 1994	89
December 1994	100

Source: Treaty of Asunción (1991).

high degree of automaticity in the integration process within MERCOSUR, and second, the total time frame allowed for integration is significantly shorter than those attempted previously (Edwards and Savastano, 1988). These features of the Asunción Treaty clearly indicate that, even in an agreement dominated by a not fully enthusiastic reformer such as Brazil, the rules governing opening up are quite aggressive and dynamic. An important, and as yet unresolved question, however, is whether this ambitious automatic intraregional liberalization program can be sustained in the presence of major macroeconomic imbalances in Brazil.

Revival of the Andean Pact

In November 1990, more than two decades after its initial launching, the Andean Pact was renewed by the presidents of Bolivia, Colombia, Ecuador, Peru, and Venezuela.[54] The new agreement, which came to be known as the Act of La Paz, established a number of ambitious targets, including[55] (1) the implementation of a free trade zone in the region by 1992; (2) an agreement on the level and structure of the CET by December 1991; (3) the implementation of the CET by December 1995; (4) the liberalization of maritime and air transportation; and (5) the facilitation of foreign investment and capital mobility within the Andean Group.

It is important to notice that there is great heterogeneity among the countries in the pact (see Table 7.16), with respect to the economic structure and to macroeconomic policy. For instance, while Bolivia and Peru are moving steadily toward low inflation and price stability, Venezuela continues to struggle in the area of macroeconomic management. Despite large increases during 1992 and 1993, the volume of intraregional trade remains somewhat limited (see Table 7.19) because factor endowments are rather similar across these countries and because there have

---

[54]Chile, an original signatory of the pact, declined to participate.

[55]Nogués and Quintanilla (1992) provide a detailed account of the Act of La Paz.

Table 7.19. Trade Among Andean Pact Countries, 1992

Country	Exports (percent)	Value (million U.S. dollars)
Bolivia	13	90
Colombia	13	920
Ecuador	3	90
Peru	8	270
Venezuela	3	510

Source: IMF, *Direction of Trade Statistics*.

been significant impediments to intraregional trade. These have been re-lated both to administrative and commercial regulations and to an ex-tremely poor land transportation system within the countries in the region. The low level of current intraregional trade suggests, in fact, that there is a possibility of significant trade diversion once the customs union is launched. Whether the union actually happens will depend largely on the level and structure of the common external tariff. The tariff, in fact, has become highly controversial and is currently threatening the future of the pact.

As the above discussion on the extent of the reforms showed, the An-dean Pact nations have a significantly more homogeneous structure of protection than the MERCOSUR countries (Table 7.2). Nonetheless, there are still some important differences regarding the objectives of overall trade policy. Bolivia and Peru pursued aggressive free trade reforms, whereas Colombia and Venezuela, arguing that higher tariffs are still nec-essary to encourage the formation of a strong industrial base, have main-tained a more protectionist stance. More recently, however, the Colombian government has been more inclined to accelerate the opening of its economy and its integration into the global economy. The differ-ences on commercial policies have already generated serious friction among the signatories of the Act of La Paz, with Peru's authorities threat-ening to abandon the pact altogether if the common external tariff is set at a rate considered to be excessively protectionist.[56]

In December 1991, in accordance with the Act of La Paz, a new agree-ment was signed by the Andean Group's political authorities. The Act of Barahona established free trade zones between Bolivia, Colombia, and Venezuela, starting on January 1, 1992. Ecuador and Peru were expected to join the free trade zone in July 1992. With respect to the common ex-ternal tariff, the Act of Barahona established an extremely cumbersome mechanism, with exceptions across both countries and goods. According

[56]The new political development in Peru, and especially the Fujimori "coup," have added considerable uncertainty to the integrationist process.

to this act, the CET would have four levels (0, 5, 10, and 15 percent), except for Bolivia, which would only have levels of 5 percent and 10 percent. There were also exceptions for agricultural goods, automobiles, and noncompeting regional products, for which the tariff levels are still to be determined. From the beginning, this agreement on CET suffered serious shortcomings, including that the rules of origin were not determined. For all practical purposes, it is possible that the lowest tariffs (those of Bolivia) will become the *effective* CET for the region as a whole.

In May 1992, only a few months after the CET agreement, the future of the Andean Pact suffered a blow, when Peru unilaterally decided to suspend the preferential treatment granted to imports from member countries. This action was part of a general Peruvian policy aimed at forcing on the pact a lower CET. The governments of Colombia and Venezuela consequently decided to suspend negotiations with Peru on the common external tariff. It is too early to say whether the Andean integrationist movement will continue to move forward or whether it will die a second death. Although negotiations at the diplomatic level are still under way, the individual pact members have proceeded with their respective policies.

Revitalization of the Central American Common Market

During the early and mid-1980s, the Central American Common Market (CACM) began to break down, largely as a result of the international debt crisis. Most countries in the area responded to the debt crisis by imposing massive nontariff barriers, including multiple exchange rates. The most important consequence of this increase in protectionism was that the CACM common external tariff soon ceased to be relevant because the different members had different implicit tariffs for imports coming from outside the region. In 1986, the CACM received a fatal blow when the Central American payments clearing mechanism collapsed.[57]

In July 1991, after several years of independently undertaking trade adjustment, the presidents of the Central American nations decided to revitalize the CACM.[58] Three important features of the renewed CACM are worth noting: first, the agreed-upon common external tariff contemplates a range of between 5 percent and 20 percent. This is significantly lower than the tariff structure most Central American countries have had until recently and represents a clear move toward trade liberalization (see Table 7.20). Second, the newly revitalized CACM includes two new countries: Panama, which never joined the original agreement, and Honduras, which had withdrawn in 1969. Third, in recent years the members of the

---

[57] This collapse was partially the result of Nicaragua's accumulation of a very large debt. See Saborio and Michalopoulos (1992).

[58] The details of the agreement appear in the Declaration of San Salvador, July 17, 1991.

Table 7.20. Tariff Structures in the Central American Common Market

(In percent)

Country	Prereform Average Tariffs[1]	Average Legal Tariff, 1987	1991 Range	1993 Range	1995 Range
Costa Rica	52	26	10–50	5–30	5–20
El Salvador	48	23	5–35	5–25	5–20
Guatemala	50	25	5–37	5–20	5–20
Honduras	41	20	4–35	5–20	5–20
Nicaragua	54	21	5–20	5–20	5–20

Source: Saborio and Michalopoulos (1992).
[1]Ad valorem equivalent of average external tariff.

CACM have actively used export-promotion schemes as a way to diversify and increase exports (see, for example, Saborio and Michalopoulos, 1992). Although it is still too early to know how successful these schemes have been, recent evidence presented by Saborio and Michalopoulos suggests that they have been costly from a fiscal perspective, without having had a significant impact on export expansion over and above what has been obtained through more competitive real exchange rates.

The renewed CACM is a far cry from the agreement originally enacted in the 1960s. Instead of promoting an inefficient and forced industrialization process behind protective walls, the countries in the region are now joining forces to compete internationally and to expand exports more rapidly.

North American Free Trade Agreement

As in most of Latin America, Mexico's trade policy was characterized for decades by significant protectionism and inward orientation. As discussed above, in late 1985 Mexico embarked on an ambitious unilateral trade liberalization program as a component of a major structural adjustment plan. Import tariffs were halved, and import licenses were reduced to 20 percent from 92 percent.

After almost a decade of intensive, and often confrontational, trade negotiations, the United States and Mexico agreed in November 1990 to move toward a free trade agreement. In February 1991, Canada, Mexico, and the United States decided to start negotiating NAFTA, and later that year the U.S. Congress approved the "fast track" treatment of the agreement. On August 12, 1992, the three parties announced that they had come to an understanding on the exact nature of the proposed agreement.

Both the U.S. and Mexican negotiators originally expected the U.S. government to submit the agreement to Congress in the summer of 1992. However, U.S. presidential politics, plus deep dissension about certain details of the agreement, delayed its submission until late 1993. The most important areas of contention between U.S. and Mexican negotiators were (1) defining rules of origin for specific products, including automobiles; (2) establishing the rules for agricultural trade; (3) determining the treatment that would be given to automobiles; (4) workers' protection in Mexico; and (5) environmental rules in Mexico, especially on the border. Of these, perhaps the most important problem was defining rules of origin. After a grueling debate, and the hasty implementation of a number of side agreements, the U.S. Congress finally passed NAFTA in November 1993. The agreement establishes different speeds of liberalization for different sectors. For example, according to the final text, in order for motor vehicles to be subject to free trade within NAFTA, their regional value added should initially be at least 50 percent. This figure, however, will increase slowly over eight years until it reaches 62.5 percent. Regarding the agriculture sector, the agreement proposes that tariffs be eliminated over a 15-year period for most items.

A number of authors have argued that NAFTA will have a severe, negative effect on Mexico's agricultural sector (Instituto Tecnológico Autónomo de México/McGraw-Hill, 1994). In fact, the January 1993 uprising in Chiapas was, at least in part, the result of the perception that NAFTA would wipe out traditional agriculture in that state. A recent study by Vélez and Rubio (1994) indicates that production of most grains in Mexico—sorghum, wheat, barley, soybeans, beans, and maize—will suffer considerably from the implementation of the free trade agreement. Grain production in Mexico is highly inefficient and subject to a significant degree of protection. To avoid the devastating impact of free trade on Mexican agriculture, NAFTA considered the implementation of high initial tariffs, at a level that would replicate the protection granted by traditional licenses. These tariffs would be phased out gradually. For instance, the agreement established an initial import tariff on barley of 128 percent, which would be eliminated over ten years. Maize is perhaps the most dramatic example of inefficient production. Mexico's average yields are approximately 1.7 tons a hectare, barely one-fourth of average U.S. yields. NAFTA established a tariff quota for maize imports into Mexico. Initially, it will be possible to import 2.5 million tons free of duty. During the first year of NAFTA, imports above that level will be subject to a tariff of 215 percent, which would be completely liberalized in 15 years.

As Nogués and Quintanilla (1992) have argued, the heavy media coverage received by NAFTA negotiations has tended to overshadow the broader commitment made by the Mexican government toward freer trade. In fact, after becoming a member of GATT in 1986, Mexico has consistently and systematically pursued freer trade policies, as manifested in the reduction of trade impediments, the signing of bilateral trade agree-

Table 7.21. Nontariff Barrier Coverage of OECD Countries Against Latin American Exports, mid-1980s

(In percent)

Country	Import-Weighted Level of the NTB
Argentina	63.0
Brazil	38.3
Chile	23.8
Mexico	8.4
Peru	12.8
Uruguay	23.2
Venezuela	3.2
Central America	17.1
Average for Latin America and the Caribbean	28.6

Source: Leamer (1990).

ments with Chile (1991), and the current discussions to sign free trade agreements with Venezuela (1993), Colombia, and Central America. The recent negotiations to become a member of the Organization for Economic Cooperation and Development also underlie the Mexican government vision of the importance of freer trade as a fundamental component of the national development strategy for the next several decades. However, for this policy position to be translated into additional gains in productivity and welfare, it will be necessary to further reduce tariffs and license coverage, and, as discussed in the preceding sections, to effectively broaden the reforms to all areas of the economy, especially agriculture. Although Mexico has come a long way, it still has a long way to go to achieve a protective structure similar to that of its most important trade partners, including the United States and Canada.

GATT and the Prospects for Global Trade Liberalization

There is little doubt that Latin America has embarked on one of the most substantial *unilateral* trade liberalization reforms in modern economic history. However, a serious concern among the region's political leaders has been the industrial countries' lack of reciprocity. While the Latin American countries have greatly opened up their trade sector to foreign competition, most industrial nations have continued to follow protectionist practices. In fact, as captured in Table 7.21, the industrial countries have traditionally imposed significant restrictions on Latin American exports. These trade impediments have primarily taken the form of nontariff barriers, including quotas, prohibitions, and licenses. The approval of GATT's Uruguay Round package in December 1993 provides some hope that in the years to come multilateralism could result in a more open world trade system. (See Table 7.22 for a summary of the Uruguay Round's most important implications for Latin America.)

Before 1947, when the first round of multilateral trade negotiations was held in Geneva, average tariff protection in industrial countries was above 100 percent.[59] Fueled by the Smoot-Hawley Tariff Act of 1930, protectionist ideas grew during the first decades of the century, leading the world economy into the Great Depression. By 1993, after seven rounds of GATT-sponsored negotiations, average tariffs had been reduced to 5 percent. However, in spite of this lowering of import tariffs, most industrial countries continued to use extensively an array of nontariff barriers that effectively raised the degree of protectionism. By 1993, developing country imports into some industrial countries were, for all practical purposes, prohibited.

The liberalization of world trade contemplated in the Uruguay Round will be implemented gradually over a ten-year period. From an institutional point of view, one of the most important elements of the agreement is the creation of the World Trade Organization (WTO), which is to replace GATT in 1995. Market access negotiations, which will largely determine the actual extent of the liberalization effort, are expected to be completed at the Morocco ministerial meeting of April 1994.

Some authors (Corden, 1984, for example) have argued that regional integration schemes will serve as intermediate steps toward a more perfect multilateral system based on GATT and, subsequently, the WTO. There are, however, some problems with this idea. The current structure of trading blocs is not cooperative across groups, so that the gains from more trade within blocs have to be compared with the losses from less trade between groups. Moreover, the United States is currently pushing forward a policy of reciprocity rather than one of free trade.

The Uruguay Round covers trade in agriculture and textiles, services, and investment regulations. Overall, according to the agreement, industrial countries' average trade-weighted tariffs on developing country exports will have to be reduced by 34 percent in ten years (from 6.4 percent to 4 percent). Developing countries, in turn, have committed themselves to increasing the coverage of bound duties and to remove export subsidies. In some cases, the reduction is expected to be impressive; Brazil, for instance, committed itself to lowering import tariffs from a maximum of 105 percent to a ceiling of 35 percent. Trade-distorting investment measures, such as local content requirements, are also to be eliminated in five to seven years.

The streamlining of intellectual property protection is expected to help some developing countries that have started exporting knowledge-intensive goods, such as software and agriculture-related technology.

---

[59]This paragraph and those that follow are based on Losada (1994).

Table 7.22. Significance of the Uruguay Round for Latin American Countries

Area	Results
Market access	Overall cut of 33 percent in import tariffs on industrial products, reductions in peaks and escalation. Tariffs reduced in five equal annual steps, starting when the World Trade Organization (WTO) comes into effect. Weighted average tariff down from 6.4 percent to 4.0 percent in industrial countries. Share of duty-free imports from 20 percent to 43 percent in industrial countries. Developing country tariff bindings increased from 12 percent to 56 percent of imports.
	Lower-than-average tariff cuts made in "sensitive" sectors, such as textiles, clothing, footwear, and transport equipment.
	42 percent reduction in tariffs on tropical agricultural products and 57 percent on tropical industrial products in industrial countries. Some developing countries will experience erosion of preference margins.
	34 percent cut in tariffs on natural-resource-based products. Larger-than-average gains in some metals and minerals, lower gains for fish.
	Developing countries with high per capita income are required to phase out subsidies within eight years.
Agriculture	Gradual liberalization process in the sector—over six years for industrial countries and ten years for developing countries. Bindings on agricultural tariffs increased from 81 percent to 95 percent of imports in industrial countries and from 23 percent to 90 percent in developing countries; virtual elimination of all NTBs. Minimum tariff cut of 15 percent on all tariff lines by industrial countries, average tariff reduction of 36 percent over six years from a 1986–88 base. Restrictions against imports subject to a tariffication commitment.
	Reduction in export subsidies by 36 percent in value and 21 percent in volume over the implementation period. Reduction of domestic support programs by 20 percent.
	Special safeguard provisions permit the imposition of additional duties up to certain limits, triggered by both price and volume clauses.
Textiles and clothing	Four-step phaseout of the Multifiber Arrangement over ten years. Gradual integration of the sector into the WTO. Expansion of outstanding quota restrictions. Provisions to redistribute quotas in favor of quota-constrained and efficient exporters. Developing countries' exporters accounting for less than 3 percent of a country's imports of a product are exempted from safeguard action, provided that all developing members with less than 3 percent share account for less than 9 percent overall.
Intellectual property rights	National treatment and most-favored-nation clauses are to apply in respect of all intellectual property rights. Subsidies to research activities are declared nonactionable. Provision of minimum standards for copyrights, trademarks, industrial design, and patents.
	Patent protection for 20 years in all areas of technology, including pharmaceuticals.
	One-year delay for the implementation of trade-related intellectual property rights after the establishment of the WTO. The delay for developing and transition economies is extended to five years, except for the most-favored-nation and national treatment clauses.

Table 7.22 (concluded)

Area	Results
Services	Extension of multilateral rules to a large segment of world trade (20 percent). The General Agreement on Trade in Services establishes the nondiscrimination principle, including most of the GATT-type provisions.
	Framework for establishing and maintaining liberalization commitments. Continuing negotiations related to safeguards, subsidies, and government procurement. Special annexes address specificity of sectors.

However, the liberalization measures agreed upon in December 1993 are rather timid in some areas—especially in agriculture—and the implementation timetable is too lengthy. Safeguard rules are expected to be softened and could be introduced in the future in a discriminatory way and without compensation. It is possible that these antidumping measures will give rise to a new form of disguised protectionism.

The successful completion of the Uruguay Round is expected to provide both static and dynamic gains to the world economy. The developing countries' share of these gains will be about one-third. Trade is expected to grow by 12 percent in the next ten years, owing exclusively to the Uruguay Round. Developing countries, however, will not receive a significant share of the dynamic gains because economies of scale and technological spillovers through greater innovation are likely to accrue to exporters of industrial goods.

Appendix. Productivity Growth and Commercial Policy: An Econometric Analysis

A number of researchers have found that factor accumulation explains between one-half and two-thirds of long-run growth (Fischer, 1988). The large unexplained residual in growth-accounting exercises has been attributed to "technological progress" or "productivity gains." From a policy perspective, a key question is what determines these productivity improvements. In particular, it is important to understand whether national domestic policies—including financial and trade policies—can affect the pace of productivity growth. If this is the case, policymakers will have additional degrees of freedom to pursue those avenues that will enhance long-run performance.[60]

The recent interest in endogenous growth models has generated a revival in applied research on the determinants of growth. Some authors have emphasized the role of openness in determining the pace at which countries can absorb technological progress originating in the rest of the world (Grossman and Helpman, 1991). Edwards (1992) has recently assumed that there are two sources of TFP growth: (1) a purely domestic source stemming from local technological improvements (innovation); and (2) a foreign source related to the absorption of inventions generated in other countries (imitation). More specifically, assume that a country's ability to appropriate or imitate world technical innovations depends on two factors: positively on the degree of openness (y) of the economy and, also positively, on the gap between the country's level of TFP and the world's stock of TFP. The first channel is the "openness effect" discussed by Lewis (1955). more open countries have an advantage in absorbing new ideas generated in the rest of the world. In this context "more open" should be interpreted as referring to a less distorted foreign trade sector. The second channel is a "catch-up" effect common to growth models based on "convergence" notions.

If the aggregate production function is defined as $y_t = Af(K_t, L_t)$, then total factor productivity is $A_t = y_t/f(\cdot)$, and total productivity growth is $(\dot{A}/A)$. The role of the two sources of technical progress discussed above—innovation and imitation—can be captured by the following, simple expression:

$$\frac{\dot{A}}{A} = \alpha + \left[\beta\omega + \gamma\left(\frac{A^* - A}{A}\right)\right], \tag{A.1}$$

where α and γ are parameters, A^* is the level of world's appropriable TFP, and ω is the rate of growth of the world's TFP (that is $A_t^* = A_0^* e^{\omega t}$). β is a parameter between zero and one that measures the country's ability to absorb productivity improvements originating in the rest of the world

---

[60]This appendix is based partially on Edwards (1992).

and is assumed to be a negative function of the level of trade distortions in the economy (δ).

$$\beta = \beta(\delta); \; \beta' < 0, \tag{A.2}$$

where δ is an index of trade distortions that takes a higher value when international trade, both in imports and/or exports, becomes more distorted.

Parameter α is the basic rate of domestic productivity growth or innovation, which, for simplicity, is assumed to be exogenous. On the other hand, $(\gamma(A^* - A)/A)$ is the catch-up term that says that domestic productivity growth will be faster in countries where the stock of knowledge lags further behind the world's accumulated stock of appropriable knowledge.[61]

In this setting, the path through time of domestic TFP will be given by[62]

$$A_t = \left[A_0 - \left(\frac{\gamma}{\gamma + \omega (1 - \beta) - \alpha} \right) A_0^* \right] e^{-(\gamma - \alpha - \beta\omega)t}$$
$$+ \left(\frac{\gamma}{\gamma + \omega (1 - \beta) - \alpha} \right) A_0^* e^{\omega t}. \tag{A.3}$$

It follows from equation (A.3) that the long-run rate of growth of domestic TFP will depend on whether $(\gamma - \alpha - \beta\omega) \gtrless 0$. If $(\gamma - \alpha - \beta\omega) > 0$ in the steady state, TFP will grow at the rate of the world's productivity ω. This means that the level of domestic TFP (and of GDP) will be a function of the degree of trade intervention, with higher trade distortions resulting in a lower level of real income. A key implication of this result is that countries that engage in trade liberalization programs will be characterized, during the transition between two steady states, by higher rates of productivity growth and thus by faster rates of GDP growth.

A second case appears when $(\gamma - \alpha - \beta\omega) < 0$. Long-run TFP growth ($\dot{A}/A$) will depend on how large the world's rate of growth of TFP (ω) is relative to the domestic rate of productivity improvement. If $\omega > (\alpha - \delta)/(1 - \beta)$, domestic TFP will grow in the steady state at the world rate ω. If, however, $\omega < (\alpha - \gamma)/(1 - \beta)$, and $(\gamma - \alpha - \beta\omega) < 0$, the long-run equilibrium rate of TFP growth will be equal to $(\alpha + \beta\omega - \delta)$[63] and will depend negatively on δ, the country's level of trade distortions. That is, in this case more open countries (those with low δ) will grow faster during steady-state equilibrium. This is because in this case the domestic source

---

[61]It is assumed that not all inventions generated in the world can be freely appropriated. In that sense, A^* could be interpreted as the accumulated stock of innovations in the more advanced countries that have spilled over to the rest of the world.

[62]This, of course, is the solution to differential equation (A.1).

[63]Of course in this case $(\alpha + \beta\omega - \delta) > \omega$.

of technological inventions is strong enough, even in the steady state, to drive the aggregate rate of technological innovations.[64]

The model developed above suggests that TFP growth will depend on the degree of trade distortions in the economy and on a catch-up term that measures the gap between the country's and the world's level of productivity. A cross-country data set was used to test these implications of this model. More specifically, equations of the following type can be estimated:

$$\rho_n = b_0 + b_1 \delta_n + b_2 g_n + \Sigma a_i x_{in} + \mu_n, \tag{A.4}$$

where ρ_n is the average rate of growth of TFP in country n; δ_n is, as before, an index of trade distortions; g_n is the catch-up term; the x_i's are other possible determinants of TFP growth; and μ is an error term.

Recently, Barro (1991), Edwards (1992), and Roubini and Sala-i-Martin (1992), among others, have suggested that in addition to the degree of openness, productivity growth will also be affected by the following factors: (1) human capital, usually measured by level of education; (2) the importance of government in the economy measured by the ratio of government expenditure to GDP; (3) the degree of political instability; and (4) the inflation rate. In the estimations of equation (A.4) reported above, these variables have been incorporated as possible determinants of productivity growth. Variables were defined in the following way:

TFP growth: A problem with estimating equations of the type of (A.4) is the measurement of TFP growth. In particular, it is difficult to obtain long time series of capital stocks for a large number of countries. In this appendix, three measures of TFP growth constructed by Edwards (1992) are used.

Trade distortions: Traditionally, studies that have investigated the relationship between trade policy and economic performance have had difficulties measuring the extent of trade distortions. This analysis uses two variables: first, in most of the basic estimates the ratio of total taxes on foreign trade—import tariffs plus export taxes—to total trade is used as a proxy for trade distortions. This variable is measured as an average for 1971–82. Since this variable, denoted TRADETAX, measures the "true" extent of trade distortions with error, in the estimation of the TFP growth equation, an instrumental variable technique that tries to correct for measurement error is also used. The second proxy is the 1971–82 average trade dependency ratio—imports plus exports as a percentage of GDP. These two indices of trade distortions were constructed with raw data obtained from the IMF.

---

[64]In Grossman and Helpman's (1990) micro model of technological progress, it is also possible that, under some circumstances, more open economies will exhibit higher long-run growth.

Catch-up term: Following the recent literature on endogenous growth (Barro 1991; Edwards, 1992), initial GDP per capita—for 1971 in this case—represents the gap between a particular country's level of productivity and that of the world. This variable is denoted as GDP71; the data were obtained from Summers and Heston (1988). The coefficient of this variable is expected to be negative.

Human capital: Two indices are used. The first one is the attainment of secondary education in 1981. The second one is the increase in secondary education coverage between 1961 and 1981. When alternative indices, such as secondary and higher education, were used, the results obtained were not altered. The data were obtained from the World Bank's *World Development Report*. The coefficient of this variable is expected to be positive.

Role of government: This index is defined as the share of government in GDP and is taken from Summers and Heston (1988). Barro (1991) has argued that this coefficient should be negative, capturing the effect that greater government activities tend, in general, to crowd out the private sector.

Political instability: This variable was defined as the average perceived probability of government change and was obtained from Cukierman, Edwards, and Tabellini (1992).[65] Its coefficient in the TFP growth equations is expected to be negative, reflecting the fact that in politically unstable situations economic agents do not devote their full energies to pursuing economic objectives.

Inflation tax: This variable was defined as the average collection of the inflation tax for 1971–82 and was computed as πm, where π is the rate of inflation and m is the ratio of M1 to GDP. The coefficient of this variable is expected to be negative, reflecting the effects of higher inflation on uncertainty and economic activity.

Tables 7.A1 and 7.A2 summarize the results obtained from the estimation of several versions of equation (A.4). Table 7.A1 contains weighted least-squares estimates—with population in 1971 as weight—for all three measures of TFP growth;[66] Table 7.A2 presents instrumental variable regressions for the *TFP*1 definition of productivity growth. (When the other two indices were used, the results were not altered significantly.)

As can be seen from these tables, the results are highly satisfactory. Almost every coefficient has the expected sign and is significant at conventional levels. Particularly important for the discussion pursued in this paper is the fact that in every regression the proxies for trade distortions and openness are highly significant. Moreover, the computation of

---

[65]These authors computed this index from a probit analysis on government change using pooled data for 1948-81.

[66]In simple, ordinary least-squares estimates, heteroscedasticity was detected. Barro (1991) and Edwards (1992), among others, also use weighted least squares in equations of this type.

Table 7.A1. TFP Growth Regressions, Cross-Country Results

Variable	Eq.1 TFP1	Eq.2 TFP1	Eq.3 TFP2	Eq.4 TFP2	Eq.5 TFP3	Eq.6 TFP3
Constant	−0.013 (−1.041)	−0.012 (−1.326)	−0.018 (−1.418)	−0.005 (−0.439)	0.074 (6.163)	0.030 (1.772)
GDP71	−1.85E-06 (−3.433)	−7.28E-07 (−1.929)	−1.8E-06 (−2.960)	−1.08-06 (−2.451)	−3.69E-06 (−3.673)	−1.48E-06 (−2.187)
TRADETAX	−0.076 (−3.033)	—	−0.074 (−2.620)	—	−0.199 (−4.902)	—
Trade dependency	—	0.017 (3.147)	—	0.025 (3.910)	—	0.025 (2.480)
Government	−6.14E-04 (−2.429)	−4.20E-04 (−1.708)	−6.50E-04 (−2.292)	−4.10E-04 (−1.433)	−2.00E-03 (−5.157)	−2.00E-03 (−4.827)
Education	1.19E-04 (1.536)	1.56E-07 (2.130)	5.9E-06 (0.675)	1.30E-04 (1.560)	—	1.20E-04 (0.895)
ΔEducation	—	—	—	—	1.60E-04 (1.453)	—
Political instability	−0.017 (−2.117)	−0.017 (−2.480)	−0.026 (−2.846)	−0.043 (−5.253)	−0.014 (−1.670)	−0.023 (−1.802)
Inflation tax	—	8.3E-05 (0.540)	—	8.8E-05 (0.487)	—	−2.7E-05 (−0.921)
R2	0.400	0.351	0.492	0.487	0.598	0.416
N	54	52	54	52	52	52

Note: For exact explanations on how TFP1, TFP2, and TFP3 were constructed, see Edwards (1992). *t*-statistics are in parentheses; N is the number of observations; and R2 is the coefficient of determination.

standardized beta coefficients indicates that, after the catch-up term, trade impediments are the second most important explanatory variable of TFP growth.[67]

As pointed out above, both the TRADETAX coefficient and the trade dependency ratio are imperfect proxies of trade distortions. In particular, they do not directly capture the role of quantitative restrictions on trade. To deal with this measurement error problem, instrumental variable versions of some of these equations were also estimated. In re-estimating equations (A.4.1) and (A.4.2), the trade penetration ratio of imports to GDP was used as an instrument for TRADETAX.[68] The results obtained are

---

[67]In equation (4) the standardized beta coefficient of taxes on trade is -0.75; that of GDP71 is -0.78.

[68] The instruments themselves do not have to be measured free of error. Of course, the use of instrumental variables is not the only way of dealing with measurement error. Edwards (1992) used reversed regressions to construct intervals for a different proxy of openness in standard growth equations.

Table 7.A2. TFP Growth Regressions

(Dependent variable—TFP1)

Instrumental Variable	Equation 7	Equation 8
Constant	0.036 (1.689)	0.050 (2.037)
GDP71	−3.4E-06 (−2.766)	−3.7E-06 (−2.677)
TRADETAX	−0.171 (−2.432)	−0.185 (−2.314)
Government	−4.9E-04 (−1.708)	−5.5E-04 (−2.292)
Education	3.00E-05 (2.130)	4.80E-05 (0.675)
Political instability	−0.029 (−2.333)	−0.040 (−2.823)
Inflation tax	−8.1E-05 (−0.766)	−2.5E-05 (−0.939)
R2	0.248	0.392
N	52	52

Note: t-statistics are in parentheses; N is the number of observations; and R2 is the coefficient of determination. Equations are weighted by population in 1971.

presented in Table 7.A2. They confirm the results discussed previously and provide additional support for the view that, after controlling for other factors, countries with more open and less distorted foreign trade sectors have tended to exhibit a faster rate of growth of total factor productivity, over the long run, than those countries with a more distorted external sector.

References

Agacino, R., G. Rivas, and E. Román, "Apertura y Eficiencia Productiva: La Experiencia Chilena, 1975–1989," Working Paper No. 113 (Washington: Inter-American Development Bank, 1992).

Balassa, Bela, *The Structure of Protection in Developing Countries* (Baltimore: Johns Hopkins Press, 1971).

——, *Development Strategies in Semi-industrial Economies* (Baltimore: Johns Hopkins Press, 1982).

Baldinelli, Elvio, "Armonización de Políticas Crediticias, Fiscales, y de Promoción de Exportaciones," *Integración Latinoamericana*, Vol. 16 (May 1991), pp. 3–17.

Barro, Robert, "Economic Growth in a Cross Section of Countries," *Quarterly Journal of Economics*, Vol. 106 (May 1991), pp. 407–43.

Bhagwati, Jagdish, *Anatomy and Consequences of Exchange Control Regimes,* Vol. 2, *Foreign Trade Regimes and Economic Development* (Cambridge, Massachusetts: Ballinger, 1978).

Bianchi, Andrés, and Takahashi Nohara, eds., *A Comparative Study on Economic Development Between Asia and Latin America* (Tokyo: Institute of Developing Economies, 1988).

Bonelli, Regis, "Growth and Productivity in Brazilian Industries: Impacts of Trade Orientation," *Journal of Development Economics,* Vol. 39 (July 1992), pp. 85–109.

Bruton, Henry, "Import Substitution," in *Handbook of Development Economics,* Vol. 2, ed. by Hollis Chenery and T. N. Srinivasan (Amsterdam; New York: North-Holland, 1989).

Calvo, Guillermo, Leonardo Leiderman, and Carmen Reinhart, "Capital Inflows and Real Exchange Rate Appreciation," IMF Working Paper 94/62 (Washington: International Monetary Fund, 1992).

Cardoso, Eliana A., and Ann Helwege, *Latin America's Economy: Diversity, Trends, and Conflicts* (Cambridge, Massachusetts: MIT Press, 1992).

Castro, Antonio Barros de, and Carlos Lessa, *Introducción a la Economía: Un Enfoque Estructuralista* (Santiago: Editorial Universitaria, 1969).

Coes, Donald, "Brazil," in *Liberalizing Foreign Trade,* Vol. 7, *Lessons of Experience in the Developing World,* ed. by Michael Michaely, Demetris Papageorgiou, and Armeane Choksi (New York: Basil Blackwell, 1991).

Corbo, Vittorio, Timothy Condon, and Jaime De Melo, "Productivity Growth, External Shocks, and Capital Inflows in Chile: A General Equilibrium Analysis," *Journal of Policy Modeling,* Vol. 7 (Fall 1985), pp. 379–405.

Corden, W. Max, "The Structure of a Tariff System and the Effective Protection Rate," *Journal of Political Economy,* Vol. 74 (June 1966).

———, "The Normative Theory of International Trade," in *Handbook of International Economics,* Vol. 1, ed. by Ronald Jones and Peter Kenen (Amsterdam: North-Holland, 1984).

Cukierman, Alex, Sebastián Edwards, and Guido Tabellini, "Seigniorage and Political Instability," *American Economic Review,* Vol. 82 (June 1992).

De Gregorio, José, "Economic Growth in Latin America," *Journal of Development Economics,* Vol. 39 (July 1992), pp. 59–84.

Díaz-Alejandro, Carlos, *Essays on the Economic History of the Argentine Republic* (New Haven: Yale University Press, 1970).

———, *Colombia: Foreign Trade Regimes and Economic Development* (New York: National Bureau of Economic Research, 1976).

———, "Southern Cone Stabilization Plans," in *Economic Stabilization in Developing Countries,* ed. by William Cline and Sidney Weintraub (Washington: Brookings Institution, 1981).

Dixit, Avinash, "Tax Policy in Open Economies," in *Handbook of Public Economics,* Vol. 1, ed. by Alan Auerbach and Martin Feldstein (Amsterdam; New York: North-Holland, 1985).

Dornbusch, Rudiger, "Los Costes y Beneficios de la Integración Económica Regional: Una Revisión," *Pensamiento Iberoamericano*, No. 15 (January-June 1989), pp. 25-54.

———, "Policies to Move from Stabilization to Growth," in *Proceedings of the World Bank Annual Conference on Development Economics* (Washington: World Bank, 1990).

———, and Sebastián Edwards, "Macroeconomic Populism," *Journal of Development Economics*, Vol. 32 (April 1990), pp. 247-77.

Edwards, Sebastián, "The Order of Liberalization of the External Sector in Developing Countries," Princeton Essays in International Finance No. 156 (Princeton, New Jersey: Princeton University, 1984).

———, "Stabilization with Liberalization: An Evaluation of Ten Years of Chile's Experiment with Free Market Policies, 1973-1983," *Economic Development and Cultural Change*, Vol. 33 (January 1985), pp. 223-54.

———, *Exchange Rate Misalignment in Developing Countries* (Baltimore: Johns Hopkins University Press, 1988).

———, *Real Exchange Rates, Devaluation, and Adjustment: Exchange Rate Policy in Developing Countries* (Cambridge, Massachusetts: MIT Press, 1989).

———, "Trade Orientation, Distortions, and Growth in Developing Countries," *Journal of Development Economics*, Vol. 39 (July 1992), pp. 31-57.

——— (1993a), "Exchange Rates as Nominal Anchors," *Weltwirtschaftliches Archiv*, Vol. 129, pp. 1-32.

——— (1993b), "Openness, Trade Liberalization, and Growth in Developing Countries," *Journal of Economic Literature*, Vol. 31 (September), pp. 1358-93.

———, and Alejandra Edwards, *Monetarism and Liberalization: The Chilean Experiment* (Chicago: University of Chicago Press, 1991).

Edwards, Sebastian, and Miguel Savastano, "Latin America's Intraregional Trade: Evolution and Future Prospects," NBER Working Paper No. 2738 (Cambridge, Massachusetts: National Bureau of Economic Research, 1988).

Elías, Victor, *Sources of Growth: A Study of Seven Latin American Economies* (San Francisco: ICS Press, 1992).

Erzan, Refik, Kiroaki Kuwahara, Saratino Marchese, and Rene Vossenar, "The Profile of Protection in Developing Countries," *UNCTAD Review*, Vol. 1 (1989), pp. 29-49.

Ffrench-Davis, Ricardo, and Thomas Griffin, *Teoría del Comercio Internacional* (Mexico City: Fondo de Cultura Económica, 1967).

Fischer, Stanley, "Issues in Medium-Term Macroeconomic Adjustment," *World Bank Research Observer*, Vol. 1 (July 1986), pp. 163-82.

———, "Recent Developments in Macroeconomics," *Economic Journal*, Vol. 98 (June 1988), pp. 294-339.

Fishlow, Albert, "Revisiting the Great Debt Crisis of 1982," in *Debt and Development in Latin America*, ed. by Kwang Suk Kim and David Ruccio (Notre Dame: University of Notre Dame Press, 1985).

————, "Liberalization in Latin America," in *Economic Liberalization: No Panacea*, ed. by Tariq Banuri (Oxford: Clarendon Press, 1991).

Furtado, Celso, *La Economía Latinoamericana Desde la Conquista Ibérica Hasta la Revolución Cubana* (Santiago: Editorial Universitaria, 1969).

Griffith-Jones, Stefany, and Osvaldo Sunkel, *Debt and Development Crises in Latin America: The End of an Illusion* (New York: Oxford University Press, 1986).

Grossman, Gene, and Elhanan Helpman, *Innovation and Growth in the Global Economy* (Cambridge, Massachusetts: MIT Press, 1991).

Hanson, James, "Opening the Capital Account," World Bank Policy Research Working Paper No. 901 (Washington: World Bank, 1992).

Harberger, Arnold, "The Chilean Economy in the 1970s: Crisis, Stabilization, Liberalization, Reform," in *Economic Policy in a World of Change*, ed. by Karl Brunner and Allan Metzler, *Carnegie-Rochester Conference Series on Public Policy*, Vol. 17 (Amsterdam: North-Holland, 1982).

————, "Observations on the Chilean Economy, 1973-1983," *Economic Development and Cultural Change*, Vol. 33 (April 1985), pp. 451-62.

————, "Towards a Uniform Tariff Structure" (Chicago: University of Chicago, Department of Economics, 1990).

Heitger, Bernhard, "Import Protection and Export Performance: Their Impact on Economic Growth," *Weltwirtschaftliches Archiv*, Vol. 123 (1987), pp. 249-61.

Hirschman, Albert, "The Political Economy of Import-Substituting Industrialization in Latin America," *Quarterly Journal of Economics*, Vol. 82 (February 1968), pp. 1-32.

Ibarra, Luis, "Credibility of Trade Policy Reform: The Mexican Experience" (Ph.D. dissertation; Los Angeles: UCLA, Department of Economics, 1992).

Iglesias, Enrique, *Reflections on Economic Development: Toward a New Latin American Consensus* (Washington: Inter-American Development Bank, 1992).

Instituto Tecnológico Autónomo de México/McGraw-Hill, *Lo Negociado del Tratado de Libre Comercio* (Mexico City, 1994).

Jaspersen, Frederick, "External Resource Flows to Latin America: Recent Developments and Prospects," Working Paper No. 116 (Washington: Inter-American Development Bank, 1992).

Kim, Kwang Suk, "Korea," in *Liberalizing Foreign Trade*, Vol. 7, *Lessons of Experience in the Developing World*, ed. by Michael Michaely, Demetris Papageorgiou, and Armeane Choksi (New York: Basil Blackwell, 1991).

Krueger, Anne, *Foreign Trade Regimes and Economic Development: Liberalization Attempts and Consequences* (Cambridge, Massachusetts: Ballinger, 1978).

————, "Trade Policy as an Input to Development," *American Economic Review, Papers and Proceedings of the Ninety-Second Annual Meeting of the American Economic Association*, Vol. 70 (May 1980), pp. 288-92.

————, *Trade and Employment in Developing Countries* (Chicago: University of Chicago Press, 1981).

————, *Exchange Rate Determination* (New York: Cambridge University Press, 1983).

Lal, Deepak, "The Real Effects of Stabilization and Structural Adjustment Policies: An Extension of the Australian Adjustment Model," World Bank Staff Working Paper No. 636 (Washington: World Bank, 1985).

Leamer, Edward, "Latin America as a Target of Trade Barriers Erected by the Major Developed Countries in 1983," *Journal of Development Economics*, Vol. 32 (April 1990), pp. 337-68.

Leff, Nathaniel, *Economic Policymaking and Development in Brazil, 1947-1964* (New York: Wiley, 1969).

Lewis, William A., *The Theory of Economic Growth* (London: Allen and Unwin, 1955).

Lin, Ching-Yuan, "East Asia and Latin America as Contrasting Models," *Economic Development and Cultural Change*, Vol. 36 (April 1988), pp. S153-97.

Little, Ian, Tibor Scitovsky, and Maurice Scott, *Industry and Trade in Some Developing Countries: A Comparative Study* (London; New York: Oxford University Press, 1970).

Losada, Fernando, "Partners, Neighbors and Distant Cousins: Explaining Bilateral Trade Flows in Latin America" (Unpublished; Los Angeles: UCLA, 1993).

——, "The Uruguay Round, GATT and Regionalism" (Unpublished; Washington: World Bank, Latin America and Caribbean Region, Office of the Chief Economist, 1994).

Lucas, Robert, "On the Mechanics of Economic Development," *Journal of Monetary Economics*, Vol. 22 (July 1988), pp. 3-42.

Lustig, Nora, "The Future of Trade Policy in Latin America," Working Paper (Washington: Brookings Institution, 1994).

Martin, Ricardo D., "Sources of Growth in Latin America" (Unpublished; Washington: World Bank, Latin America and Caribbean Region, 1992).

McKinnon, Ronald, "The Order of Economic Liberalization: Lessons from Chile and Argentina," in *Economic Policy in a World of Change*, ed. by Karl Brunner and Allan Metzler, *Carnegie-Rochester Conference Series on Public Policy*, Vol. 17 (Amsterdam: North-Holland, 1982).

Michaely, Michael, "The Demand for Protection Against Exports of Newly Industrialized Countries," *Journal of Policy Modeling*, Vol. 7 (Spring 1985), pp. 123-32.

——, Demetris Papageorgiou, and Armeane Choksi, eds., *Liberalizing Foreign Trade* (New York: Basil Blackwell, 1991).

Mill, John Stuart, *Principles of Political Economy* (New York: Appleton and Co., 1848).

Nogués, Julio, "The Experience of Latin America with Export Subsidies," *Weltwirtschaftliches Archiv*, Vol. 126 (1990), pp. 97-115.

——, and Neera Gulati, "Economic Policies and Performance Under Alternative Trade Regimes: Latin America During the 1980s," LAC Technical Department Report No. 16 (Washington: World Bank, 1992).

Nogués, Julio, and Rosalinda Quintanilla, "Latin America's Integration and the Multilateral Trading System," paper presented at the World Bank/CEPR Conference on New Dimensions in Regional Integration (Washington: World Bank, 1992).

Ocampo, José Antonio, "Determinants and Prospects for Medium-Term Growth in Colombia," paper presented at the Lehigh University Conference on the Colombian Economy: Issues of Debt, Trade, and Development (Bethlehem, Pennsylvania: Lehigh University, 1991).

Paz, Pedro, and Osvaldo Sunkel, *El Subdesarrollo Latinoamericano y la Teoría del Desarrollo* (Madrid: Siglo Veintiuno de España, 1st ed., 1970).

Prebisch, Raúl, "Commercial Policy in the Underdeveloped Countries," *American Economic Review*, Vol. 40 (May 1950).

———, "Five Stages in My Thinking on Development," in *Pioneers in Development*, ed. by Gerald M. Meier and Dudley Seers (Oxford: Oxford University Press, 1984).

Rabello de Castro, Paulo, and Mauricio Ronci, "Sixty Years of Populism in Brazil," in *The Macroeconomics of Populism in Latin America*, ed. by Rudiger Dornbusch and Sebastián Edwards (Chicago: University of Chicago Press, 1991).

Rodríguez, Carlos, "The Argentine Stabilization Plan of December 20th," *World Development*, Vol. 10 (September 1982), pp. 801-11.

Romer, Paul, "Capital Accumulation in the Theory of Long-Run Growth," in *Modern Business Cycle Theory*, ed. by Robert Barro (Cambridge, Massachusetts: Harvard University Press, 1989).

Roubini, Nouriel, and Xavier Sala-i-Martin, "Financial Repression and Economic Growth," *Journal of Development Economics,* Vol. 39 (July 1992), pp. 5-30.

Saborio, Sylvia, and Constantine Michalopoulos, "Central America at a Crossroads," Policy Research Working Paper No. 922 (Washington: World Bank, 1992).

Sachs, Jeffrey, "Trade and Exchange Rate Policies in Growth-Oriented Adjustment Programs," in *Growth-Oriented Adjustment Programs*, ed. by Vittorio Corbo, Morris Goldstein, and Mohsin Khan (Washington: International Monetary Fund and World Bank, 1987).

———, "Conditionality, Debt Relief, and the Developing Country Debt Crisis," NBER Working Paper No. 2644 (Cambridge, Massachusetts: National Bureau of Economic Research, 1988).

Sánchez, Manuel, "Entorno Macroeconómico Frente al Tratado de Libre Comercio," in *Mexico y el Tratado Trilateral de Libre Comercio* (Mexico City: Instituto Tecnológico Autónomo de México/McGraw-Hill, 1992).

Schott, Jeffrey, "Trading Blocs and the World Trading System," *The World Economy*, Vol. 14 (March 1991), pp. 1-17.

Sheahan, John, *Patterns of Development in Latin America: Poverty, Repression, and Economic Strategy* (Princeton, New Jersey: Princeton University Press, 1987).

Singer, Hans, "The Distribution of Gains Between Investing and Borrowing Countries," *American Economic Review*, Vol. 40 (May 1950).

Solís, Leopoldo, "Raúl Prebisch at ECLA: Years of Creative Intellectual Effort," ICEG Occasional Paper No. 10 (San Francisco: International Center for Economic Growth, 1988).

Stockman, Alan, "Comment," in *Economic Policy in a World of Change*, ed. by Karl Brunner and Allan Metzler, *Carnegie-Rochester Conference Series on Public Policy*, Vol. 17 (Amsterdam: North-Holland, 1982).

Sturzenegger, Federico, "Bolivia: Stabilization and Growth" (Unpublished; Los Angeles: UCLA, Department of Economics, 1992).

Summers, Robert, and Alan Heston, "A New Set of International Comparisons of Real Product and Price Level Estimates for 130 Countries, 1950-1985," *Review of Income and Wealth*, Vol. 34 (March 1988), pp. 1-26.

Sunkel, Osvaldo, "Inflation in Chile: An Unorthodox Approach," *International Economic Papers*, Vol. 10 (August 1960).

Taylor, Lance, "Economic Openness: Problems to the Century's End," in *Economic Liberalization: No Panacea*, ed. by Tariq Banuri (New York: Clarendon Press, 1991).

Thorp, Rosemary, "A Reappraisal of the Origins of Import-Substitution Industrialization, 1930-1950," *Journal of Latin American Studies*, Vol. 24, supplement (1992), pp. 181-95.

Tybout, James, "Linking Trade and Productivity: New Research Directions," *World Bank Economic Review*, Vol. 6 (May 1992), pp. 189-211.

United Nations, Economic Commission for Latin America and the Caribbean, *Balance Preliminar de la Economía de América Latina y el Caribe* (Santiago, Chile, 1991).

——, *Equidad y Transformación Productiva: Un Enfoque Integrado* (Santiago, Chile, 1992).

Valdés, Alberto, "The Performance of the Agricultural Sector in Latin America" (Washington: World Bank, Latin America and Caribbean Region, 1992).

Velez, Félix, and Gloria Rubio, "El Impacto del Tratado de Libre Comercio en el Campo Mexicano," in *Lo Negociado del Tratado de Libre Comercio* (Mexico City: Instituto Tecnológica Autónoma de México/McGraw-Hill, 1994).

Vuskovic, Pedro, "Distribución del Ingreso y Opciones de Desarrollo," *Cuadernos de la Realidad Nacional*, Vol. 7 (September 1970).

Weiss, John, "Trade Policy Reform and Performance in Manufacturing: Mexico, 1975-88," *Journal of Development Studies*, Vol. 29 (October 1992), pp. 1-23.

World Bank, *World Development Report 1987* (New York: Oxford University Press, 1987).

—— (1993a), *The Asian Economic Miracle: Economic Growth and Public Policy* (New York: Oxford University Press).

—— (1993b), *Latin America a Decade After the Debt Crisis*, report prepared for the Office of the Vice President, Latin America and the Caribbean, The World Bank (Washington: World Bank).

Comment

S.J. Anjaria

I am very grateful to Sebastian Edwards for his paper, which covers a lot of ground in the area of trade and capital movements and exchange rate policy. I am glad he concluded on the note of the General Agreement on Tariffs and Trade (GATT), because I would like to begin at that point in my comments.

It is useful to remind ourselves that all of the discussion of regional trade arrangements today in Latin America as well as elsewhere is taking place in the context of an existing multilateral trade and payments system. Of course, as a staff member of the IMF, I am particularly aware of the IMF's role in promoting an open, multilateral system, even though on the trade side the GATT has primary responsibility. As we have just discussed, the Uruguay Round of multilateral trade negotiations has been completed, and the implementation of the agreements will strengthen and make more liberal the multilateral trading system. The first point I would like to make is that when we look at any issue dealing with regional arrangements to expand trade, we are not writing on a blank slate but are elaborating on the existing system. Therefore, we must assess the impact that regional arrangements would have on the existing system. I will come back to this later.

Second, I think everyone will agree that the Uruguay Round is a major step forward. The fact that it took seven years to negotiate and caused a great deal of difficulty is indicative of the negotiating and political pain and suffering that went into it. No complete assessment of the effects of the Uruguay Round is available so far, to my knowledge. However, its results are notable both for the success in reducing trade and nontariff barriers and for certain other accomplishments that many thought, even until the last hours or minutes, it could not achieve. I am referring, obviously, to trade in agriculture and trade in services.

Let me add a personal note. I happened to be present as an IMF representative at the Punta del Este conference that launched the Uruguay Round in September 1986. Upon returning to Washington, I had to write a report to our Executive Board about what had happened at the conference. I remember agonizing over how to describe what had been agreed upon as the objectives of the Uruguay Round negotiations in the area of services. Even at the end of the Punta del Este conference, there remained a sharp division between the developing countries, or at least the larger developing countries, and most of the industrial countries on whether trade in services should or should not form part of the negotiations. That was seven years ago. Today there is an agreement on trade in services, and all countries who participated in the negotiations are part of it. There are no dissenting views. This is some indication of the degree to which the mood has changed in all countries about the need to strengthen and extend the multilateral system.

One or two words now about Latin America, very well described and portrayed in the paper by Mr. Edwards. The progress on trade liberalization that has taken place has been well documented. Much of this liberalization took place on a multilateral basis. The best kind of outward-oriented strategy is the kind that is outward-oriented on a multilateral basis rather than on a regional basis. At the same time that they pursued multilateral trade liberalization, Latin American countries have made progress with regional arrangements. The North American Free Trade Agreement (NAFTA) is of course the most recent, spectacular example of this progress—again something that was fought over very actively. Other regional arrangements, as the paper points out, are being put in place or being considered from the standpoint of whether they fulfill the criterion of outward orientation rather than that of inward orientation.

There are two or three questions that we should ask ourselves, in a sort of forward-looking spirit. The first question is whether we have come to the end of trade liberalization in Latin America. The evidence in Table 7.2 of Mr. Edwards' paper suggests that there is still some way to go toward fuller liberalization before Latin American countries can achieve the level of openness in trade regimes that is typical of the industrial countries. While different countries in Latin America are in different positions, trade liberalization is still an issue and must be pursued.

Second, and in this context, what is the future of regionalism in Latin America? As I said before, some of the new arrangements are outward looking. I think the earlier difficulty with using regional arrangements to promote intraregional trade was that there was a fundamental conflict between the objectives of regional trade liberalization and the objectives of, or the approach to, inward-looking trade policies. One called for more liberalization, the other called for less liberalization, and that conflict, in effect, was resolved too often in favor of inward-looking policies.

If that approach is to be changed, then, indeed, regionalism does have a future. It is essential, however, that regionalism be completely consistent with the multilateral and open trade regime that has just been strengthened under the Uruguay Round. In this respect, one or two suggestions may be useful. One is that if trade is to be liberalized under a regional arrangement, the liberalization schedule should be as automatic as possible. In the past, the experience was that nonautomaticity in the trade liberalization schedule led to difficulties and pressures for protection that delayed liberalization and gave precedence to inward-oriented strategies. Second, and even more important because the issue is usually neglected, regional arrangements, to be consistent with the multilateral framework—particularly Article XXIV of the GATT—must involve liberalization that is as comprehensive as possible. Obviously, the risk of trade diversion is greater in a regime that is selective in the sectors it liberalizes. In brief, if there is automaticity, and if across-the-board actions can be incorporated in the agreement, then, yes, there is a future for regional arrangements.

Finally, one word on exchange rate policy and future trade liberalization. I think if we agree that there is scope for trade liberalization in the future, then for any region as a whole—for Latin America as a whole—we must ask ourselves if some of the discussions that we have had on nominal anchors are somewhat premature. In those countries where future trade liberalization will require compensating real exchange rate adjustments, clearly the possibility of fixing the nominal exchange rate beforehand becomes problematic. I hope we will come back to this point later in our discussion.

Comment

Jaime Ros

For the sake of brevity and comparative advantage, my comments on this paper will focus on some gray areas where I disagree with the author. This means not doing full justice to a paper that I consider to be generally clear and comprehensive. In particular, I will not address the author's informative discussion of the speed and sequence of trade reforms and his comments on the recent regional free trade agreement initiatives in the hemisphere.

Assessment of the Historic Experience of Latin America

The paper rightly recognizes that the postwar trade system in Latin America was not so much exclusively an import-substitution regime as a hybrid one that combined domestic market protection with export promotion through subsidies, preferential credits, and tariff exemptions. Since the early or mid-1960s, an increasing number of countries (notably, Brazil, Colombia, and Mexico) have implemented these types of export-promotion policies in addition to domestic market protection.

A key question raised in the paper is why these export-promotion policies were less successful in Latin America than in East Asia. In addition to the differences in macroeconomic policy management that influenced the effectiveness of trade policies, the author's response is that the approach taken by the Latin American countries targeted selected industries instead of rewarding export activity in general, as the Asian countries did. I am not sure that this response is convincing because Korea appears to have used a sectoral approach as well. But, more than the response, I am challenging the very basis of the question: When we consider the differences in saving and investment rates and macroeconomic policy management in the two regions, were the Latin American experiences really less successful?

What I wish to suggest is that there was not a fundamental difference between Latin America and East Asia but a continuum of policies and results in which the differences between the Latin American countries (Brazil and Chile, for example) were as great as or greater than those between East Asia and some Latin American countries (for example, Brazil and Korea). In this connection, it should be recalled that in the Krueger and Bhagwati studies of the

1970s,[1] the Brazilian case was considered to be one of export-led growth similar to the Korean experience. In general, no one thought to broach the topic of substantial differences in the trade regimes adopted by those two countries or their growth performance at that time. This is not merely an academic point or an attempt to dispute the desirability of a trade regime that is more transparent, less distorted, and less prone to corruption than the prevailing regime in Latin America in the past. Rather, it is a case of understanding that only so much can be expected of trade reform. If too much is expected of it, the result could be distraction from more important tasks for the recovery of growth.

Results Expected from Trade Reform and Recent Experience

This brings me to the following comments on the results of trade reform. I shall concentrate on the dynamic effects on productivity and exports.

My first comment is that my reading of the bibliography on trade openness and dynamic effects on growth and productivity leaves me with a somewhat different impression from the one conveyed by Mr. Edwards. My impression—taking into account the contributions of Bhagwati, Pack, Rodrik, and Tybout, for example—is that the theoretical arguments and empirical research are not conclusive with regard to the possible orientation of these effects. It might be interesting to recall some of the quotations on the subject:

> Although the arguments for the success of the EP [export promotion] strategy based on economies of scale and X-efficiency are plausible, empirical support for them is not available. The arguments on savings and innovation provide a less than compelling case for showing that EP is necessarily better on their account than IS [import substitution].[2]
>
> . . . to date, there is no clear confirmation of the hypothesis that countries with an external orientation benefit from greater growth in technical efficiency in the component sectors of manufacturing.[3]
>
> . . . if truth-in-advertising were to apply to policy advice, each prescription for trade liberalization would be accompanied with a disclaimer:

---

[1]See Anne O. Krueger, *Liberalization Attempts and Consequences* (Cambridge, Massachusetts: Ballinger, 1978) and Jagdish Bhagwati, *Anatomy and Consequences of Exchange Control Regimes*, Vol. 2, *Foreign Trade Regimes and Economic Development* (Cambridge, Massachusetts: Ballinger, 1978).

[2]Jagdish Bhagwati, "Export-Promoting Trade Strategy: Issues and Evidence," *World Bank Research Observer*, Vol. 3 (January 1988), p. 40.

[3]Howard Pack, "Industrialization and Trade," in *Handbook of Development Economics*, ed. by H. Chenery and T.N. Srinivasan (Amsterdam; New York: North-Holland, 1988), p. 38.

"Warning! Trade liberalization cannot be shown to enhance technical efficiency; nor has it been empirically demonstrated to do so."[4]

Even though the World Bank is much more adamant about this, it
recognizes that "a degree of skepticism is warranted."[5]

My second comment refers to the specific experience of Mexico in recent times. Like the author, I will begin by making a distinction between
developments in the manufacturing industry and in the economy as a
whole. Labor productivity growth has been spectacular in manufacturing,
rising to about 5 percent a year in 1989 (after the second phase of trade
opening) and above the historical average. As the paper indicates, the evidence of overall factor productivity in the manufacturing sector also
points to this. It is debatable how much of the productivity increase is
due to trade reform and how much to other factors, such as the impact of
privatization or the response of enterprises to the decline in profitability,
because of the appreciation of the currency, of the sectors producing internationally tradable goods. The main problem, in my opinion, is that
these increases in productivity have not led to a recovery of economic
growth or an improvement in the productivity performance of the economy as a whole. As the paper shows, the overall productivity growth in
the economy was below its historical level in the period prior to trade
opening.

In a recent paper, I attempted to break down this performance into
three sources: (1) productivity growth in high-productivity sectors (including manufacturing); (2) growth attributable to low-productivity sectors (agriculture and services, mainly); and (3) growth associated with the
redeployment of jobs from the high- to the low-productivity sectors. The
conclusions are clear: the increased productivity growth in the high-
productivity sectors was nullified by the flagging performance of the agricultural and services sectors and, to a large extent, by the transfer of jobs
from the high-productivity to the low-productivity sectors, related to the
reduction in employment in manufacturing and widespread underem-
ployment in agriculture and the services industry. The results suggest that
the decline in productivity growth in the economy as a whole is a macroeconomic and endogenous phenomenon linked to the slow pace of GDP
growth and, ultimately, to low rates of savings and investment in physical
and human capital (in comparison with the historical average), which
have characterized the Mexican economy in recent years. This interpretation, which attributes the poor performance of productivity to the lack

---

[4]Dani Rodrik, "Closing the Productivity Gap: Does Trade Liberalization Really Help?" in
Trade Policy, Industrialization and Development: New Perspectives, ed. by G.K. Helleiner
(Oxford, England: Clarendon Press, 1992), p. 172.

[5]World Bank, *World Development Report 1991* (New York: Oxford University Press,
1991), p. 98.

(until very recently) of reforms (commercial or regulatory) in the agricultural and services sectors, is at variance with that of Edwards. Although this may have led to lower productivity growth than there might have been, it does not, in my opinion, explain the marked decline in productivity performance in relation to the past.

By contrast, export performance since trade has been opened is particularly impressive because of the non-oil export boom the economy has been able to sustain throughout the exchange appreciation of recent years. However, in conclusion, I must add a word of caution. The boom in non-oil exports since the beginning of the 1980s has been associated, to a large extent, with two phenomena: (1) booming exports from the automobile industry, one of the few sectors in which the domestic market remained protected throughout the 1980s and where export growth is linked to changes in the investment and export strategies of North American corporations in the sector under the old industrial and trade policy regime; and (2) the rapid growth of exports from the offshore processing industry, in which trade reform had no impact on the policy regime in effect since the mid-1960s.

Participants

Moderator

André Lara Resende
Pontifícia Universidade Católica (Rio de Janeiro)
Brazil

Authors

Edward J. Amadeo
Pontifícia Universidade Católica (Rio de Janeiro)
Brazil

Tomás J.T. Baliño
International Monetary Fund

Sebastián Edwards
World Bank

Ricardo López Murphy
Fundación de Investigaciones Económicas Latinoamericanas (FIEL)
Argentina

Parthasarathi Shome
International Monetary Fund

Roberto Steiner
Fundación para la Educación Superior y el Desarrollo (FEDESARROLLO)
Colombia

Discussants

S.J. Anjaria
International Monetary Fund

Guillermo A. Calvo
University of Maryland
United States

Ricardo Ffrench-Davis
United Nations Commission for Latin America and the Caribbean (ECLAC)
Chile

Note: The affiliations are those as of the time of the conference.

Ricardo Hausmann
Inter-American Development Bank (IDB)

Roberto Junguito
Banco de la República
Colombia

Felipe Larraín
Pontificia Universidad Católica de Chile
Chile

Carlos Noriega
Ministerio de Hacienda
Mexico

Miguel Rodríguez
Consultant
Venezuela

Mário Henrique Simonsen
Fundação Getúlio Vargas
Brazil

Luis Viana
Compañía Forestal Uruguaya S.A.
Uruguay

Sérgio Werlang
Fundação Getúlio Vargas
Brazil

Participants

Frits Van Beek
International Monetary Fund

Miguel Bonangelino
International Monetary Fund

Armínio Fraga Neto
Soros Fund Management
United States

Roberto Frenkel
Centro de Estudios de Estado y Sociedad (CEDES)
Argentina

Santiago Herrera
Ministerio de Hacienda y Crédito Público
Colombia

Gustavo Márquez
Instituto de Estudios Superiores de Administración (IESA)
Venezuela

Celso Luiz Martone
Consultant
Brazil

Patricio Meller
Corporación de Investigaciones Económicas para Latinoamerica
    (CIEPLAN)
Chile

Felipe Morandé
Instituto Latinoamericano de Doctrinas y Estudios Sociales (ILADES)
Chile

Hernán Puentes
International Monetary Fund

Jaime Ros
University of Notre Dame
United States

Luiz Afonso Simoens da Silva
Banco Central
Brazil

Dante Simone
Consultant
Argentina

Ernesto Talvi
Banco Central
Uruguay

José Toro
Universidad Metropolitana
Venezuela

Observers

Ana Cláudia Duarte de Além
Banco Nacional do Desenvolvimento Econômico e Social (BNDES)
Brazil

Monica Baer
Centro Brasileiro de Análise e Planejamento (CEBRAP)
Brazil

Alexandra Barone
Instituto de Economia do Setor Público
Brazil

Sérgio Caruso
Banco Central
Brazil

Carlos Augusto Dias de Carvalho
Banco Central
Brazil

Vicente de Paulo Diniz
Banco Central
Brazil

Eduardo Fernandes
Banco Central
Brazil

José Augusto Coelho Fernandes
Confederação Nacional da Indústria (CNI)
Brazil

Roberto Brito Fernandes
Banco Central
Brazil

Carlos Eduardo de Freitas
Fundação Getúlio Vargas
Brazil

Fernando Antonio Gomes
Banco Central
Brazil

Ricardo Gottschalk
Fundação do Desenvolvimento Administrativo (FUNDAP)
Brazil

Sérgio Ruffoni Guedes
Banco Central
Brazil

Gerson Pereira Lima
Casa Civil da Presidencia da República
Brazil

Márcio Cartier Marques
Banco Central
Brazil

Ana Paula Fernandes Mendes
Banco Nacional do Desenvolvimento Econômico e Social (BNDES)
Brazil

Arno Meyer
Fundação do Desenvolvimento Administrativo (FUNDAP)
Brazil

Yoshiaki Nakano
Fundação Getúlio Vargas
Brazil

Elba Cristina Lima Rêgo
Banco Nacional do Desenvolvimento Econômico e Social (BNDES)
Brazil

João Carlos Scandiuzzi
Pontifícia Universidade Católica (Rio de Janeiro)
Brazil

Mary de Melo Sousa
Instituto de Pesquisas Econômicas Aplicadas (IPEA)
Brazil